REVOLUTION

Volume 13

GRENADA

GRENADA

Revolution and Invasion

ANTHONY PAYNE, PAUL SUTTON
and
TONY THORNDIKE

LONDON AND NEW YORK

First published in 1984 by Croom Helm Ltd

This edition first published in 2022
by Routledge
4 Park Square, Milton Park, Abingdon, Oxon OX14 4RN

and by Routledge
605 Third Avenue, New York, NY 10158

Routledge is an imprint of the Taylor & Francis Group, an informa business

© 1984 Anthony Payne, Paul Sutton and Tony Thorndike

All rights reserved. No part of this book may be reprinted or reproduced or utilised in any form or by any electronic, mechanical, or other means, now known or hereafter invented, including photocopying and recording, or in any information storage or retrieval system, without permission in writing from the publishers.

Trademark notice: Product or corporate names may be trademarks or registered trademarks, and are used only for identification and explanation without intent to infringe.

British Library Cataloguing in Publication Data
A catalogue record for this book is available from the British Library

ISBN: 978-1-032-12623-4 (Set)
ISBN: 978-1-003-26095-0 (Set) (ebk)
ISBN: 978-1-032-12770-5 (Volume 13) (hbk)
ISBN: 978-1-032-12773-6 (Volume 13) (pbk)
ISBN: 978-1-003-22618-5 (Volume 13) (ebk)

DOI: 10.4324/9781003226185

Publisher's Note
The publisher has gone to great lengths to ensure the quality of this reprint but points out that some imperfections in the original copies may be apparent.

Disclaimer
The publisher has made every effort to trace copyright holders and would welcome correspondence from those they have been unable to trace.

GRENADA
REVOLUTION AND INVASION

ANTHONY PAYNE, PAUL SUTTON
and TONY THORNDIKE

CROOM HELM
London & Sydney

© 1984 Anthony Payne, Paul Sutton and Tony Thorndike
Croom Helm Ltd, Provident House, Burrell Row,
Beckenham, Kent BR3 1AT
Croom Helm Australia Pty Ltd, First Floor,
139 King Street, Sydney, NSW 2001, Australia

British Library Cataloguing in Publication Data

Payne, Anthony, *1952-*
   Grenada: revolution and invasion.
   1. Grenada — Politics and government
   I. Title   II. Sutton, Paul
   III. Thorndike, Tony
   972.98'45   F2056

ISBN 0-7099-2080-6

Typeset by Mayhew Typesetting, Bristol
Printed and bound in Great Britain

CONTENTS

Preface

Introduction

Part I: The Revolution and its Impact

1. The Gairy Years — 1
2. The People's Revolutionary Government: Political Strategies and Development Priorities — 18
3. United States Policy towards the Caribbean Basin — 43
4. Cuba and the Caribbean — 71
5. The Commonwealth Caribbean Dimension — 89

Part II: The Invasion and its Aftermath — 103

6. The Internal Struggle for Power — 105
7. The US Invasion — 148
8. International Reaction — 168
9. Grenada under the Governor General — 178
10. The Invasion and Caribbean Politics — 198

Select Bibliography — 227

Index — 229

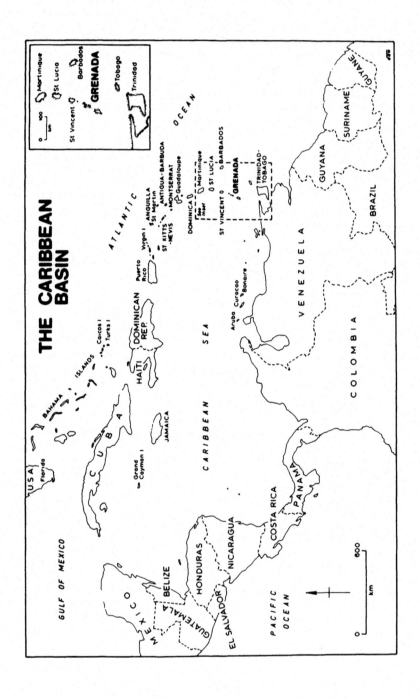

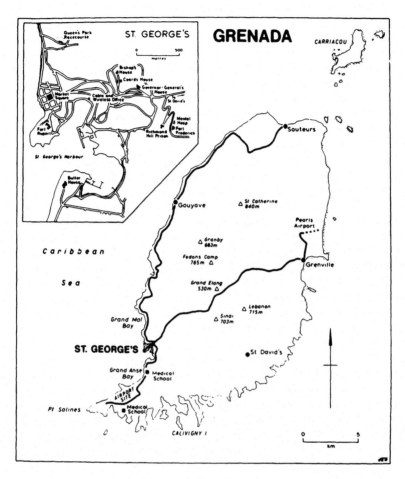

Small as we are, and poor as we are, as a people and as a country we insist on the fundamental principles of legal equality, mutual respect for sovereignty, non-interference in our internal affairs, and the right to build our own process free from outside interference, free from intimidation, free from bullying, free from the use or threat of force. We say this is our right as a country and as a people and we will fight and die for that right.

Maurice Bishop, St George's, Grenada,
13 March 1980

PREFACE

In a speech to a regional meeting of the Socialist International in July 1981, Maurice Bishop, the murdered leader of the Grenadian revolution, demanded: 'Not only when the marines land must there be outcries.' His reference then was to mobilising international public opinion against covert interference in the affairs of countries seeking to follow a non-capitalist path of economic development and social change. This book is written with the knowledge that the marines did land and from a perspective which shares with Bishop a belief that international public opinion should be alerted to and question very closely the wisdom, let alone the legitimacy, of such acts. To do so such an opinion must be informed, a need which this book seeks to meet. It sets out the background to the revolution in Grenada and details the course of its progress, examining the reasons why latterly it faltered and then stalled. International factors played no small part in these events, setting the agenda for, and to a considerable degree conditioning, the internal processes of the revolution and ultimately, of course, bringing it to an end. They have been given due prominence. But at the end of the day it was a revolution carried out by the Grenadians themselves, the first of its kind in the Commonwealth Caribbean and therefore both a potential point of departure and a unique experiment in its own right. Why this was so, and what the consequences have been, are recurring themes throughout the book.

In producing it the authors must directly thank Richard Hart for his help in securing the minutes of the Central Committee of the New Jewel Movement and Derek Waite for his skill in drawing the maps. More indirectly, but no less sincerely, we are grateful to our respective families, who once again have tolerated our absences with their customary understanding and good grace. Finally, and most importantly, we wish to thank the many Grenadians who over the years have helped us to understand the significance of their revolution and appreciate the beauty of their island. They include some who tragically are now dead; some who presently are in prison; and some who thankfully are free. Although we have not omitted to be critical where it has seemed to us that mistakes were made, the book nevertheless stands as an appreciation and an acknowledgement of the efforts and the will of all those

Preface

who have laboured in the last few years to bring about constructive change in Grenada.

Anthony Payne
Paul Sutton
Tony Thorndike
February 1984

INTRODUCTION

By the most tragic of means Grenada has now acquired a prominence in world affairs greater than at any previous time in its history. For a couple of weeks in October 1983 international attention suddenly focused upon this tiny Caribbean island and, not surprisingly, found it difficult to understand the extraordinary events taking place there. These were undeniably dramatic — the house arrest and eventual execution of the Prime Minister, the creation of a military government, the dawn invasion of the island by troops from the United States and other Commonwealth Caribbean territories and the subsequent war of words which broke out between all the contending parties once the actual fighting was over. The question that was uppermost in people's minds was simply why? Why was a seemingly popular leader shot so brutally? Why did other Caribbean states take up arms against Grenada so promptly? Above all, why was the world's greatest power invading an island just 133 square miles in size, with a mere 110,000 inhabitants, whose best-known export was nutmeg? It all seemed somehow beyond belief.

The answers to these questions are to be found originally in the peculiar character of Grenadian and Commonwealth Caribbean history. Central to this is the long and bitter experience of imperialism which all the islands of the region had to endure during the course of several centuries. The pure plantation economies of the eighteenth century may themselves have been superseded and sugar is certainly no longer king. But none of the various attempts of the last 150 years to diversify the Commonwealth Caribbean economy — first the establishment of a peasant agricultural sector growing food and new export crops such as bananas, cocoa, coffee and spices, and latterly the development of light manufacturing, mineral and tourist sectors — have succeeded in banishing from the region the dependency syndrome so familiar throughout the Third World. The postwar era of Commonwealth Caribbean history has thus witnessed in abundance all the problems usually associated with peripheral status within the world economy — growing populations, narrow vulnerable structures of production, high levels of foreign investment and ownership, increasing unemployment, widening inequality and ultimately rising discontent.

There was also engendered, especially in the smaller territories like

Introduction

Grenada, a deep-rooted sense of psychological dependency. This can be defined as a deep attachment to the metropole, its economic, social and political institutions, and all the ideological attachments that went with them. This attitude derived from the length and totality of the imperial experience suffered by the people of the Commonwealth Caribbean, who were originally brought to the region over 300 years ago as slaves and subsequently deliberately stripped of all cultural identity. For decades, even centuries, the legacy of this past generated a powerful sense of inadequacy which rendered the Commonwealth Caribbean seemingly the most colonised of all the colonial regions.

Even the modern politics of nationalism threatened for a long while to pass the region by. Following a brief outburst of popular violence in several of the islands in the 1930s, the major states of the Commonwealth Caribbean proceeded peacefully towards self-government by a series of discrete constitutional changes culminating in the achievement of independence in the early to mid-1960s. Jamaica and Trinidad and Tobago acquired this status in 1962 and Barbados and Guyana in 1966. A year later, the smaller territories, including Grenada, were granted, and accepted, so-called Associate Statehood, an arrangement which conceded full internal self-government but kept responsibility for defence and foreign affairs in the hands of the British government. For the most part, the transition was effected in an orderly, collaborative style with little of the sense of struggle against colonialism which has accompanied and sustained nationalist politics in other parts of the Third World.

In the early years of independence too, the new states of the Commonwealth Caribbean all followed conventionally pro-Western economic policies which generally produced satisfactory rates of economic growth but less impressive levels of social and economic development. The inherited Westminster system of representative democracy was also accepted throughout the region without substantial amendment. However, during the 1970s, under the pressure of deteriorating international economic conditions, several countries in the area became increasingly critical of colonial and neo-colonial values and began to search around for new strategies of economic development and new models of political organisation. Guyana started to experiment in 1970 with a form of 'co-operative socialism', which involved both the assertion of state control over the various foreign interests that traditionally had dominated the Guyanese economy and the prosecution of a radical and non-aligned foreign policy; Trinidad experienced in the same year major Black Power demonstrations which briefly appeared as if they might

Introduction

lead to the fall of the government; and Jamaica in 1974 announced its espousal of 'democratic socialism', embarking upon a series of populist and egalitarian reforms in both domestic and foreign policy. None of these moves reflected a strong commitment to radical politics in the Commonwealth Caribbean but they did indicate that a process of change had at last been inaugurated in the region. It embraced initially only the larger territories, but potentially even the smaller islands were susceptible given that in the 1970s they too had begun to break the psychological hold of colonialism and were proceeding, one by one, to independence.

In this context the significance of Grenada – also the first of the Associated States to secure the 'political kingdom' – is that there came to power in that country on 13 March 1979 a People's Revolutionary Government (PRG), led by Maurice Bishop and other members of the New Jewel Movement, which quickly showed itself to be determined to challenge the legacy of dependency in all its many forms. By that stage the other reform movements in the region had fallen by the wayside. Guyanese socialism had been revealed to be nothing more than a strategy for aggrandisement by an avaricious party elite, Trinidadian discontent had been effectively assuaged by the liberal conservatism of Eric Williams and an ample supply of oil, and the Jamaican populist nationalism of Michael Manley had been broken on the back of the intransigence of the International Monetary Fund with which the government had cumulatively become embroiled. By contrast, the Grenadian revolution appeared to be a much more substantive affair. Sustained by a firm grasp of the problem of dependency, staffed by committed party activists and able civil servants, and led with vigour and true inspiration by Bishop, Grenada was the only place in the Commonwealth Caribbean where at the beginning of the 1980s serious economic and political change was being pursued.

Its potential as a model was all the greater because of its size. From the mid-1960s the conventional wisdom in the Commonwealth Caribbean had been that smallness of itself was a powerful independent constraint upon the development potential of a state. Although the university community in the region always had some reservations about the applicability of the argument, it was undoubtedly a major influence upon the politicians and policy-makers of the area, rendering them notably hesitant and deferential in the face of powerful external obstacles to the fulfilment of the potential of Commonwealth Caribbean nationalism. Grenada shattered whatever remaining intellectual credibility this notion had. By its resolute pursuit of social and

Introduction

economic independence and the tangible achievements soon garnered, the PRG seemed to reverse for all territories in the region, including the smallest, the vision of permanent dependency which was to such a large extent part of the Commonwealth Caribbean's psyche. The lesson was obvious: if Grenada could do it, then so could everyone.

This also partly explains the international opprobium which the Grenadian revolution immediately attracted from some quarters. From the very outset, the opposition of the United States was both persistent and virulent. From the geopolitical point of view, all of the Commonwealth Caribbean states are unavoidably located in the American sphere of influence. When they finally emerged from the formal protection of British colonialism to gain their political independence, it had been assumed by all concerned that they would automatically fall in with the traditional model of US political and economic hegemony over the whole Caribbean area. Grenada's attempted escape from dependency after 1979 was thus a direct challenge to the power of the United States, as well as the more impersonal forces that control the international economy.

It came, moreover, at a time when US hegemony in the area was being threatened more seriously than ever before. The United States has traditionally defined the Caribbean to include Central America and all the non-British territories, as well as the Commonwealth Caribbean, a definition which it has lately made specific with its designation of the whole region as the Caribbean basin. Although the Cuban revolution had no successor in the basin for 20 years, there developed from 1979 onwards a whole series of breakdowns in the traditional order of the region: the overthrow of Somoza in Nicaragua by the Sandinista revolutionaries in July of that year; civil war in El Salvador between the ruling military junta and the Farabundo Marti Liberation Front insurrectionary army; growing guerrilla activity in Honduras and Guatemala; and even some violent *independentista* protests in Puerto Rico. In European-dominated parts of the region too, there were similar disturbances of the *status quo*, including a *coup* and a sharp move to the left in Suriname after 1980 and some sporadic outbreaks of nationalist violence in the French territories of Guadeloupe and Martinique. All of these developments the United States instinctively attributed to Cuban subversive activity, rather than the nature of social and political conditions in the region. Cuban foreign policy in the Caribbean in the 1970s had been much more active than ever before, but scarcely so efficacious as to generate widespread political change on its own. Nevertheless, it was happy to establish friendly relations with

Introduction

new left-wing governments where they had emerged and with Grenada developed a close working bond. In short, from Washington's point of view Grenada was not only part of an alarming sequence of fallen or falling dominoes which, if allowed to continue, would ultimately imperil US control of its backyard, the foundation on which its credibility as a global power was in turn constructed, but was also a further stimulant to its long-standing paranoia about Cuba. In this perception of regional politics Grenada's particular problem was that its small size must always have made it appear to the United States as the place where US policy could most easily begin to roll back the tide.

The chemistry was thus complete. The elements which ultimately exploded into conflict on 25 October 1983 were in place: a determination to confront dependency and imperialism on the part of the revolutionary regime in Grenada, and a determination to reassert their country's traditional dominance over the Caribbean on the part of an increasingly reactionary government in the United States. Looking back, perhaps only the particular circumstances and timing of the final conflict were unpredictable. The Grenadian revolution and invasion thus jointly constitute one of the most seminal episodes of modern Caribbean history. The nature of politics in the Caribbean has been changed so fundamentally as a consequence that one can truthfully say that nothing will ever be the same again.

PART 1

The Revolution and its Impact

1 THE GAIRY YEARS

Grenada and the Grenadines were discovered for Europe by Columbus during his third voyage in 1498. Although the native Carib Indians made full use of the mountainous terrain and dense bush to repel would-be colonisers in an era when the tiny Caribbean island of Nevis was worth more in terms of value of produce than the nascent New York state, their eventual defeat was inevitable. This was accomplished by the French after a bloody war in 1651 which ended when the Carib leadership jumped over a cliff into the sea, preferring death to slavery. The name of the nearby village, Sauteurs, or 'leapers', bears witness to this defiance to the present day. War between Britain and France led to Grenada's formal annexation by the British in 1763. Slaves from Africa had first been imported in the late seventeenth century and, by the time of the British take-over, totalled nearly 12,000 as against 1,250 Europeans. By 1934, as many as 23,600 transplanted Africans toiled in the hot sun of Grenada.

Anglo-French rivalry in the Caribbean did not cease with the end of the Seven Years War; indeed, it was given added impetus by the reverberations of the French and Haitian revolutions. From their headquarters in Guadeloupe, the French revolutionaries planned the recapture of Grenada through subversion and insurrection. A revolutionary edict of 1792 had declared the equality of all races: it was not therefore surprising that slaves supported a rebellion raised by Julien Fédon, a French coloured planter. For two years his forces held the north and east of the island, being defeated only when the British called upon Spanish assistance from Trinidad. Although Fédon's struggle was essentially against the hated British, he was later venerated as a campaigner for the rights of the slaves, although none were ever formally freed. Popular resistance, although sporadic, did not stop with emancipation in 1834. In 1848, wage reductions consequent upon sharp falls in the London sugar price triggered revolt in the island, as did unemployment and destitution for returning soldiers who, in 1920, tried to destroy the capital, St George's, by fire.

These developing political and economic pressures, exacerbated in the inter-war years by world economic depression, prompted two Grenadians, Uriah 'Buzz' Butler and T. Albert Marryshow, to take action. Although born only a decade apart — in 1897 and 1887 respectively —

these modern precursors of change, development and cultural pride came from quite different backgrounds, and their paths rarely crossed. Whereas Butler was a man of working-class background who, in 1921, had migrated to Trinidad in search of work in the expanding oil industry, the middle-class Marryshow was a journalist, debater and essayist. Butler soon became the spokesman of the oilfield workers, articulating their discontent through the British Empire Workers and Citizen Home Rule Party. A key figure in the riots of June and July 1937 in Trinidad, he was to suffer several terms of imprisonment before his seminal role in the development of trade unionism in the Caribbean was finally recognised. Whereas Butler had gone to Trinidad, Marryshow, a champion of West Indian unity, had remained in Grenada. Intellectually versatile, he campaigned vigorously against the subjugation of the black masses by both the commercial and bureaucratic elites. He pressed particularly for more representative government in the colony. Although he refused steadfastly either to form or join a political party, his election to the Legislative Council in 1925 launched a parliamentary career which, by his skilful exploitation of successive colonial constitutions, marked the beginning of modern politics in Grenada and was to contribute significantly to the political awakening of the colony.

The Political Awakening of Grenada

Butler and Marryshow and their followers were campaigning against a deep-rooted dependency that went far beyond political subservience to London. Colonialism in the Caribbean was built around the profitable export of sugar. Although the gradual decline in prices and the growing disinclination of workers to cultivate sugar led to its replacement by cocoa as the main crop in Grenada in the 1850s and then bananas after their introduction in the 1930s, the end result was the same. Prices for these crops and the nutmeg and mace which Grenada also produced, as well as the prices of imports, were all entirely determined elsewhere. Admittedly, the impact of this situation on the living standards of ordinary people was lessened because, from the early 1840s onwards, many sugar plantations had failed and peasant farming had begun to develop. In fact, even in the days of slavery, the large amount of land unsuitable for sugar had given slaves opportunities to grow food for themselves and the markets. By 1843, this continuing process had led to 5 per cent of the population, or 1,360 people, becoming freeholders owning and working two-and-a-half acres or less. By 1881, the peasant sector numbered 3,000 (8 per cent); by 1911, 6,332 (11 per cent)[1] and by 1982, 8,202 (9 per cent). More significantly, it was then estimated that peasants and their dependants totalled some 22,000 or 24 per cent of the population.[2] In many cases, economic necessity had forced them to work on the remaining plantations on an occasional basis. Although they had little choice but to accept the very poor wages, they were better off than the 2,000 or more agricultural workers who owned no land. The emergence of a Grenadian peasantry also promoted a degree of pride and independent-mindedness in the population and prevented a drift away from the land towards the towns as happened in neighbouring islands more topographically suited to sugar cultivation such as Antigua, St Kitts and Barbados. In these countries, the working class continued to be heavily dependent upon imported food and estate employment.

Another consequence of the slave past was the racialism of a rigid colour-class dichotomy. A strong correlation developed between skin colour and social status. At the top of the social order were the tiny number of whites, followed by the mixed-race coloureds and, at the base of the pyramid, the black masses. There were exceptions, notably those of 'associational colour', whereby if a black was employed in a job normally undertaken by one of paler skin, he or she would assume the higher status. Poor whites were also to be found, but always had their colour to fall back on. For generations, such a group, genetically degenerate, existed in self-imposed isolation near St George's, descendants of those shipped to Grenada from Barbados by a planter- and merchant-dominated government, embarrassed by their presence after emancipation. These cases apart, the broad correlation of colour and class was the dominant feature of colonial society in Grenada and was maintained even as a measure of representative government was won by the efforts of men like Marryshow. Political concessions such as those granted by Britain in the 1925 constitution were welcomed by the coloured merchant and professional classes so long as a restricted franchise was established. Based on a minimum property ownership, this effectively excluded the predominantly black peasantry and reinforced the privileged position of the coloured element alongside the remnants of the old white plantocracy.

Ironically, it was the existence of a large peasant class which excluded Grenada from the wave of popular disturbances that swept through much of the region after 1935. Nevertheless, the appointment of a Royal Commission under Lord Moyne's chairmanship to 'investigate social and economic conditions' in Britain's West Indian colonies, and make recommendations, applied to Grenada no less than the others. The Commission's report, finally published in 1945, advocated 'the largest measure of constitutional reform which is thought to be judicious in existing circumstances',[3] but argued against self-government on the grounds that it was necessary for the Colonial Secretary to retain controls over local finances in order to prevent potentially irresponsible spending by elected members. Although note was taken of the frustration of the middle-class representatives in the Legislative Council which expressed itself in constant bickering, the report's only practical recommendation was an increase in the degree of local representation in the Executive and Legislative Councils. In sum, the proposed changes did not add up to a significant constitutional breakthrough. The fact that better co-operation between the colonial government and local representatives was subsequently achieved was due more to a greater sense of tact and enlightenment by British officials, particularly during the administration of Sir Arthur Grimble who served as Governor from 1942 to 1948. Britain certainly recognised the dominant social position of the Grenadian middle classes in this period and gave official support to their resistance to demands, led by Marryshow, for universal suffrage. The result was that

> political goals and style were set within certain fundamental British-colonial values such as imperial loyalty, the myth of racial harmony, a respect for British institutions and acceptance of gradualist evolution to higher constitutional status, and, generally, a disposition to accept that the 'uncultured' black strata were unqualified for rights of political participation and representation.[4]

In fact, there was to be no threat to the Moyne settlement for a further five years. The report had elsewhere recommended the encouragement of trade unions to help alleviate working-class poverty. The employers reluctantly recognised the first weak attempts to move in this direction, and wage agreements were reached despite union membership remaining very small. Thereafter, the government enforced minimum wage legislation. The workers remained largely non-unionised, in sharp contrast to those in other Eastern Caribbean islands where dynamic leaders, such as Vere Bird (Antigua), Robert Bradshaw (St Kitts) and Ebenezer Joshua (St Vincent), had emerged to press workers' demands. In fact, the by then ageing Marryshow retarded developments for a while by echoing the insistence of the Colonial

Office and the local middle classes upon the divorce of trade unionism and political activity. However, in the circumstances of the Caribbean, where social, economic and political subjugation were inextricably linked, such a separation proved impossible to uphold for long.

'Hurricane Gairy'

The catalyst for change was the return to Grenada in 1949 of Eric Gairy, expelled from the Dutch island of Aruba for union activities. A former primary school teacher, Gairy first attracted attention in 1950 by successfully claiming compensation for some tenant farmers who had been evicted from an estate. He next registered the Grenada Manual and Mental Workers Union (GMMWU) and demanded a wage increase for the sugar workers. A strike was called and, before the dispute could be settled, a claim was lodged for all workers in the agricultural sector. The employers responded by refusing to recognise the GMMWU, preferring to negotiate with the remnants of the early unions with whom they shared a common concern to arrest Gairy's growing dominance in industrial relations. His reply was a general strike, called in February 1951 and involving by this time workers in both agriculture and the public works department. Lasting a month, it led to violence, the declaration of a state of emergency, the despatch of British troops and Gairy's detention. The strike was, however, highly successful as significant wage increases were eventually conceded. This represented a fundamental change in Grenadian politics in that the power of the old planter elite to maintain its long-standing domination over the black masses was irrevocably broken. The crisis thus went far beyond a mere industrial dispute, as a visiting anthropologist observed

> Violence is done to planter class values if workers lay claim to equality in the bargaining process, if workers share in the making of economic decisions, and if their bargaining representatives are, like themselves, black and of lower-class origin ... The violent, personal tones in which planters refer to the union leaders indicates that they are concerned with something a good deal more fundamental than wage demands.[5]

Furthermore, the advance was to be permanent, for the politicisation of the black working class, encouraged by the sudden emergence of the labour movement, was paralleled and reinforced by the simultaneous grant of universal suffrage. Together, these developments dramatically altered the nature and scope of government as Gairy, following in the footsteps of union leaders elsewhere in the region, fashioned a political arm of the GMMWU. Originally called the Grenada People's Party, it was soon renamed the Grenada United Labour Party (GULP). The indivisibility of union and party was highly effective: in the 1951 general election, GULP won 64 per cent of the vote and six of the eight seats in the Legislative Council, devastating the old middle-class 'citizens' associations' which were simply no match for the new-style political party.

Gairy's success stemmed from his flamboyant defiance of the commercial and bureaucratic elites whose attitudes were deeply offensive to the independent-minded black peasants and agricultural workers. Their grievances went far beyond wages to matters such as greater access to cultivable lands and credit. As late as 1972, it was calculated that farms under five acres accounted for nearly 90 per cent of total landholdings but only 45 per cent of cultivable land. By contrast, farms over 100 acres (0.5 per cent of landholdings) occupied nearly 50 per cent, including the most fertile areas.[6] Worse still, many of the peasant holdings were fragmented due to archaic inheritance laws. By contrast, since many larger farms were owned by absentee landlords who had emigrated, much cultivable land lay idle. With such little security, bank credit for peasant farmers to expand operations was rarely granted. They were also to find that income from the marketing associations, dominated by the commercial elite, declined as greater deductions were made for 'administrative' and 'transport' costs. For example, whereas in 1970 nutmeg growers received about 87 per cent of total receipts, this had fallen to 60 per cent by 1977.[7]

In these conditions Gairy was able to consolidate his position by an energetic programme of land reform. However, as it was not accompanied by any semblance of planning, agricultural production fell as a consequence. The elected marketing boards were replaced by bodies with nominees of his choosing. His charm and sartorial elegance further advanced his position in the minds of the masses, although it did not give him the social recognition for which he craved from the elite, who wanted to keep him in his place. There was also Gairy's mysticism to consider. In a country deeply attached to Christianity, this was taken seriously. In one famous instance, in late 1952, Gairy called upon God to send a sign that He favoured a strike.

That night there was a downpour, heavy even by Grenadian standards. The road between St George's and Gouyave was blocked by fallen rock, which many regarded as a sign of divine support ... The Public Works Department tackled this roadblock with unusual energy, but took a fortnight to remove it. With Gairy's divine sign, and a wave of awe sweeping Grenada, police took up protective positions ...[8]

His hold on the working classes was undoubtedly highly individualistic, likened to that of the 'hero' in front of the 'crowd'.[9] His ability to mesmerise, to channel the crowd's emotions and to direct its anger was exploited to the full. But it was not long before he changed course. The first evidence of this surfaced in 1957 when, after leading another strike and being imprisoned by an increasingly exasperated colonial administration, he secured his release by suddenly allying himself with the government and offering to use his influence to bring the disturbances to an end. His reward was a greater ease of access to Government House and the social calendar associated with it.

Gairy's ever more unpredictable behaviour and growing involvement with various business enterprises, from which he gathered an increasing income, led GULP to obtain only 46 per cent of the votes cast in the 1954 election. His rule was further challenged by the founding of the Grenada National Party (GNP) in 1956. Representing a shaken but by now reorganised middle class, its leader, barrister Herbert Blaize from Carriacou, was lacklustre. None the less, it combined with other opposition groups to replace GULP as the governing party by the next year. Gairy skilfully exploited the GNP's lack of direction and, repeating his promises to the working class, was returned to power in 1961. Soon afterwards he was himself forcibly removed from office for 'squandermania'.[10] Accused of corrupt handling of public funds, unauthorised expenditure and intimidation of civil servants, Gairy denied the charges, but the incident helped lead to a resumption of GNP rule until 1967.

Once again, his return to power followed a virtually complete lack of response by the GNP government to working-class demands and expectations, concerned as it was with efficient and accountable administration rather than development for the population as a whole. For Gairy the difference after 1967 was that he was able to enjoy the fruits of the new 'Associated Statehood' constitution which had been ushered in in that year and which provided, in effect, for full 'internal independence', leaving only foreign affairs and defence in British hands. Gairy had campaigned vigorously against it on the grounds that Blaize and the GNP had advocated a form of union with Trinidad, although this initiative failed due to Trinidadian opposition. He therefore argued that no mandate existed for the GNP to be party to what he insisted was just another manifestation of British colonialism. His strident attacks on Blaize and Britain went as far as the UN General Assembly, where, for the first time, he attracted worldwide attention.

On Gairy's return to office, however, no more was heard of these complaints, nor of his election promises to the working class. In fact, Gairy's dominance among his erstwhile supporters steadily weakened as fewer and fewer slices of a diminishing economic cake were allocated to them in the wake of marked economic decline. He also began to distance himself socially and politically from his supporters, encouraged by many of the middle class who gave him lip service support because of his widespread powers of patronage. His became a virtual personal rule, with the constant conjuring of the image of a messiah sent to deliver his people. In the aftermath of a Black Power solidarity rally in May 1970, he buttressed his position by an Emergency Powers Act. At the same time, special squads of armed ruffians were established. Soon to be named by the people as the 'Mongoose Men' with another group known as the 'Night Ambush Squad', their infamous activities, combined with Gairy's superstition and his interest in the occult, led to unflattering comparison with Haiti's *tontons macoute*.

The 1970 demonstration marked a new departure in Grenadian politics, the full effect of which was not to be realised for several years. The disturbances in nearby Trinidad and the assertion of demands by the poor and deprived which Black Power represented found a ready echo in Grenada, particularly among the young who constituted a high proportion of the near 50 per cent of the population who were unemployed. Although the Black Power movement itself had confused ends, being a mixture of racial nationalism and anti-capitalism, it was leavened by the activities of young intellectuals who, during their studies in universities in Britain and North America, had embraced socialist theory and been active in protest movements. Many had listened to Malcolm X (*né* Little) — himself a Grenadian — during his overseas speaking tours and had noted the experiences of what appeared to be successful experiments in socialism in other parts of the Third World, such as Cuba and Tanzania. Gairy was dismissive of them: 'these irresponsible malcontents, these disgruntled political frustrates coming from abroad, coming here, metaphorically and literally hot and sweaty, and shouting "Power to the People" '.[11] Surrounded by a coterie who owed their positions entirely to him, he failed to recognise that the new movement was beginning to meet the needs and demands of the very people who had once given him their allegiance.

The New Jewel Arises

One of those intellectuals, a newly-qualified lawyer called Maurice Bishop, had returned in February 1970. In the aftermath of the Black Power disturbances, he helped found FORUM, a discussion group of young radical professionals in St George's. This was succeeded by the Movement for the Advancement of Community Effort (MACE) which stressed political research and education among the urban population. By this stage Bishop had been joined by fellow lawyer Kenrick Radix, both of whom worked assiduously in the local courts for working-class clients. Another young Grenadian, Bernard Coard, who had returned to the Caribbean from study in Britain to become a lecturer in International Relations at the Trinidadian campus of the University of the West Indies, made occasional visits to his homeland and thus maintained contact with these new political organisations. Also established in St George's was the Committee of Concerned Citizens (CCC). Its membership was largely drawn from the younger members of the commercial elite and it had hitherto allied itself with the GNP for tactical electoral purposes. In the country, in St David's parish, ex-GNP candidate Unison Whiteman had established JEWEL, the 'Joint Endeavour for the Welfare, Education and Liberation of the People'. Founded one month after the February 1972 elections which reconfirmed Gairy in power, it was based upon a farming co-operative and sought, with moderate success, to mobilise the agricultural workers.

The diversity and spontaneity of these various groups was expressive of a widespread frustration in Grenada. Gradually, they came together. First, the MACE and the CCC merged to form the Movement for Assemblies of the People (MAP). It made clear its objective of political organisation aimed at the defeat of Gairyism and the abolition of the two-party system of the Westminster model in favour of a 'participatory democracy' of 'people's assemblies'. Modelled on the *ujamaa* villages of Tanzania, it would readily permit mass participation in decision-making. As its leader Bishop explained,

> We envisage a system which would have village assemblies and workers' assemblies. In other words, politics where you live and

politics where you work . . . elections in the sense of the elections we now know would be replaced by Assemblies at different levels.[12]

In this scheme, a national assembly made up of representatives from lower level assemblies would elect a council to put its decisions into practice. Members of this council would sit on committees designed to head and oversee government departments. This system, Grenadians were later assured, 'would end the deep divisions and victimisation of the people found under the party system'.[13] Finally, MAP and JEWEL themselves came together in March 1973 after both co-operated in a demonstration against the action of a British landowner who had blocked public rights of way to a beach. The new group was christened the New Jewel Movement (NJM) and attracted international attention within a month when it was involved in a three-day demonstration during which the airport was closed. The protestors were angered by the killing of a local youth by a policeman.

As forecast by the objectives of the MAP, the New Jewel Movement was not conceived as a political party in the traditional Commonwealth Caribbean — or British — mould. It adhered to the participatory philosophy of the MAP, but enjoyed an even broader and more dynamic popular base with the involvement of such working-class activists as Selwyn Strachan and George Louison. It was, however, forced to participate in the existing system by the need to speak up for those harassed by the increasing excesses of the Mongoose Men, which were having the effect of arousing and entrenching opposition to Gairy. From this struggle and out of persecution was shaped a party. Although outwardly conforming to a conventional British model, there was always, even in these early years, a deeper underlying thrust to the New Jewel's approach to politics. Strachan later summarised its early development in these words:

> [The NJM] started off as what we would call a revolutionary party, a revolutionary democratic party. We never called ourselves socialist at the beginning. [It] was engaged in revolutionary politics, trying to raise the consciousness of the people, and — fundamentally — raising democratic issues amongst the masses and trying to get them to struggle with us for democratic rights and freedoms . . . As we got more and more mature, we were able to work out a clearer, ideological position. It didn't come artificially, it was the result of struggle, in a concrete way.[14]

From its genesis, the NJM had as its core a Political Bureau. Responsible for ensuring theoretical development and consistency, it formulated what were termed 'principled positions', but which in fact rather uneasily combined elements of racial and national pride, rastafarianism, 'popular power' and 'participatory democracy' with social reformist zeal. Only later, in 1976-7, did aspects of socialist and Marxist theory emerge. It was at the same time organisationally loose, possessing much of the atmosphere of a discussion group and tending to create institutions only in response to, or after, events. For example, unlike other Marxist-influenced parties, there was for a long while no Central Committee to oversee the work of the Political Bureau and the party as a whole. The pragmatism of the NJM also extended to a readiness to work with other groups, particularly the commercial elite, although always from a position of leadership. Recognising the class structure of Grenadian society, such co-operation was more than a matter of tactics, since the party considered national unity to be an essential prerequisite of development. As it happened, it proved easy for the NJM to assume leadership of the anti-Gairy opposition since the GNP was weakly led and organised and could not cope adequately with the major new crisis which had emerged in the country. It centred upon independence.

The Independence Crisis

From 1969 onwards Gairy had made public his dissatisfaction with Associated Statehood. The difficulty facing him was that the West Indies Act stipulated that if an 'associate' wanted to proceed to independence without British consent, then a referendum involving a two-thirds majority would be required. This condition would be waived only if some or all of the associates were to seek independence as a federation. Since the Colonial Office had planned the constitutions to be long-term arrangements for the Leeward and Windward Islands, which at the time were thought to be insufficiently viable to support independence, it was reasonable for Gairy to assume British scepticism, if not opposition, to any independence proposal.

Gairy began to argue, however, that independence, far from being an economic burden, in fact opened the doors of international financial institutions and encouraged potential aid donors. His new maxim was the slogan 'Independence will support Grenada, the people of Grenada do not have to support independence'. Quite apart from this practical consideration, he also insisted that independence was Grenada's right and, in common with the leaders of all the other Associated States after him, refused demands for a referendum. Other British colonies with less advanced constitutions had not been forced to submit to what he termed 'this miserable indignity': so why should Grenada? In any case, a referendum was unknown in West Indian political experience. Inevitably, in the highly politicised societies of the Commonwealth Caribbean, it would be impossible to isolate the issue in question, and defeat could mortally wound his government. Accordingly, he sought independence first through a federation with Trinidad and Tobago, and thereafter with all the other Associated States together with Guyana and finally with neighbouring St Lucia and St Vincent alone. When all these initiatives failed, he was apparently informed by Britain in early 1972 that if an election was won on a manifesto that promised independence, then such a request would be sympathetically considered.[15]

Despite this, his manifesto, issued just prior to polling in February 1972, made scant reference to any such possibility. Therefore, when he announced in October that he would seek independence without a referendum, protests erupted. Whereas the GNP and its allies, the Chamber of Commerce and the Employers' Federation, argued that Grenada's economy was too precarious to support independence, the NJM saw it as a means to promote national identity and higher standards of living, which had not been achieved under Gairy. However, it perceived his quest as 'an insecure opportunist move designed to strengthen the grip of tyranny and corruption'.[16] By mid-1973, strikes were widespread and petitions sent to London. All was in vain as, at the end of the Constitutional Conference in May, Britain made clear its acquiescence. A few months earlier, a study had been commissioned by the British Cabinet to assess, on a cost-benefit analysis, the options available to Britain for its remaining dependencies. It strongly recommended accelerated decolonisation. In any event, Britain was anxious to leave the Caribbean, its possessions being but a heritage of an almost forgotten history whose future defence could safely be left to the United States.

The disturbances in Grenada were met fiercely by Gairy who urged his police aides to 'cinderise' his opponents. His actions not only alarmed Grenadians but also considerably embarrassed other Commonwealth Caribbean governments, who realised that such behaviour unavoidably brought the whole area into disrepute. The NJM reacted quickly to the deteriorating situation. It led other opposition groups into an anti-government 'Committee of Twenty-two', but made clear its own progressive intentions with the publication of its manifesto, with 'We'll be Free in '73' as the slogan. The document's concluding words contained the warning that 'when a government ceases to serve the people and instead steals from and exploits the people at every turn, the people are entitled to dissolve it and replace it by any means necessary'.[17]

Following the success of its 'Independence Convention', the NJM called openly for Gairy's resignation. A general strike was threatened and scheduled to begin on 18 November 1973. This date subsequently became known in Grenada as 'Bloody Sunday', marking the fact that Bishop, Whiteman, Strachan and others were arrested and severely beaten in the Grenville police cells.[18] Some weeks later, Bishop's father, Rupert, was murdered and several other NJM supporters suffered the same fate. By Independence Day itself, 7 February 1974, the party's entire leadership was imprisoned. As one onlooker recalled, albeit with the benefit of hindsight,

> Shortly before midnight, we assembled on the battlements of Fort George, overlooking the harbour for the lowering of the Union Jack. On the roof before us stood an escort of British bluejackets . . . Under our feet, quite literally, sat the opposition: safely locked in their cells following the afternoon round-up. Gairy made a preposterous speech in which he declared, 'We are now completely free, liberated, independent. In spite of a wicked, malicious, obstructive, destructive minority of noise-making self-publicists. God has heard our prayers. God has been merciful. God has triumphed.' A British sailor sealed the occasion by blowing the last post before the navy marched away to the quayside. With huge sighs of relief . . . we, the British, had knowingly delivered Grenada into the hands of a lunatic.[19]

The Inevitable Coup

After independence, of course, Grenada was on its own with Gairy. Strong regional pressure forced the publication of the Duffus Report which catalogued the brutality of the Mongooses and some policemen during the protests and demonstrations, but little response was made by Gairy either in the way of reparation or reform. Indeed, further repression followed, Gairy now stressing anti-communism as justification for the persecution of the NJM. Opponents occasionally and mysteriously disappeared. As for the preservation of other basic freedoms, eleven categories of workers were subjected to a ban on industrial action during 1977 and 1978. By the beginning of 1979, less than 30 per cent of the workforce was unionised, the employers being able to exploit a variety of ordinances and laws relating to recognition of trade unions to prevent their effective operation. In accordance with domestic trends, Grenada's foreign policy also began to assume sinister proportions as arms deals were signed with General Pinochet of Chile.

For its part, the economy, already dangerously weakened by several years of mismanagement, never recovered from the independence crisis and stagnated for the rest of the decade. By 1979, more than 16,000 people — approximately 50 per cent of the island's workforce — were without jobs, and even this official rate of unemployment disguised a 69 per cent rate for women and a devastating 80 per cent for young people under 25 years of age.[20] The government's finances collapsed into chaos, the Treasury becoming virtually denuded of funds. The country's trade deficit rose to over EC$50 million thanks to a huge import bill and the national debt to some EC$60 million thanks to indiscriminate government borrowing. Capital aid flows and aid funds more or less dried up within a year of the winning of independence and, since population growth was not abated, *per capita* incomes fell in real terms by some 3 per cent per annum between 1974 and 1979. The prospect of starvation for many of the people was, in fact, only averted because of peasant subsistence agriculture.

This appalling economic record was manifested in the steady decline of the country's basic infrastructure in such areas as roads, water and electricity supply, telephones, housing and health. Piped water supplies in rural areas often broke down due to lack of maintenance, in some instances remaining unrepaired for up to five years; no sheets, pillow cases or medicines — even aspirins — were to be found in the hospitals. The infant mortality rate climbed to 29.5 per 1,000 live births. School buildings collapsed and were abandoned and school books became non-existent. Functional illiteracy rose to 40 per cent. As one of the NJM leaders later put, Grenada was in 'an unbelievable mess'.[21]

Against this background, the NJM sharpened its opposition by focusing upon a constant stream of anti-government issues. Its statements and analyses became steadily more socialist in content and Marxist in tone, particularly following the return to Grenada of Bernard Coard in September 1976 in time to fight the elections in December. But even then it was not primarily an anti-capitalist party, being concerned more to mobilise the population against Gairyism and to argue for an alternative form of government by and for the people. Part of this strategy was the decision to form a People's Alliance to fight the 1976 election. The NJM and the GNP had been joined in their opposition to Gairy by a section of the business community organised within the United People's Party (UPP). Originally founded in 1974 by Leslie Pierre, the UPP represented dissatisfaction both with the ineffectual GNP and with Gairy's 'onemanism'. Winston Whyte, a young and articulate businessman who had been one of the very few effective GULP ministers after his election and appointment in 1969, assumed its leadership soon after its emergence. He, Bishop and Blaize brought their parties together in a common cause by early 1976 and, despite alleged ballot-rigging, the People's Alliance won six of the 15 seats — three for the NJM (Bishop, named the official Leader of the Opposition, Coard and Whiteman), two for the GNP and one for Whyte. Although co-operation between the three parties ceased by mid-1977, due to the opposition of the GNP, and Whyte in particular, to what was perceived as 'NJM domination' and 'extremism', they continued to vote in a bloc in the House of Assembly and the Senate.

After this election, the first divisions also began to appear in the NJM. Two prominent NJM members, George Brizan, the architect of the People's Alliance manifesto, and Lloyd Noel were among those who voiced their opposition to the increasingly Marxist stance of the NJM's 'principled positions'. As a result, Noel was expelled from the Political Bureau. There were also rumours — never substantiated — that at least two assassinations of alleged opponents of Gairy attributed to the Mongooses were, in fact, the work of the NJM, which by 1978 had developed a clandestine wing. Notwithstanding these suspicions, grass-roots support became widespread as violence and job victimisation grew and the Mongoose gangs, under the leadership of Willie Bishop, cousin to Maurice, stepped up their activities. In February 1979, a strike of Barclays Bank employees was forcibly broken by them, leading more of the middle class to support the NJM and further isolating the Gairy regime in terms of popular support. The inevitable end was in sight.

Nevertheless, Gairy's belief in his mystical powers — he was 'appointed by God to lead Grenada' — was such that he travelled confidently to New York in mid-March to persuade United Nations Secretary-General Kurt Waldheim to create a UN agency to investigate cosmic phenomena, one of his long-standing interests. He had, however, come to realise that the power of the NJM had to be broken and so gave orders on his departure for the indefinite imprisonment of its leaders. The clandestine insurrectionist section of the party, the embryonic People's Revolutionary Army (PRA), was alerted once this information was received by a prison officer sympathetic to the New Jewel Movement. It was by this time quite clear that parliamentary democracy in a deeply corrupt political system could not defeat Gairy and that force was the only answer. Armed with weapons smuggled in from the United States in oil drums, 45 party members led by Hudson Austin, a corporal in Gairy's army who had first met Bishop in 1973 when a guard at the prison where Bishop was being detained, mounted a dawn attack on 13 March 1979 upon the army headquarters at True Blue. The 'green beasts', so named because of their Chilean uniforms, were overwhelmed. Twelve hours later, and with the help of many ordinary Grenadians, the island was completely in the hands of the NJM. Only two of Gairy's men lost their lives in the fighting, whilst another died in an accident. The newly promoted General Austin joined Bishop, Coard and other party leaders in proclaiming the formation of the Provisional (later renamed People's) Revolutionary Government. There were few in Grenada who did not greet the news with enthusiasm.

Notes and References

1. E. Gittens Knight, *The Grenada Handbook and Directory 1946* (Advocate Company, Bridgetown, 1946), p. 43.
2. *Grenada Employment Census* (Government of Grenada, St George's, mimeo, April 1982).
3. *West India Royal Commission, 1938-39, Report*, Cmnd. 6607 (HMSO, London, 1945), p. 373.
4. P. Emmanuel, *Crown Colony Politics in Grenada, 1917-1951* (Institute of Social and Economic Research, University of the West Indies, Cave Hill, Barbados, 1978), p. 184.
5. S. Rottenberg, 'Labour Relations in an Underdeveloped Economy', *Caribbean Quarterly*, vol. 4, no. 1 (1955), p. 54.
6. W.R. Jacobs and R.I. Jacobs, *Grenada: The Route to Revolution* (Casa de las Americas, Havana, 1980), p. 143.
7. G. Brizan, *The Nutmeg Industry: Grenada's Black Gold* (n.d.), cited in F. Ambursley, 'Grenada: The New Jewel Revolution' in F. Ambursley and R. Cohen (eds.), *Crisis in the Caribbean* (Heinemann, London, 1983), p. 196.
8. M.G. Smith, *Plural Society in the British West Indies* (University of the West Indies, Kingston, Jamaica, 1965), p. 290.
9. See A.W. Singham, *The Hero and the Crowd in a Colonial Polity* (Yale University Press, New Haven, 1968), p. 10.
10. *Report of the Commission of Enquiry into the Control of Public Expenditure in Grenada During 1961 and Subsequently*, Cmnd. 1735 (HMSO, London, 1962).
11. Quoted in C. Searle, *Grenada: The Struggle Against Destabilization* (Writers and Readers, London, 1983), p. 15.

12. Jacobs and Jacobs, *Grenada*, p. 76.
13. 'The Manifesto of the New Jewel Movement', reproduced in Institute of International Relations, University of the West Indies, *Independence for Grenada: Myth or Reality?* (Institute of International Relations, St Augustine, 1974), p. 154.
14. An interview with the *Intercontinental Press*, 17 December 1979, quoted in M. Bishop, *Forward Ever! Three Years of the Grenadian Revolution* (Pathfinder Press, Sydney, 1982), p. 21.
15. R.I. Jacobs, 'The Movement Towards Independence' in Institute of International Relations, *Independence for Grenada*, p. 22.
16. *The New Jewel* (Grenada), 18 May 1973.
17. 'Manifesto of the New Jewel Movement' in Institute of International Relations, *Independence for Grenada*, p. 156.
18. The bloodstained clothes which they were wearing were later displayed in the National Museum in St George's.
19. M. Hastings, 'Black Comedy in Grenada', *Spectator*, 29 October 1983.
20. Rita Joseph, 'The Significance of the Grenada Revolution to Women in Grenada', *Bulletin of Eastern Caribbean Affairs*, vol. 7, no. 1 (1981), p. 16.
21. C. Searle, 'Grenada's Revolution: An Interview with Bernard Coard', *Race and Class*, vol. 21, no. 2 (1979), p. 179.

2 THE PEOPLE'S REVOLUTIONARY GOVERNMENT: POLITICAL STRATEGIES AND DEVELOPMENT PRIORITIES

From its inception, the People's Revolutionary Government (PRG) rejected the model of government bequeathed to Grenada by Britain in 1974. It was not so much that it had been open to abuse, although that was bitterly recalled, or even that it was regarded as impractical for a numerically small population coexisting in a limited area, although that too was said. Rather, these factors were overshadowed by something which the NJM considered to be fundamental: namely, that it critically undermined any programme of meaningful development — social, political and cultural as well as economic — for and by the people.

The Struggle Against Dependency

By the indefinite suspension of the constitution, the NJM made clear to the world that the events of 13 March 1979 were designed to do much more than just replace a dictator in order to return to the forms of representative democracy drawn up for Grenada by Whitehall civil servants and lawyers. It was to be a continuing revolution, in thought as well as deed. In the view of the New Jewel Movement, the constitution held little meaning for Grenadians and was part and parcel of the dependency relationship which clearly existed between Grenada and the rich and powerful capitalist states, which were simultaneously the main source of its imports and the major market for its exports. This relationship accounted for Grenada's underdevelopment and amounted to imperialist exploitation. Bishop set out the party's thinking in these terms:

> We contend, comrades, that the real problem is not the question of smallness per se, but [that] of imperialism. The real problem that small countries like ours face is that on a day-by-day basis we come up against an international system that is organised and geared towards ensuring the continuing exploitation, domination and rape of our economies, our countries and our peoples. That, to us, is the fundamental problem.[1]

Pledged to contest vigorously both the cause and the effect of this relationship, the new government made popular mobilisation a high priority. In particular, the PRG was anxious to do what had never before been attempted in the Commonwealth Caribbean, let alone Grenada: to change deep-rooted prejudices and values planted by the slave experience and nourished by colonialism. In short, it planned nothing less than the creation of a new sense of Grenadian identity, patriotism and pride, for 'a people united will never be defeated'. To do this, every Grenadian was expected individually to identify with the revolution and be part of the decision-making process. The inherited 'independence' constitution positively prevented this; indeed, it conditioned the population to accept dependency as a normal state of affairs by cloaking it with a sense of legitimacy. In other words, the people experienced a form of 'false consciousness'. In such circumstances, the Westminster system appeared to be the only way in which political activity and thought could be conducted, with the consequence that any alternative designed by the people to suit themselves and their goals was automatically to be distrusted. The elimination of these highly restrictive modes of thought was thus central to the whole strategy of the revolution.

> The New Jewel Movement was born . . . as a reaction to and repudiation of old-style rum-and-corned beef politics, the politics of bribery and corruption . . . a process that consciously sought to divide the people into two warring camps, the 'ins' and the 'outs'. The Government can only mobilise half the people [for national development] with the other half being by definition completely opposed to it . . . So with these kinds of violent divisions, you can't get a small parish or community united, let alone a people nationally. Out of that context of political tribalism . . . the New Jewel Movement developed . . . Its most fundamental [principle] is that whatever the task that confronts us, whether political . . . economic . . . or . . . defence . . . the people must be involved.[2]

This challenge to psychological dependency was paralleled by a similar determination to combat economic dependency. It was recognised that it was impossible to control export prices and the costs of imported manufactures and food. Furthermore, the scope for moving the economy away from export crop production as the main source of foreign exchange earnings was clearly limited given Grenada's human and physical resources. The battle to restructure the economy was therefore conducted on two fronts. The first objective was to diversify. As Deputy Prime Minister and Finance Minister Bernard Coard stressed shortly after the *coup*,

> For us the most important aspect in building an economically independent country (which is the only way that you can truly say that you are politically independent) is the method of diversification — in all ways and in all respects. First, diversification of agricultural production, secondly, diversification of the markets that we sell these products to, thirdly, diversification of the sources of our tourism, the variety of countries from which our tourists come. The maximum of diversification, the minimum of reliance upon one country or a handful of countries means the greater your independence, the less able certain people are able to squeeze you, pressurise you and blackmail you.[3]

In line with this, food production was to be increased for both domestic and regional consumption. Efforts were also made to establish a small manufacturing sector. A building materials plant (the 'Sandino') was set up to supply the local construction industry, while new textile and processed food factories began to develop export markets.

The other thrust of the PRG's economic policy was to tackle some of the consequences of dependency. This had left a legacy of deprivation for the labouring classes, freeholders and wage-earners alike, which the PRG argued was perpetuated by the exploitative behaviour of the small pro-Gairy 'comprador bourgeoisie' of merchants and bankers who were substantially dependent upon North American and Western European interests. Curbing their activities and restricting their influence, albeit not to the point of opposition and persecution, went together with increased welfare expenditure in which great stress was put upon education, health, housing, road repair and other social services.

Since the development and evolution of dependency is ultimately shaped by external forces, they too had to be challenged. The existing international division of labour, created and maintained by the actions of the core or dominant economies, was thus identified and denounced by the PRG which rapidly came to the forefront of those articulating Third World demands for a 'new international economic order'. Consistent with this was a total commitment to the principles of the Non-Aligned Movement — quickly recognised by Grenada's election to the organisation's Co-ordinating Bureau in September 1979. As Bishop told the movement in his maiden address, 'the fundamental principles of the movement have had a most dramatic impact upon the development of our own revolution in Grenada'.[4] In particular, as he was later to indicate, it was essential that the sovereign rights of all states were respected:

> That small as we are, and poor as we are, as a people and as a country we insist on the fundamental principles of legal equality, mutual respect for sovereignty, non-interference in our internal affairs and the right to build our own process free from outside interference, free from bullying, free from the use or threat of force.[5]

In the view of the PRG, certain principles of foreign policy were logically derived from this firm position. First and foremost was the need to designate the Caribbean Sea and those states along its shores as a zone of peace. Such an act would give progressive forces in the region a measure of protection against US intervention. This was followed by demands for the recognition of the right of self-determination for all peoples in the region, particularly in the non-independent territories such as Puerto Rico; the acceptance of the principle of ideological pluralism and an end to propaganda and 'economic and violent' destabilisation; an end to the arming and financing of counter-revolutionaries and 'anti-progressive' regimes; respect for the sovereignty, legal equality and territorial integrity of all countries in the region; and freedom to join whatever international organisations or regional or sub-regional groups were deemed to be in the best interests of the people.[6]

Economic Achievements

Away from the glare of international publicity which quickly attached itself to the PRG's implementation of these foreign policy principles, the new regime embarked upon its programme of reconstruction and reform. Although it was made clear that the PRG would especially favour and encourage the growth of state enterprises — 'which would lead the development process'[7] — they had nevertheless to coexist alongside, and compete with, the private sector. By these means, it was believed that the inefficient government monopolies which plagued many socialist countries would be avoided. The same principle applied to the small co-operative sector. While the government would provide aid and encouragement, the economics of the market place were to be respected, except where the public interest was manifestly at stake. Consequently, there was little nationalisation. Management shortcomings prompted the take-over of the Electricity Corporation and Telephone Company. Hotels and nightclubs owned by Gairy and his Attorney General Derek Knight were sequestrated. The Canadian Imperial Bank of Commerce decided to cease operations and was taken over and renamed the National Commercial Bank. The Holiday Inn was also purchased but only after it had been badly damaged by fire and its owners had indicated a disinclination to rebuild.

With the above in mind, the PRG saw its duty as to provide efficient central planning machinery, impose selective import and price controls, and purchase certain commodities directly bypassing the merchants. For example, through the auspices of the Marketing and National Importing Board, Cuban cement was purchased at below cost price. Drugs and hospital supplies, fertilisers and powdered milk were similarly acquired from Cuba as well as from other sources, notably the United States, Britain and the EEC. These activities led to the relative decline of the private sector, and by 1981, according to the Chamber of Commerce, an absolute fall in its activities.[8] More importantly, private sector investment fell by over 25 per cent in 1981.[9] An alarmed Coard announced concessions and tax reductions for those companies, whether Grenadian or foreign owned, which invested in approved activities. Together with other incentives announced in 1979, they resulted in a 10 per cent rise in production in this sector by 1982 and a corresponding increase in company tax revenue. The National Development Bank lent to 191 private sector projects in 1981 (amounting to EC$740,000), rising to 238 in 1982 (EC$1.5 million), the bulk of which were linked to peasant agriculture.[10] By such methods the private sector was protected, if not nurtured, by the government. Coard justified this on the grounds that the private sector was a benefit, not a threat, to Grenada's economic and political development. The small size and limited resource endowment of the country meant that no multinational companies operated there and so, by and large, private sector investment and activity was indigenous, and the more acceptable to the government for that.

The considerable emphasis placed on agriculture by the PRG was deliberate. While the peasants were encouraged to diversify, idle land was taken over compulsorily on ten-year lease arrangements. An estimated 33 per cent of cultivable land was unused in 1979, and the Land Utilisation Act, one of the many 'People's Laws', released hundreds of acres. Some were allocated by the Land Reform Commission to the 23 state farms of the Grenada Farms Corporation, others to unemployed youths who wanted to become small farmers. Within four years, some 2,000 did so, while another 1,500 found work in the new industries, public works and construction. This made considerable inroads into unemployment: by early 1982 it had fallen to 14 per cent, mainly benefiting youth and women, and was estimated to be 10 per cent by late 1983. Overall, over 3,500 jobs were created over four years.

Food production also rose rapidly because of investment in new feeder roads and reform of the marketing system. Despite widespread hurricane damage, export earnings of fruit and vegetables rose dramatically: from 1981 to 1982 by 314.5 per cent, a rise in revenue from EC$1.5 million to EC$4.5 million. The result was that Trinidad and Tobago, the main food market, became second only to Britain as Grenada's best customer, taking 31 per cent of its products by value in 1982. Britain still took 36 per cent.[11] However, the PRG was concerned that, on both state farms and many private estates, the value of labour productivity was on average two or three times less than the wage. Reasons advanced to account for this phenomenon, common to many poor agricultural economies, were primitive technology, inadequate health and nutrition, low educational levels and 'very poor' organisation and management.

Success in agriculture was seen as essential to help feed the people, of whom there were on average 700 square mile, thereby making Grenada one of the most densely populated agricultural countries in the world. In terms of import substitutions, there was limited success: the percentage of food in the import bill fell from 30.6 per cent to 27.5 per cent between 1979 and 1982. Greater impact was made with the diversification programme. Whereas in 1979, 93 per cent of exports were traditional — bananas, cocoa and nutmeg — this sector accounted for only 63.4 per cent in 1982. This was partly due to the new industries. While the two agro-industrial plants were only in the early stages of production by October 1983, those relating to flour and wheat products, and clothing, marked up increases in income of 7.8 per cent and 10.6 per cent respectively from 1981 to 1982, or nearly EC$2 million and EC$6.6 million. The record of the National Fisheries Company, although equipped by Cuban boats, was by contrast very disappointing, meeting only 16 per cent of its 1982 production target.

Another setback was hurricane and flood damage. The disasters of August 1979 and January 1980 destroyed 27 per cent of the nutmegs, 40 per cent of banana production and 19 per cent of the cocoa crop, together worth US$27 million. Damage to feeder roads was also widespread. Since the traditional tree crops, except bananas, took longer to mature, the effect continued to be felt up to 1983. These problems were compounded by falls in world prices, notably for cocoa (15 per cent) and nutmeg (12.6 per cent). On average, export prices fell 13 per cent between 1980 and 1982, while prices of imports rose by 15 per cent. Banana production fell 12.2 per cent in 1982, from 11,384 tonnes to 9,996 tonnes; that for cocoa dropped 21.7 per cent, from 1,214 tonnes in 1981 to 951 tonnes. Nutmeg production increased, but one million lb were still left unsold in early 1983 despite increased exports.[12] Although a commitment was made to purchase some of this by the Soviet Union as part of a wide-ranging cultural and trade agreement signed in mid-1982, the deal was never finalised. As regards mace, the outer skin of the nutmeg, a production increase more than made up for a fall in price.

Overall, increased economic activity reversed the negative growth rate of the economy of the last years of the Gairy regime, for which the average was minus 3.2 per cent. The figure climbed to 2.1 per cent in 1979 and to 3 per cent for both 1980 and 1981, reaching 5.5 per cent in 1982. In terms of income *per capita*, the rise was from US$450 in 1978 to US$870 in 1983. In the last complete financial year of PRG rule, tax revenue was nearly 10 per cent higher than estimated (EC$67.6 million to EC$74.1 million). Taking inflation at 7 per cent into account − the lowest rate in all the Commonwealth Caribbean − real living standards rose 3 per cent. Only 3.7 per cent of export earnings, or 3 per cent of production, had to be allocated in debt servicing, reflecting the fact that Grenada had one of the lowest debt ratios in the world.[13] In short, it is not surprising that the World Bank should have given a glowing report on the economy in August 1982. It recognised Grenada's growth and commented favourably on its credit-worthiness and the impressive development of most sectors of the economy. It stressed the need for more exports and tourist arrivals to promote continued growth which, in turn, would attract 'additional concessional capital as well as private investment flows'. In this connection, it projected that, if the PRG's plans were largely fulfilled and world price levels for the traditional exports stabilised, 'the share of exports in Gross Domestic Product (GDP) would rise gradually from 38 percent in 1982 to about 47 percent in 1986, most of the improvement occurring in 1985 and 1986'.[14] Until then, Grenada's capacity to import would continue to depend largely on its ability to attract foreign savings.

Another testament to the regime's economic achievements was an equally favourable report from the International Monetary Fund (IMF). Despite strong US opposition, the IMF agreed to a stand-by loan of US$14.1 million in August 1983 and, in sharp contrast to its previous harsh treatment of other Commonwealth Caribbean countries, imposed no conditions except to say that it expected an 'improvement' in the foreign exchange position through increased exports and tourist receipts. It was the alleged inability of the PRG to do this that was at the core of US opposition to the loan. It pointed out that the 1982 import bill was $150.9 million, offset by only EC$50 million worth of exports, which had fallen by nearly 5 per cent in value since 1981. It also pointed out that tourist arrivals had fallen for the fourth successive year: 24,864 in 1982 compared to 32,101 in 1979, a drop of a quarter. Coard, in reply, made clear that although import and export prices were outside his government's control, the new airport would boost tourist earnings; also, arrivals in the first four months of 1983 had increased by over 40 per cent over the same period in 1982 — and those of Americans by 20 per cent — despite continuing US propaganda directed against the Grenadian tourist industry.[15] In fact, a visitor survey conducted by the Barbados-based Caribbean Tourism Research Centre in December 1982 showed that US visitors were still the largest contingent, at 27 per cent, followed by Canadians (19 per cent), British, Continental European and West Indian (15 per cent each) and others (9 per cent). But relatively few were on package holidays, there being a high proportion of vacationing Grenadian-born citizens of other countries and visitors who owned property on the island.[16]

Coard's trump card in the increasingly acrimonious exchanges with the US government on the issue of the loan was the ability of the PRG to undertake a capital expenditure programme totalling nearly EC$237 million over three years, nearly all of which was financed by soft loans and grants from the EEC, the UN Development Programme, OPEC and several other countries, notably France, Mexico and Venezuela. As Coard could proudly boast,

> This massive amount of investment achieved in only four years stands on its own as a remarkable achievement, and it completely overshadows the tiny amounts spent on capital projects during all of Gairy's 25-year dictatorship . . . [It] reflects the growing confidence which other Governments and International Organisations now have in our people and Revolution, and in the ability of the Government to manage the economy.[17]

It should not be forgotten either that this planning achievement and the associated skilful manipulation of monetary and fiscal levels in the economy took place using a currency, the Eastern Caribbean dollar (EC$), administered by a currency board, and used by seven other neighbouring territories. The PRG was in the forefront of those who pressed for the establishment of a common central bank to safeguard the international value of the currency and in July 1983 joined with the other Eastern Caribbean governments in signing an agreement to create such a body.

Social Advances

The PRG particularly welcomed the non-interference by the IMF in its social programmes and general pattern of public expenditure. Over 22 per cent and 14 per cent of the 1982-3 budget were allocated to education and health respectively, the highest proportions anywhere in the Commonwealth Caribbean; only 6 per cent was earmarked for defence, mainly, of course, as a consequence of the extensive provision of external military aid. By mid-1983, many Grenadians were studying abroad in institutions of higher education, a number of them in Cuba, and most enjoying free scholarships donated by the host countries. All the large outstanding debt accumulated by the Gairy regime to the University of the West Indies was paid off, thus enabling Grenadians to study there again.

Greater emphasis, however, was put upon the rebuilding of the school system, particularly at primary level. As most teachers were untrained, the National In-Service Teacher Education Programme (NISTEP) was launched in October 1980. Since it was impossible to finance an in-college full-time course for over 500 employed teachers, the programme centred upon tutors and 'teacher-partners', whereby experienced teachers were attached to a group of co-operating untrained colleagues to develop their skills for two days per week. Innovative as it was, Grenada's overall lack of resources and frequently inefficient administrative machinery at middle management level and below led to co-ordination problems. Tutors who had undergone a traditional training course also tended to be too academic in their approach and complaints of project relevance were often heard. None the less, standards were raised and recognition given to the importance of 'creole', as opposed to 'proper', English, children being taught in both versions.

When their teachers were away on the NISTEP scheme, pupils participated in the complementary Community Day School Programme (CDSP). This had two inter-related aims: first, to develop closer community-school relationships and, second, to introduce a work-study approach. Together, they emphasised the importance of practical education in agriculture, health, nutrition, arts and crafts and sports, utilising the skills of the local community who were expected to volunteer their help. As a specialist in education commented: 'Work-study is experience based and aims not only in helping pupils to find satisfaction in manual skills and technical knowledge but to acquire certain knowledge, values and behaviour patterns.'[18] The experience of similar models in other countries, particularly the People's Republic of China and Cuba, was extensively drawn upon. Once again, however, administrative inefficiency took its toll. Indifference and resistance to the programme, especially at local level, where little or no tradition of community involvement existed, sometimes undermined its overall effectiveness. Also, where it worked, it tended to continue the 'two-track' problem in schools. Because secondary education was – and continued to be under the PRG – open only to those who passed the entrance examination, slower pupils in many primary schools were allocated to gardening, woodwork and home economics lessons, while their brighter colleagues pursued more academic subjects. Under the CDSP, those schools – nearly all rural – who had the most untrained teachers became, in effect, 'half-work, half-study' establishments in sharp contrast to those better endowed. By 1983, concern about this was beginning to be expressed. However, those at secondary school enjoyed free education by 1981.

More successful – and very popular – was the Centre for Popular Education (CPE). Through its activities, hundreds of adults were made functionally literate and others broadened their education. It also had a definite political aim: to instil new values, attitudes and habits. Teaching materials, some based upon similar programmes in Cuba, traced the purpose and process of revolution in Grenada and elsewhere. Said Bishop,

> It is . . . going to have tremendous relevance to the success of building a deeper and greater sense of national unity, and raising the national consciousness . . . it will be much easier for them not to be misled . . . it will be so much easier for them to understand *Imperialism*. It will be much easier for them to understand what we mean when we talk of *de-stabilisation*, what we mean when we say that

the Revolution is for the people, and that the people *are* the Revolution.[19]

In short, 'work and study are part of the same dynamic, the same process, the same dialectic'. One letter of invitation to workers to a CPE seminar spelt out what it was concerned with.

> Why is our country poor? Are there no social classes in Grenada, and if there are classes, to which social class do the workers belong? Will there always be rich and poor? Why must we as workers try to produce more? When were our trade unions formed and for what reasons? Have there always been trade unions? And finally, how does our economy work? And much, much more.[20]

Political education classes then became compulsory for civil servants, as is commonplace in Guyana. Resistance was encountered whereupon the Minister for National Mobilisation, Selwyn Strachan, warned that non-attendance would be 'viewed most seriously' by the government.

Post-school youth programmes were many and varied. The National Youth Organisation, one of the mass organisations, and the Young Pioneers were responsible for much voluntary work, and sports competitions were a regular occurrence. Political and practical education were always featured. Many youths joined either the PRA or the Militia, became farmers or were employed in public works programmes. The 1982 report on the economy laid claim to the government's achievements in this respect with these words:

> Where are the youths who used to be seen in our wellknown limingspots, on walls and streetcorners all over the country during working hours? They are working on the Eastern Main Road in St. David's; they are building farm roads . . . putting up the new Telephone Company buildings . . . rebuilding the Careenage in St. George's.[21]

In the area of health, the emphasis was upon the preventative rather than the curative. This was realistic, given the extremely low resource base which existed at the time of the *coup*. This went hand in hand with administrative reorganisation, an end to corrupt practices, the recruitment of Cuban medical personnel — especially dentists, as there had been no government dental service for years — and the return to Grenada of several trained nationals who had left in search of opportunities overseas. To attract local doctors into the new system of public health and the community-based health centres — normally at Parish Council and village levels — private practice was permitted on the condition that doctors scheduled their public service clinics at the hospitals and health centres and their private practice at their private offices, a distinction not always observed in the past. Health and associated workers outside the wards concentrated upon health education, nutrition and family planning. Mobile teams in rural areas were soon a regular feature.

There was also assistance from the St George's University, a US offshore medical school which was established in 1978 with two campuses, one at True Blue and the other at Grand Anse. Set up for American students who were unsuccessful in their attempts to enrol in mainland US medical schools, the university not only encouraged its specialist clinical staff to advise their Grenadian counterparts but the students themselves spent some of their periods of practical training in hospitals both in St George's and in neighbouring St Vincent.

Health education and provision also played an important role in the improvement of the position of women. The Women's Desk in the Ministry of Education and Social Services gave a strong lead in the promotion of greater job opportunities for women, the dissemination of new skills, the removal of forms of discrimination and the establishment of pre-school and daycare centres. In particular, the problem of low-income young mothers with illegitimate children — a feature common to poor societies and, to an extent, a legacy of slavery where stable unions were discouraged — was tackled by these and other means. Not only were they given a second chance through education, but also cash benefits to help them with the cost of school uniforms and other expenses. Another very popular innovation designed to help women was maternity leave, introduced in October 1980. Applicable to all, it included domestic servants who form a relatively large and economically depressed sector of working women in Grenada. Less successful, however, was the implementation of a policy declaration on equal pay made in the immediate aftermath of the March 1979 *coup*. In agriculture, different types of work were traditionally undertaken by men and women and the equal pay proposal met with considerable resistance. Much time had to be spent by the Women's Desk to determine through consultation with women which types of work were of equal value.[22]

Another aspect of the involvement of women in the revolution was the work of the National Women's Organisation (NWO), led by Phyllis Coard, wife of Bernard Coard. One of the mass organisations, its work included education, both practical (for instance, sewing, first aid, cooking, childcare) and political, sport, culture, community development, the encouragement of women's co-operatives and defence. It also became critically important in the distribution of free dried milk — nearly 10,000 lb per month — and cooking oil to the needy, the provision of much-need material and other support for rural schools and the production of crafts and other goods at home.[23] By mid-1983 it had nearly 12,000 members.

The impact of the revolution upon culture was harder to judge inasmuch as calypso, a traditional form of expression, had for long been a political statement set to music both in Grenada and its original home of Trinidad. After the revolution this characteristic did perhaps become sharper with the lyrics of such calypsonians as 'The Mighty Survivor', 'The Flying Turkey', 'Lord Melody' and 'Explainer'. As 'The Flying Turkey' exclaimed,

> People want to hear you come out in defence of the Revolution, people want to hear you come out and rage hostility upon imperialism, rage hostility upon Reagan and American interventionist attitudes . . . 'The Lion' from Carriacou . . . he came out and he blaze imperialism! Or the fellow from Gouyave, 'Awful', and his 'No Dictator, No Way'![24]

What was significant, however, was the far greater access to, and participation in, forms of cultural expression such as poetry. The Minister of Health, Chris 'Kojo' de Riggs, was one of those foremost in this field, as was George Peters ('The Mighty Survivor') and Garvin Stuart, whose poems often appeared in the post-revolution paper, the *Free West Indian*.

A different form of social advance was trade union reform. Anti-worker ordinances were removed from the statute book and the Trade Union (Recognition) Act (People's Law no. 29, 1979) was passed in May 1979. Its principal architect was Vincent Noel whose struggle to force Barclays Bank to recognise the Bank and General Workers' Union in February 1979 helped set the scene for the consequent *coup*. Its critical provision was section 3(1), whereby if a union claimed that a majority of workers in a bargaining unit wanted it to be their bargaining agent, the Minister of Labour was obliged to organise a poll. If positive, and subject to appeal, the decision of the poll was final so far as the employer was concerned.[25] Not surprisingly, trade union membership rose from 30 per cent to 80 per cent of the workforce within six months of the *coup*. From the point of view of the revolution, this did, however, have some negative effects. From late 1980, substantial wage demands were made by the Public Workers' Union, the Grenada Union of Teachers and the Technical and Allied Workers' Union. A 90 per cent salary increase was demanded at first, but was then watered down to an 'irreducible minimum' of 37.5 per cent for 1981 and 25 per cent for 1982. The PRG replied that only 12 and 5 per cent respectively was available and, as virtually all the government's employees were involved, invited the union leaders to inspect the state accounts. The Public Workers' Union was particularly stubborn and its pressure eventually resulted in most of the claim being met by an angry Coard. He declared himself 'astonished' at the 'sheer selfishness and avarice' of 'privileged civil servants and state employees in comfortable jobs' who wanted 'to take money away from the peasants and the working class'. Others in the PRG made similar remarks. Although it helped restore spending power — there had been no salary increase since 1973 — it created a climate of distrust and disharmony between the party and civil servants which did little to encourage administrative efficiency and enthusiasm.

Finally, there were also opportunities to rebuild houses with National House Repair Programme grants. Supplemented by the work of voluntary labour, particularly in the aftermath of the hurricanes and floods of 1979 and 1980, over 2,000 houses were repaired during the four years of the revolution.

The International Airport

Of all the many economic and social development projects embarked upon by the PRG, the boldest and most visible was without doubt the building of a new international airport in Grenada. This was to be located at Point Salines in the south-west of the island. The idea of an airport situated in this area of relatively uninhabited and unproductive saltponds and bush was, in fact, first conceived in 1926. However, the physical problems involved in its construction led the British to construct cheaply an airstrip at Pearls, which opened in January 1943. This was progressively lengthened to a 5,250 ft (1,600 m) runway, but could not be expanded further due to the surrounding topography on three sides and the sea on the fourth. As well as making night flying impossible, the fact that its width was also restricted forced pilots to use a visual, rather than an instrument, approach, always assuming weather conditions permitted. The prevailing winds further made the construction of a 'crosswind' runway impossible, although flat land was available. Thus Pearls, its aged terminal building described as 'a squalid leftover from colonial days which looks for all the world like a Victorian railway station transported to the tropics',[26] could only accommodate Avro 748 turbo-prop aircraft carrying up to 48 passengers. All these many difficulties meant that many tourists wanting to visit Grenada had to overnight, at considerable expense, in Barbados; not surprisingly, many did not think it worthwhile. Even on landing at Pearls, which is situated on the north-east coast of Grenada some 16 miles from the capital and over 20 miles from the Grand Anse tourist area, access to the town and beach entailed negotiating a 2,000 ft mountain with innumerable hairpin bends. The extraordinary natural beauty and clean, empty beaches of Grenada made the journey worthwhile, but it is easy to see why the island was designated a 'highly desirable' but 'touristically disadvantaged' destination by the regional tourist authorities.

Something manifestly had to be done if tourism and its associated industries were to be fully developed in Grenada. The first serious survey of the Point Salines site was undertaken in 1955 when the British consultants, Scott, Wilson, Kirkpatrick and Partners, recommended the construction of a new airport there. This was followed by another positive recommendation by the former West Indies Federation in 1960. In 1966, a 'Tripartite Economic Commission', established by Britain, the United States and Canada to survey the development needs of the Commonwealth Leeward and Windward Islands, also supported the project. As a follow-up, the Canadian government undertook a further study and found the economic case proved. Finally, the original consultants were again commissioned by the British government: they reported favourably once more in January 1969. When, therefore, the World Bank recommended in 1976 yet another examination, Grenada's patience was understandably beginning to wear thin. As Coard was later to put it,

> There are many thousands of people who earn their livelihood in writing economic and technical feasibility studies continuously ever and ever into the future. It is an industry all by itself . . . I plan personally to write a study about the politics of construction of international airports in the Caribbean, and Grenada's will be a case study in imperialism.[27]

On coming to power in 1979, the PRG decided to press ahead on its own initiative and commence construction of what was by far the biggest project undertaken in Grenada's history. Although the NJM's original manifesto in 1973 had not favoured the building of a new airport — at the time it was a Gairy scheme — the party leadership later changed its mind. At a major co-financing conference at the EEC Commission in Brussels, Coard stressed that 'in many countries the critical factor at a particular historical moment is to identify the major bottleneck, the major fetter to further rapid economic development and growth of a particular country'.[28] In the case of the United States, it was the railroads that created 'the big push forward'; in Grenada's case, it was to be the Point Salines airport. New feasibility studies confirmed the conclusions of all the previous reports, and once Cuba had agreed to supply US$40 million worth of labour and machinery, work was able to start on the site in January 1980.

However, as the total project was costed at US$71 million, Grenada had to seek assistance elsewhere both for finance and specialist expertise. Since airline operators had moved to wide-bodied aircraft quicker than expected, it was decided to construct a 2,750 m runway (9,000 ft) in one complete phase. That was later extended to 3,000 m (9,800 ft), the length necessary to permit operation by fully loaded Boeing 747 aircraft including substantial lengths of unpaved safety areas at each end. Contracts were placed with the specialist Layne Dredging Company of Miami to fill in the salt ponds, Norwich Engineering of Fort Lauderdale, also in Florida, to design the fuel storage complex and a British company, Plessey, to supply and construct all radio and radar apparatus, landing lights and associated electrical equipment in the control tower, to specifications produced in Havana. A Finnish company was also involved in terminal building work. A cash-flow analysis was made, using only 'the most incredibly conservative and limited calculations', to show that the airport would generate enough income to enable a surplus to be made after five years of operation and to repay loans thereafter. It assumed that Grenada's share in total Caribbean tourism would move from 0.4 per cent (1981) to 1 per cent in 1990 and offered a low (5 per cent growth in tourism) and high (8 per cent) scenario. This affected forecasts for hotel rooms needed by 1990, necessitating an increase from 437 to 661. But, although it was admitted in 1981 that the 'very magnitude of the required expansion in hotel plant over the next ten years is at least as much or more than the investment in the airport itself',[29] it was pointed out that there already existed a 40 per cent excess capacity, that 'concrete

34 The People's Revolutionary Government

proposals' had been received from prospective hoteliers and that the infrastructure on that part of the island, near as it was to the existing Grand Anse beach area and St George's itself, would need little improvement.

There is, however, no doubt that the Point Salines project stretched Grenada's financial resources to their limit and perhaps beyond. Less money than had been hoped for was obtained from the EEC as a consequence of US and British opposition. A further US$4 million promised by Libya and Iraq did not, for the most part, materialise. France, Mexico and Canada could not be persuaded to supply aid directly for the airport, but did continue to include Grenada in their development programmes, thereby releasing other capital funds within the state sector for expenditure on the airport. Even so, the PRG was left to find a lot of money from its own resources. For example, the 1983 budget allowed for a capital expenditure of EC$15.6 million on the project, out of a total of EC$50.6 million that had to be found for the airport in that financial year.[30] The situation unavoidably created pressing cash-flow problems for the government and necessitated the establishment of progressively stricter expenditure control. For obvious political reasons, the PRG was anxious not to seek Soviet aid for Point Salines, although the growing desperation of its financial plight did lead eventually to the making of a request for EC$15 million, which was still under consideration in Moscow in October 1983. Clearly, the international airport was more seriously conceived than some of the grandiose 'prestige' projects which Third World governments have embarked on over the years. Yet its sheer scale *vis-à-vis* Grenada's own economic resources, combined with the hostile attention it generated, made it an enormously costly burden for the revolution to carry in its formative phase.

People's Power

Although valuable and praiseworthy, the PRG's rebuilding of the Grenadian economy after the devastation caused by Gairy, its provision of more extensive social services and even its daring scheme to build a new airport were all clearly reformist in political character. So where was the revolution? The answer was that it lay, above all, in the widespread challenge to psychological dependency. In the attempt to create a patriotic, politically aware and educated Grenada, great emphasis was put by the regime upon state mobilisation campaigns, rallies and solidarity celebrations. The PRG was declared to be 'a worker's government which has exactly the same wishes and goals as all militant and progressive trade unionists'. Production Committees were established, composed of management and union representatives, and planned for every workplace. Responsible for drafting, discussing and putting into action agreed work plans, and for monitoring management to prevent 'abuse of power', they were to be paralleled by Disciplinary, Education and Emulation Committees. The latter would agree production targets, 'devise and organise brotherly and sisterly competition' and give much publicity to the efforts of exemplary workers.[31] Although few were fully established by October 1983, the framework was in place. One problem was that many workplaces were small, often family operated, and not amenable to such organisation. Discussions had taken place within the Ministry of National Mobilisation on the possibility of establishing networks of committees over several such workplaces involved in similar work, but the practical difficulties were such that the plan was temporarily shelved. Supplementing the role of these committees in the meantime was the work of the mass organisations and that of the national literacy campaign, the CPE. The National Women's Organisation, the Young Pioneers, the National Students Council, the National Youth Organisation and the trade unions, all encouraged popular participation in development and promoted much voluntary work.

This revolution of attitudes was part and parcel of the structure of 'People's Power' which the NJM, and earlier, the MAP, had always argued was a prerequisite of the construction of a new Grenada. Bishop and his colleagues repeatedly denounced the 'superficial' democracy of the 'discredited' Westminster model. They argued that 'the type of democracy where people walk into a ballot box and vote for five seconds every five years is not real democracy at all'.[32] Further, it constituted a 'Tweedledum and Tweedledee situation' with 'two parties which were two sides of the same coin' simply replacing each other.[33] Bishop had nevertheless promised an early poll soon after the *coup*,[34] but subsequently rebuffed all assaults upon this 'principled position' by external critics who demanded elections for the sake of legitimacy. In one speech he said specifically:

> We want to say to Reagan here and now that the kind of democracy that he speaks of and the kind of democracy that he practises — we in Grenada are not in the least bit interested in that kind of democracy. A democracy that fires 10 million workers . . . which cuts

social benefits to the poorest people ... which closes down hospitals and schools ... which removes housing subsidies. That brand and version of democracy is not a democracy that we are interested in.[35]

Clearly not wishing to be seen to be responding to 'reactionary pressure, it was not until June 1983 that a five-person constitutional commission was appointed to produce a draft for popular discussion. Once amended and adopted by referendum, elections were to be organised, although no date was set. In the commission's few meetings, constitutions from a variety of countries were obtained and others requested, including that of the state of California. The one-party democracy of Tanzania attracted interest, but no formal move was made to endorse it.[36] What was desired was a formula whereby representation of all sectors of the population, particularly such influential minorities as the commercial elite and the professional classes, would be assured without deviating from three principles: democratic endorsement by the population as a whole, the vanguard position of the New Jewel Movement and democratic centralism.

The commission was especially anxious to study and exploit the post-1979 experience of 'participatory democracy' in Grenada itself. This was based upon two sets of interlinked institutions. The first was the Parish Councils, most of whose work was in late 1980 devolved to village-based Zonal Councils. Zonal Councils in each parish reported to the Parish Council, which became more of a co-ordinating link with the central government. The other was the mass organisations, including the trade unions and the Militia. The activities of both were linked through Village Co-ordinating Bureaus. Further linkage was achieved at the grassroots level by encouraging multiple membership by activists and, at the highest level, via the NJM Central Committee once it was established six months after the *coup*.

As first constituted, Parish Councils enabled local people to discuss policy with, and question, the PRG leadership, civil servants and heads of state enterprises and so permitted their views to be known on both local and national issues. In pre-revolutionary days, they were NJM local parish branches, but as the revolution began to be consolidated after the first few weeks, they were opened up to all Grenadians. The Zonal Councils were formed because of the popularity of the Parish Councils and the widespread demand for more local institutions: they fulfilled the same role as the Parish Councils, but on a smaller scale.

Each Village Co-ordinating Bureau interacted with the local NJM party organisation and support groups, passing on opinions and resolutions. Issues of importance were made known to the national party directly, which was led, as indicated, by a 14-person Central Committee, directed theoretically by the Political Bureau in accordance with the model of the Communist Party of the Soviet Union. Most of the members of the committee were also in the government, six being in the seven-person Cabinet. In the early days of the NJM, there were only eight committee members, the increase being necessary as the mass organisations grew. In accordance with party policy, only 14 of the 23-person government were full NJM members. This was to take advantage of available expertise and commitment, and signified an expression of the broad base of the revolution. Only one, the Attorney-General, Lloyd Noel, was subsequently dismissed because of his 'reactionary attitude'. Even then, as late as 1983, two senior ministers, businessmen Norris Bain and Lyden Ramdhanny, were not members of the party.

The Parish and Zonal Council structure was paralleled and complemented by the activities of the mass organisations. Covering the state as a whole, they enabled thousands to be involved in discussions on policy. Although primarily organised at village level, regular national mass meetings were held, attended by delegates. Occasionally, all the organisations came together with Parish and Zonal Council delegates in a National Conference of Delegates to debate a particular issue, such as the budget and the PRG's annual financial assessment of all the sectors and activities that made up the national economy. To the *Free West Indian*, such 'ongoing participation by the people' ensured a 'deep grasp' of what 'imperialism is in concrete terms'. Mobilisation on that scale was designed to prepare them 'for the broader objectives of building socialism'.[37] As a contemporary commentary put it,

> Today in Grenada, Parliament has moved out of town into the communities. Government has escaped . . . and spread into community centres, school buildings, street corners, market places, factories, farms and workplaces around the country. Political power has been taken out of the hands of a few privileged people and turned over to thousands of men, women and youth . . . in every nook and cranny of Grenada, Carriacou and Petit Martinique.[38]

In just the same way, popular participation in national defence was also seen as essential. Indeed, it was named as the second of the 'three pillars of the revolution', People's Power being the first and economic reconstruction the third. At a solidarity rally, Coard made its central role clear.

> A Revolution which has the support of the people but which cannot defend itself very soon would be no revolution at all ... Having the people but not having the material means for the people to defend themselves is a lesson we have to learn from [Allende's] Chile, Jamaica and other countries. But having the material means and not having the people is what Pinochet and Duvalier are all about. Therefore comrades, the people and the material means to defend the people are indispensable and interconnected in the process of the Revolution. That is why the question of arming of all our people, the involvement of all our people in the People's Militia, is of such fundamental importance.[39]

Militia manoeuvres became a common sight, giving the impression to some outsiders of a nation under arms, trained and equipped to take the struggle beyond Grenada's shores. While this was totally erroneous, it is true that the Militia was a popular and voluntary commitment and produced a situation where Grenada had a higher proportion of people in relation to population capable of using arms than any other country in the region, except Cuba. This vigilance against 'the provocations of imperialism' was colourfully praised by Strachan at the same rally.

> This voluntary people's militia, where our people are picking up guns every week to prepare to defend the benefits brought to them by people's revolutionary democracy shows their ultimate commitment to our process. For this same democracy, comrades, such as we are ... creating here in Grenada, is the greatest threat to the bogus, artificial and hypocritical lie of democracy that imperialism suspends over the world to cover up the revulsion and shame of its bloodsoaked crimes.[40]

Notwithstanding this framework, it was, however, clear that the fulcrum of power lay unambiguously with the Central Committee. Party policy was at best only marginally amended by these nascent institutions whose main purpose was more to mobilise support for development objectives, educate the masses politically, disseminate information and help defend the revolution. What emerged was a democratic centralist structure with the party in the centre, decisions being easily transmitted to, and between, the various levels. It may well have been the case that, if traditional parliamentary elections had been called soon after the *coup*, the NJM would have won virtually everywhere and thus acquired a cloak of legitimacy which ordinary Grenadians would have understood and critics and detractors abroad would not have been able to challenge. But this would then have gone against the principle of 'People's Power'. Prolonged delay in establishing the constitutional commission — 'the masses have far more important things to do, like providing enough food and shelter for everybody, to be detracted and divided by elections', said one PRG minister[41] — served only to exacerbate the sore. Another problem was the increasing need for security as external pressures upon the government mounted, including an attempted assassination of the leadership in June 1980. Bodyguards always surrounded Cabinet members when in public; they travelled in fast cars with much weaponry in evidence and their public appearances after 1981 became rarer, partly due also to pressure of work. Nevertheless, these and other measures recommended by security experts from the German Democratic Republic, tended over time to remove the image of informality which previously characterised meetings between the leadership and the public.

Revolutionary Manners

The PRG's deepening obsession with security, verging at times on the paranoid, undoubtedly led to the application of 'heavy manners' against those deemed to be against the regime. Notwithstanding the genuine commitment to People's Power, opposition came more and more to be perceived as a form of destabilisation which could be, and very occasionally was, traced back to the United States and the CIA, 'the fountainhead of lies and imperialist intrigue'.[42] Although there were no dramatic acts of revolution as experienced in some other Third World countries — no widespread collectivisation of private property or assets, no executions or forced labour — there was preventive detention without trial. During the period of NJM rule, over 3,000 people were questioned and about a tenth of these were imprisoned, the great majority only for a matter of hours or, at most days.[43] Some 100 'counter-revolutionary' political prisoners, including Winston Whyte, were in Richmond Hill prison at the time of their release on 26 October 1983; a year earlier, there had been over 120, many having been incarcerated for two years or more. A special block with very small cells – eight feet by four – was constructed and they were subject to a 'vigorous' regime. Although beatings undoubtedly took place, it was not systematic and, in the words of one ex-detainee, was 'largely the result of poor discipline and the fear many of the PRA and Militia guards had for their superiors who were over enthusiastic political sadists'.[44] Other 'security risks' were kept imprisoned by the serving of detention orders when their sentences were officially completed. More unfortunate were those such as the well-known journalist, Alister Hughes, who suffered only house arrest, temporary confiscation of property and general harassment. All detention orders were signed by Bishop in his capacity as Minister for Internal Affairs.

From the time of the *coup* strict direction was also exercised over Radio Free Grenada, access by non-NJM organisations being tightly restricted. It was responsible to Bishop for most of the PRG rule, although Phyllis Coard exercised considerable influence. The printed media took longer to control. The process was begun when in late 1979 *The Torchlight*, hitherto Grenada's main newspaper, was closed down. Owned by the Trinidad *Express*, it was consistently anti-socialist and anti-Cuban. From the regime's point of view, the final straw came when it published photographs of Bishop's security personnel and details, with maps, of all security installations, and reproduced a *Daily Gleaner* cartoon depicting Castro 'fishing' for Grenada. By 1980 the open sale of Trinidadian newspapers had also ceased although, ironically, both *Time* and *Newsweek* and the London *Times* and *Guardian* continued to be available throughout. Later in 1981, an attempt by Leslie Pierre to publish another newspaper independent of the NJM, *The Grenadian Voice*, was cut short after one issue. The 'Group of 26' who sponsored it – which included Lloyd Noel and Alister Hughes – were labelled 'the foot soldiers and parasites of imperialism' and CIA agents. While no evidence was offered by the government to support this charge, there were many who believed it, since the paper appeared to have enough capital to distribute thousands of free copies to Grenadian communities overseas. Both Pierre and Noel were condemned to indefinite preventive detention.

Thus by the end of 1981, the *Free West Indian* was the only newspaper permitted, apart from socialist papers catering, for example, for the PRA and the National Women's Organisation. To the PRG, this freed Grenada from exploitative 'hypocrites' whose actions had destroyed any notion that a 'free' press existed. To others, it revealed a disturbing feature of the Grenadian revolution – one of the paradoxes, in fact, of the whole era. Here was a government with considerable economic and social achievements to its credit, which enjoyed genuine popularity in the country, behaving more and more illiberally out of an apparently growing sense of insecurity. The common theme that recurs in all PRG defences of its actions in this regard is the CIA and its fear that the destabilisation of the revolution was being deliberately masterminded in Washington. It is now necessary, therefore, to shift the focus of analysis from the internal workings of the PRG to a direct consideration of United States policy towards Grenada and the countries of the Caribbean basin in general.

Notes and References

1. M. Bishop, 'Imperialism is the Real Problem', 13 July 1981 in M. Bishop, *Selected Speeches, 1979-1981* (Casa de las Americas, Havana, 1982), p. 190.
2. B. Coard, quoted in *To Construct from Morning: Making the People's Budget in Grenada* (Fedon Publishers, St George's, 1982), p. 150.
3. B. Coard, quoted in C. Searle, 'Grenada's Revolution: An Interview with Bernard Coard', *Race and Class*, vol. 21, no. 2 (1979), p. 179.
4. M. Bishop, 'Imperialism is not Invincible', 6 September 1979 in *Selected Speeches*, p. 47.
5. M. Bishop, 'Forward Ever Against Imperialism and Towards Genuine National Independence and Peoples Power', 13 March 1980 in ibid., p. 118.
6. For an elaboration of these principles, see U. Whiteman, 'Birth of a New Foreign Policy' in *Grenada is Not Alone* (Fedon Publishers, St George's, 1982), pp. 105-24.
7. *Report on the National Economy for 1981 and the Prospects for 1982*, Presented by Bro. Bernard Coard (Government Printing Office, St George's, mimeo, 1982), p. 64.
8. Grenada Chamber of Commerce, *Annual Report 1982* (St George's, mimeo, 1982).
9. *Report on the National Economy for 1981*, p. 9.
10. *Report on the National Economy for 1982 and the Budget-Plan for 1983 and Beyond*. Presented to the National Conference of Delegates of Mass Organisations, Thursday, 24 February 1983 (People's Revolutionary Government, St George's, 1983), p. 31.
11. Ibid., p. 29.
12. Ibid., pp. 24-8.
13. Ibid., p. 16.
14. Quoted in *Caribbean Insight*, November 1982.
15. *Washington Post*, 21 September 1983.
16. Caribbean Tourism Research Centre, *Grenada Visitor Survey: Summary* (Barbados, mimeo, 1983).
17. *Report on the National Economy for 1982*, pp. 16-17.
18. C.A. Glean, 'Reaching Beyond the Grasp: A Revolutionary Approach to Education', *Bulletin of Eastern Caribbean Affairs*, vol. 7, no. 1 (1981), p. 10.
19. M. Bishop, 'Education is a Must', 30 October 1980, in M. Bishop and C. Searle, *Education is a Must* (Education Committee of the British Grenadian Friendship Society, London, 1981), p. 39. Bishop's emphasis.
20. Quoted in C. Searle, *Grenada: The Struggle Against Destabilization* (Writers and Readers, London, 1983), p. 83.
21. *Report on the National Economy for 1982*, p. 6.

22. Rita Joseph, 'The Significance of the Grenada Revolution to Women in Grenada', *Bulletin of Eastern Caribbean Affairs*, vol. 7, no. 1 (1981), p. 19.
23. *National Women's Organisation Work-Plan for 1982* (St George's, mimeo, 15 November 1981).
24. C. Searle, 'The People's Commentator: Calypso and the Grenada Revolution', *Race and Class*, vol. 25, no. 1 (1983), p. 58.
25. L. Smith, 'Compulsory Recognition of Trade Unions in Grenada: A Critique of the Trade Unions (Recognition) Act 1979', *Bulletin of Eastern Caribbean Affairs*, vol. 5, no. 3 (1979), p. 39.
26. *Daily Telegraph*, 26 October 1983.
27. *Proceedings of Aid Donors Meeting held in Brussels at ACP House on 14 and 15 April 1981: International Airport Project – Grenada* (Embassy of Grenada, Brussels, mimeo), pp. 19-20.
28. Ibid., p. 41.
29. Ibid., p. 34.
30. *Report on the National Economy for 1982*, p. 156.
31. *To Construct From Morning*, p. 30.
32. Interview with M. Bishop in *Advocate-News*, 14 March 1981.
33. B. Coard, quoted in C. Searle, 'Grenada's Revolution', *Race and Class*, p. 174.
34. *Caribbean Contact*, May 1979.
35. M. Bishop, April 1982, quoted in M. Bishop, *Forward Ever! Three Years of the Grenadian Revolution* (Pathfinder Press, Sydney, 1982), pp. 25-6.
36. Information from interview with PRG Attorney-General Richard Hart, member of the commission, June 1983.
37. *Free West Indian*, 13 March 1981.
38. *Is Freedom We Making! The New Democracy in Grenada* (People's Revolutionary Government, Grenada, 1982), p. 22.
39. B. Coard, 'National Reconstruction and Development in the Grenadian Revolutionary Process', November 1981, in *Grenada is Not Alone*, pp. 27-8.
40. Quoted in ibid., p. 92.
41. G. Louison, quoted in *Daily Gleaner*, 28 May 1981.
42. C. Searle, *Grenada: The Struggle Against Destabilization*, p. 79.
43. Information from interview, K. Radix, November 1983.
44. Information from interview, L. Pierre, November 1983.

3 UNITED STATES POLICY TOWARDS THE CARIBBEAN BASIN

Throughout the twentieth century the policy of the United States in the Caribbean basin has been distinguished from its policy towards Latin America by the readiness, willingness and ability of the United States to intervene militarily, both overtly and covertly, in support of its interests. In the period from the Roosevelt Corollary of 1904, which announced the unilateral assumption by the United States of an 'international police power' in the Western Hemisphere to the projection of the 'Good Neighbour Policy' in 1934, US troops occupied or intervened openly in Cuba, Honduras, Panama, Haiti, Nicaragua and the Dominican Republic, as well as confirming the acquisition of Puerto Rico as a colony in all but name. During the Second World War US military power in the region was expanded considerably with the negotiation of 99-year leases from Britain for military bases in the Bahamas, Jamaica, St Lucia, Trinidad, Antigua and British Guiana, thereby confirming what was already well understood, the relative inability of Britain to defend adequately this portion of its empire. Beginning in 1954 with the adoption at the Tenth Inter-American Conference in Caracas of a resolution affirming the incompatibility of communism with the Inter-American system, an active policy of intervention was renewed, directed against Guatemala in that year, Cuba in 1961 and the Dominican Republic in 1965. Where designated, 'appropriate' policies of destabilisation, which are akin to intervention in their intent but distinguished from it by their primary reliance on local as against external forces to bring about desired ends, were fashioned, as in the case of the British Guiana 1962-4; Jamaica 1975-6; and Nicaragua and Grenada, alongside military interventionist strategies, at various times from 1979 onwards. Thus a direct and active concern with the Caribbean basin is a demonstrable facet of US foreign policy and has given rise to a corresponding image of the region in the consciousness of US decision-makers. This is expressed not in the 'if' of intervention but, as one former senior foreign policy adviser on Caribbean affairs in the State Department has candidly put it, the 'when and how'.[1]

The 'legitimacy' of such an interpretation of the Caribbean basin derives from a perception of the region as 'vital' to US national interests. The mix of various factors which at any one moment make up this constellation of interest will, of course, vary over time, though due emphasis has always been given to security and economic interests as the major and over-riding considerations. With respect to security the interest derives from geographical proximity. In recent years two major aspects have been emphasised by US officials as giving grounds for concern. The first is intimately related to the global military balance with the Soviet Union and focuses on the development of a US anti-submarine warfare capability to limit the deployment of Soviet naval forces in the Caribbean. This is done either directly, as in 1970 when Kissinger by diplomatic means prevented the construction of a putative nuclear submarine base in Cuba, or indirectly by ensuring the effective detection of Soviet submarines in the Caribbean through the operation of an underseas surveillance system (SOSUS) which in turn involves maintaining a number of US bases on Caribbean islands, notably in the Bahamas. The second focuses on the region as a maritime route for strategic and raw materials either trans-shipped through the Panama Canal or derived from within the region itself. Of these, the most important is oil. Venezuela and Mexico possess considerable proven oil reserves whilst throughout the Caribbean significant off-shore fields of oil and gas have been discovered and are being brought on-stream. As important is the Caribbean's status as an oil refining zone for crude brought from the Middle East and Africa. Some 40 to 50 per cent of the United States' oil requirements are met from external sources of which about 22 per cent is refined abroad, the greater part in Caribbean ports. In 1979, for example, of the 1,858,000 barrels per day of refined oil entering the US, no less than 1,032,900 had been refined in the Caribbean, principally in the Bahamas, the Netherlands Antilles, Puerto Rico, Trinidad and Tobago and the Virgin Islands.[2] The bauxite industry located in Jamaica, Guyana, Haiti, Suriname and the Dominican Republic has also in the recent past been of strategic importance to the US, both in terms of the volume of the mineral supplied (98 per cent of US imports in 1971) and the use to which it has been put (the provision of aluminium for the US aircraft industry).

Economic interests turn on US direct investment and the migration-tourist nexus. With respect to the first, the trend since 1945 has been for US transnational corporations to become involved in virtually every sector of the Caribbean and Central American economies. Traditional interests in export agriculture (sugar and bananas) and mining (petroleum and bauxite) have been supplemented by developments in banking, insurance, transport, construction, manufacturing and tourism. In 1980 total US direct investment in developing Western hemisphere countries stood at US $38.3 billion, of which nearly 25 per cent was located in the Central American and Caribbean region.[3] The income deriving from such investment is almost impossible to calculate. Evidence from selected countries shows it to be considerable, with investment income outflows consistently above private capital inflows, thereby reinforcing simultaneously both the dependence of the countries concerned on the US and the US balance of payments surplus. The migration-tourist nexus refers to the very considerable flow of people between the region and the United States in recent years. Hundreds of thousands of American citizens live, work and vacation in the region and even higher numbers of Caribbean and Central American people seek to visit or emigrate, legally or illegally, to the United States. Together they constitute a 'people interest'[4] which provides substantial economic benefit to the US through a variety of mechanisms, principally 'leakages' associated with high import content tourism and the provision of a ready supply of cheap labour and professional and skilled workers. Further, and just as importantly, Caribbean people, particularly via the Cuban refugee connection, constitute a vociferous and critical lobby within the US to which governments might not always defer but equally cannot electorally ignore.

While 'vital' security and economic interests provide a tangible basis for distinctive US policies within the region, they are nevertheless conducted within the wider framework of inter-American policy as a whole. Over the last 25 years this has undergone several transformations as various US administrations have reacted with higher or lower policy profiles towards Latin America according to the nature of the 'threat' perceived. Thus beginning in the very last years of the Eisenhower administration, extending throughout the Kennedy administration and into the early years of the Johnson administration, Latin America was given a high priority and specific policies fashioned accordingly, notably the Alliance for Progress intended to realise 'economic development' alongside 'security assistance' programmes to defeat insurgency. Following the invasion of the Dominican Republic in 1965 and its immediate aftermath, which ended this 'activist' phase, the US lowered its profile towards Latin America so that under the Nixon and Ford-Kissinger administrations concern was limited to specific 'crises', i.e. Chile 1970-3 and Jamaica 1975-6, rather than expressed in policy development as a whole. Indeed, so low was the profile that a former US ambassador to the Dominican Republic has described it in its Caribbean dimension as 'basically a policy of neglect' during which 'the Caribbean ceased to look to us for leadership' and instead 'looked to itself and to the Third World'.[5] Carter, on assuming office, sought to change this. Policy towards Latin America was upgraded and attempts were made to fashion specific Caribbean and Central American policies in which liberal principles would be paramount. It recalled the early Kennedy years and, just as then, quickly suffered an erosion and change of emphasis as 'vital interests' dictated a shift from economic development to military containment within the region.

The Carter Administration

The renewed interest of the US government in Caribbean basin affairs emerged forcefully in the first year of the Carter administration. In a series of initiatives in respect of Cuba, Jamaica, negotiation of the Panama Canal treaties, human rights in Central America and the promotion of collaborative economic development in the Caribbean, the administration demonstrated that it was prepared to consider, and to some degree support, changes in the region. It was also prepared to promote, in a move which certainly was novel, the development of two separate approaches to the region in conformity with a distinction between Central America and its problems on the one hand and the Caribbean islands on the other. This 'divorce' permitted political issues to come more to the fore with the attendant belief that political responses were the most practical immediate solutions to problems. In the context of the Caribbean this was manifest, above all, in the evolution of a policy identifying five principles governing US relations with the area. As set out by Philip Habib, a senior adviser on Caribbean affairs to the US Secretary of State, these were: (1) significant support for economic development; (2) firm commitment to democratic practices and human rights; (3) clear acceptance of ideological pluralism; (4) unequivocal respect for national sovereignty; and (5) strong encouragement of regional co-operation and of an active Caribbean role in world affairs.[6] Taken together, these commitments represented a considerable advance on previous US policies and, as such, were welcomed by many if not all political leaders in the region as consonant with their interests, the major exception being Dr Williams of Trinidad who spurned the leadership of the region eagerly proffered to him by Cyrus Vance, Carter's Secretary of State. In general, themes of concordance and interdependence rapidly rose to prominence in Caribbean-US affairs, finding their quintessential expression in the various Miami

Caribbean Conferences. With their feelings of goodwill and mutual understanding all round, they created for a while the shared belief that through increasing US economic assistance to the region — in 1979 nearly double that of 1976 — development for all might be realised.

At the same time as the US government marked a departure in one area, however, it was driven to affirm a consistency of policy in another. Towards Central America initiatives ran into difficulties, particularly in respect of Nicaragua and El Salvador. In the former case, for example, the attempts from 1977 to 1979 to effect the removal of the dictator Somoza, without in any way giving political credence to the principal insurgent forces ranged against him in the *Frente Sandinista de Liberacion Nacional* (FSLN), failed utterly when it was precisely these forces that eventually triumphed in July 1979. Bereft of influence as a consequence, the administration nevertheless repeated the mistake in El Salvador during the remainder of Carter's term, except that in this latter instance it was a government of the right rather than the left which finally emerged. It was apparent that the double combination of persuasion and cajolery to contain military power and open the political process to the 'middle ground' had again failed to sustain US interests as the initiative for change passed emphatically to the insurgent forces grouped together in the Democratic Revolutionary Front (FDR) and the Farabundo Marti Liberation Front (FMLN). Faced with such political failures, the over-riding imperatives of the security and economic dimensions of US policy asserted themselves more forcefully, becoming in turn the subject of vociferous criticism within the Carter administration in the final part of 1980. In a 'Dissent Paper' leaked in November, the argument for a change in policy towards support for the popular opposition forces in El Salvador was strongly stated. It also noted, prophetically:

> Misleading rationalisations of our policies have played upon domestic frustrations resulting from perceived setbacks in other theatres, and have legitimised grossly inadequate arguments in favour of military intervention. Our actions and our words have narrowed down our policy options to a single path of gradual escalation of direct military involvement in a region vital to our national interests and within a political context that gives the use of force few chances to achieve a satisfactory outcome.[7]

Carter and Cuba

Carter had also initially sought to apply his more liberal approach to Caribbean and Central American affairs to the vexed question of Cuba's place in the region. In December 1977, however, Castro committed Cuban personnel to the defence of Ethiopia. This ended definitively the hopes of the Carter administration for a linkage between Cuban withdrawal from Africa and a further relaxation of the US embargo on Cuba, as well as halting, at the official level, the new policy of *rapprochement* between the two countries. Nothing of substance transpired throughout 1978, but in 1979 the familiar pattern of hostility was renewed with Carter's 'discovery' of a 'combat brigade' of Soviet troops in Cuba. To this charge Castro reacted vigorously, accusing Carter of 'fabricating' a crisis for his own ends since all US presidents from Kennedy on had known of the existence of Soviet forces in Cuba, which had not changed 'in number, nature, or functions since 1962'.[8] Carter remained unmoved. In a nationally televised speech on 1 October he announced steps by his administration to 'neutralise' the presence of the Soviet troops. These included the establishment of a new Caribbean Joint Task Force Headquarters in Key West, Florida; the expansion of US naval exercises and forces in the Caribbean; and the stepping up of air and electronic surveillance of Cuba. He also emphasised and reaffirmed the charge that Cuba was in Africa as a proxy of the Soviet Union, utilising this as part of a general diplomatic offensive designed once more to isolate Cuba within the Western hemisphere. The culmination of this trend was the staging of military exercises under the code-name 'Operation Solid Shield' in May 1980. Led by the new Task Force it involved more than 20,000 men, 42 naval vessels and some 350 planes and was decisive in shifting the focus of military training from the eastern Atlantic, where it had previously been confined, to the Caribbean region. The head of the Task Force, Rear-Admiral McKenzie, is reliably reported at the end of the year as stating the following about his mission:

> My people aren't meant to fight the 3,000 man Russian brigade or the Cubans, but we're meant to control the force that will fight them. That's the purpose of this headquarters, to have forces assigned to us in the event of a contingency or an emergency in this part of the world . . . I've heard rumours that it was conceived because of political motivations, but whatever brought about this task force, when Mr. Carter established it, he fulfilled a longstanding

extremely valid military requirement to have a group of people focus in on the Caribbean ... We've left a rotten apple in the middle of the Caribbean basin down here, and that rotten apple is Fidel Castro.[9]

Carter and Grenada

Unfortunately for the NJM, its seizure of power in Grenada coincided with the shift of emphasis within the Carter administration away from policies favouring limited change and towards those supportive of the *status quo* in the Caribbean basin. A negative rather than positive reaction towards the revolution thus quickly emerged and was expressed in policies best summed up as 'denial and destabilisation', with an emphasis on the latter as the key technique employed by the US government to effect change.

The policy of denial by the US government was principally one of diplomatic action to limit initiatives and create difficulties for the PRG as and when appropriate. Its first and immediate manifestation was in the note handed to Bishop by the US ambassador to Barbados and the Eastern Caribbean, Frank Ortiz, only three weeks after the NJM took power. It stated:

> Although my government recognises your concerns over allegations of a possible counter-coup, it also believes it would not be in Grenada's best interests to seek assistance from a country such as Cuba to forestall such an attack. We would view with displeasure any tendency on the part of Grenada to develop closer ties with Cuba.

This drew from Bishop a stinging rebuke — 'No country has the right to tell us what to do or how to run our country, or who to be friendly with' — and the now famous phrase — 'We are not in anybody's backyard, and we are definitely not for sale'.[10] Shortly afterwards the whole episode was to be repeated, this time with the new US ambassador, Sally Shelton. In one of her first public statements on taking office she noted 'evidence' of a 'firm Cuban military presence in Grenada' and expressed the US government's 'concern'.[11] The response of the PRG was to ask her to delay presenting her credentials for nearly seven weeks, a move to which the US retaliated by pointedly excluding Grenada from a fact-finding tour of the Caribbean undertaken by Habib in August 1979. This also heralded action by the US to concert its allies to contain the political impact of the Grenadian example. In October Habib travelled to London to discuss US–British policy towards the Caribbean around which, if subsequent actions are anything to go by, substantial agreement must have been reached. In January 1980 Britain announced it would not sell two armoured cars to the Grenadian government as requested and, more significantly in the long run, began to co-operate with the United States to enhance military capability in the Eastern Caribbean among states known to be politically hostile to Grenada, notably Barbados.

The pattern of denial set by the end of 1979 continued throughout 1980. At the bilateral level relations between the US and the Grenadian government remained distant with no attempt being made on the US side to improve matters. Noteworthy in this respect was the refusal of the US government to recognise Dessima Williams, Grenada's designated ambassador to the US, on the grounds that she was too young; and the decision not to allow Sally Shelton to pay a courtesy farewell visit to Grenada in January 1981, despite an invitation extended to her by Bishop for talks aimed at restoring dialogue. Reinforcing these postures were manoeuvres by the US government to deny economic assistance to Grenada. Early in 1980 the US successfully delayed a request to the Organisation of American States (OAS) for funds following severe flooding in Grenada, and later in the year the US Agency for International Development refused to give external assistance to Grenada following hurricane damage to the banana crop, even though such aid was granted to banana-growers in the other Windward islands. This policy of deliberate exclusion of aid was also followed by the British government which provided a rationale for its action by citing 'the unattractive record of the Grenada government over civil liberties and democratic rights'.[12]

In respect of destabilisation, instances appeared early in the substance and rhetoric of Grenadian-US relations with the first reference being made by Bishop in a speech on Radio Free Grenada just one month after taking power. Then it was in the nature of a warning as to the possibility. Three weeks later Bishop was back on the air to confirm its implementation in reality. The CIA, he declared, had devised a pyramid plan 'to turn back the Grenada Revolution'. According to Bishop:

> The first part of the plan was aimed at creating dissatisfaction and unrest among our people and at wrecking our tourist industry and economy. A second level of the Pyramid involved the use of violence

and arson in the country. And if neither of these two methods of destabilizing the country worked then the plan was to move to the stage of assassinating the leadership of the country.[13]

The first two parts were already in operation, he declared, as witness the recent instances of arson and the defamation and distortion of the Grenadian revolutionary process in the foreign and local press. More would follow, with the best defence against such an attack being 'vigilance' and 'knowledge'. As it was, the pattern had been set and over the next 18 months the most obvious manifestations of destabilisation were concerned with violence and propaganda.

From the outset of the revolution the PRG was concerned to defend itself against the possibility of mercenary attack co-ordinated and directed from within the United States. Rumours of plots hatched between Gairy and various criminal figures in the US were frequent, but nothing of substance transpired until early November 1979 when the so-called 'De Raveniere Plot' was frustrated in its final stages. This envisaged a small-scale 'Bay of Pigs' type invasion with local disaffected elements (some 120 were identified) backing an invading mercenary force landing from three unidentified American ships. These never appeared and only local conspirators were detained. Their serious intent, however, was demonstrated at a press conference at which captured arms, explosives, communications equipment and written evidence were displayed. More importantly, the willingness of such elements to kill was dramatically demonstrated in two incidents in 1980. The first was an attempt to assassinate the entire leadership of the PRG by exploding a powerful time-bomb near to where they sat at a major rally on 19 June. This failed in its main object, although three young women were killed and many others were injured. Predictably the US government issued a statement denying involvement and equally predictably Bishop blamed the CIA and US imperialism. No direct link was ever discovered either way, although considerable circumstantial evidence quickly emerged to link those who planted the bomb (and another bomb a week later) with active overseas opponents of the PRG who enjoyed the sympathy and support of the US government. The other incident occurred on the night of 17 November when in two separate attacks five young men were murdered, one of them particularly savagely. This followed several shooting and bombing incidents which a month earlier had led the PRG to introduce a 'Terrorism (Prevention) Law', modelled in part on British practice in Northern Ireland. Justifying this, Bishop claimed he would have preferred not to issue such a law but had been forced to do so by

> a handful of elements . . . manipulated and funded by external enemies, including the CIA . . . who have been unable to influence the public by their vicious rumours and propaganda to rise up against the government. We are confident of the support of the great mass of Grenadians. The political criminals who are anxious to destabilize this revolution will not be allowed to succeed.[14]

Whilst destabilisation by violence was obviously disturbing, destabilisation by propaganda was perceived as immediately more damaging to Grenada and brought forth a vigorous and escalating campaign by the PRG to combat it. Constantly before the revolutionary leadership in this respect were the examples of newspapers such as *El Mercurio* in Allende's Chile and the *Daily Gleaner* in Manley's Jamaica, both of which were seen as playing leading roles in the destabilisation process in these countries. In Grenada this type of activity was attributed to *The Torchlight*, which is why it was abruptly closed down by the PRG in October 1979, as already mentioned. Attempts to re-launch it under a different guise were effectively frustrated by the passage of a law which forbade a newspaper company from publishing a paper if there were individuals in the company who owned more than 4 per cent of the shares. This was aimed at neighbouring island papers as much as at local ones and was an attempt, in particular, to limit the influence of the *Trinidad Express* group, which had taken a particularly hostile attitude to the revolution in allied publications such as the Barbados-based *Nation* and *Sun*, as well as in *The Torchlight*. In effect, though, little could be done in this area and even less to combat radio stations, such as Radio Antilles, Radio Bonaire and Radio 610, which from their nearby island bases consistently reported unfavourably on the course of the revolution.

Further afield, in papers published in the United States, Britain and West Germany, all the PRG could do was to protest to no avail. As 1980 progressed it became clear that Grenada was being subject to an ever-increasing campaign of vilification which was having the effect of isolating it both in the region and from its traditional tourist markets. The scale of this campaign should not be underestimated. In an address to journalists from the Caribbean area in April 1982, Bishop spoke as follows:

> I want to give you the benefit of some research done by our Media

Workers Association. They analysed the 19 month period from June 1980 to December 1981; to be more concrete they did a content analysis of a section of Caribbean press coverage during that period for the following newspapers 'Trinidad Guardian', 'Trinidad Express', 'Vincentian', 'Voice of St Lucia', 'Dominica Chronicle', 'Barbados Advocate', 'Barbados Nation' and occasional copies of the 'Jamaica Gleaner' and the 'Trinidad Bomb' newspapers. What this analysis showed is that during this 19 month period these papers carried some 1570 articles on Grenada and our Revolution, which works out to be an average of nearly three articles per day. Some 60 per cent of those were editorial or other comment and the remaining 40 per cent was 'straight news'. About 60 per cent of these articles were negative towards the Grenada Revolution being either downright lies or subtle and not so subtle distortions. Furthermore, 95 per cent of the PRG's rebuttals to many of these scandalous and libellous articles were never published. It is clear that no other topic has attracted such vast coverage in this section of the Caribbean press over the last three years.[15]

Incontrovertibly, Grenada was being singled out for special attention. Destabilisation having in the first instance failed, a *cordon sanitaire* had been constructed around the island and the PRG put under continuous pressure. With the return of right-wing governments in several Eastern Caribbean states during 1980, in Jamaica in the same years and, above all, in the United States itself with the election of Ronald Reagan to the presidency in November, the stage was set for the ring to be pulled tighter still.

The Reagan Administration

In the closing months of the Carter presidency, policies had clearly emerged putting into position a more traditional approach to Central American and Caribbean affairs. Stability rather than controlled change had come to be regarded as the essential prerequisite for US security, thereby effectively downgrading both the political and economic priorities which were identified at the beginning of the Carter presidency as in the best interests of the region as well as the United States. In this sense the incoming Reagan administration inherited policies already to its liking and needed only to emphasise its commitment to them to re-establish US policy in its traditional format. It chose, however, to go much further than this. In the presidential election of 1980 Reagan had campaigned very effectively on foreign policy issues, particularly as manifest in so-called 'crisis' areas of which the Central American and Caribbean region was one. On taking office, Reagan carried this perspective directly into the making of policy, elevating the Caribbean basin into a foremost concern of US policy, if not *the* foremost concern. This was a significant change from established Republican practice and suggested the influence on Reagan of what have since become identified as the ideologies of the 'new right'.

A considerable literature has lately appeared attesting to the direct influence of this group on White House policy-making for Latin America. Foremost among the figures identified has been Jeane Kirkpatrick, at present Reagan's ambassador to the United Nations and a member of the inner circle of his advisers on Central America. Her view of the issues involved is starkly simple. The principal problems in the Caribbean basin stem from the erosion of order, which is being subverted from within and without. The solution follows the diagnosis: re-establish that order at whatever cost is required. In policy terms this means a distinction between authoritarian and totalitarian regimes, with the United States committed to effective support for the former and implacable opposition to the latter. Where the Carter administration went wrong, in her opinion, was in the confusion of the solution, i.e. authoritarian regimes, with the problem, when in fact it was the other way round, i.e. it was the Carter administration itself which was the problem. In an article published just before she took office she argued:

> American policies have not only proved incapable of dealing with problems of Soviet/Cuban expansion in the area, they have positively contributed to them and to the alienation of major nations, the growth of neutralism, the destabilisation of friendly governments, the spread of Cuban influence, and the decline of US power in the region. Hence one of the first and most urgent tasks of the Reagan administration will be to review and revise the US approach to Latin America and the Caribbean.[16]

Needless to say, such a 'vision' dovetailed perfectly with Reagan's stark Cold War view of the world as a battle between the forces of 'good' (the United States) and the forces of 'evil' (the Soviet Union). In the context of Latin America this was reinforced by an unshakeable conviction that the United States itself was 'the last domino' in a

Moscow/Havana conspiracy centring presently on the Caribbean basin and destined to lead, unless checked, to the fall of the entire Western hemisphere. Nestor Sanchez, Deputy Assistant Secretary of Defense for Inter-American Affairs, has recently provided an apocalyptic account of the scenario unfolding:

> There is no doubt that if El Salvador falls, Honduras – then flanked on two sides by hostile neighbours and already the target of insurgency – will follow. The struggle might be longer and bloodier in Guatemala, but the latter would be isolated politically and militarily, and the odds of a successful resistance would be slim. Costa Rica, with no army, should be the easiest target of all. Mexico and Panama are often portrayed as being immune to Castro's depredations because of the political and other support they have given him. This may be true to an extent, but it would be naive to conclude that this good will would protect Mexico and Panama against encroachment should Moscow and Havana conclude that other conditions are propitious.
>
> Eastward but near, the Caribbean islands are weak militarily and economically. Active on many of these islands are leftist elements, bent on seizing power at any price and linked to Cuba, Libya, and others of like mind. The tiny eastern Caribbean countries could fall overnight, as did Grenada. The Dominican Republic, Haiti and Jamaica are perhaps less vulnerable, but each has serious weaknesses and each has been a target of Castro in the past. No doubt even many who share this basic assessment of Soviet and Cuban motivation and intentions will be sceptical that the prognosis can be so dark. The prospect of a communized Caribbean Basin some years down the road, however, is no less plausible than the current size and assertiveness of hostile forces in the region would have seemed to the United States 20 years ago.[17]

It followed that urgent, and necessarily military action, was a minimal response to such a nightmare possibility. And it is the insistent and mounting pressure for the exercise of such an option over and above any others which has been the most distinctive feature of the Reagan administration's Caribbean basin policy. This is particularly evident in its policy towards Central America, is implied in its policy towards Cuba and, whilst hidden for a time, eventually became the overwhelming reality for the Caribbean islands too.

Reagan and Central America

Immediately on taking office Reagan began implementing policy for tougher action in Central America. Liberals in the Foreign Service and the State Department were purged, to be replaced by ideologues of the 'new right' and veterans of covert action in Vietnam and Cambodia such as General Haig, John Negroponte and Thomas Enders, who was appointed Assistant Secretary of State for Inter-American Affairs. The last named took charge of US policy towards Central America and identified El Salvador as the principal theatre for action. He also laid down the basis of policy for the next two years (and beyond) which can be summarised as to secure no less than total victory, military and political, over the popular insurgent forces of the FDR-FMLN. Central to the achievement of this goal was increased military assistance, which was stepped up dramatically and included the sending of US military 'advisers' to work alongside the Salvadorean military in counter-insurgency campaigns. Such campaigns, however, proved less than effective and by the end of 1981 incontrovertible evidence had emerged that counter-insurgency for the Salvadorean army meant nothing less than the wholesale slaughter of civilians (over 30,000 killed from 1979 to mid-1983), which had the counter-productive but inevitable effect of increasing support for the popular forces. For their part, while they have easily been able to avoid military defeat, they have not been able to mount a decisive military initiative either, though several have been attempted. A military stalemate has thus emerged in which through a process of attrition the balance of advantage lies for the present with the popular forces, and to which the Salvadorean army responds by seeking ever greater assistance from, and ultimately the direct military involvement of, the United States.

A similar pattern has emerged with respect to the political strategy adopted by Washington. The centre-piece of this was the election held in El Salvador in March 1982. As intended, it had the effect of both dividing the constituent groups within the FDR-FMLN as to whether to participate or not, as well as disarming a considerable volume of criticism of US policy both at home and abroad. Probably unintended, however, were both the results and their consequences. Although the Christian Democrats favoured by the US government won a plurality of the vote, the right-wing parties won a majority which not only further entrenched their position within the political structures of the country but also encouraged them to react with increased intransigence to any prospect of a negotiated settlement of the conflict.

The United States thus found its policy options narrowed and directed even more towards military solutions. These were, of course, only part (albeit the crucial aspect) of a planned package as the leaked National Security Council (NSC) appraisal of April 1982 makes clear. Objectives such as 'building democratic political institutions capable of achieving domestic political support' and 'pursuing reform programmes to correct severe dislocations which foment and aid insurgency' were included as well.[18] The reality, however, as it impinged on the administration during the remainder of 1982 and early 1983, was the impossibility of realising such goals with the existing Salvadorean government and in the midst of an escalating civil war. The FDR-FMLN was thus able to gain credibility as the only viable basis for reform in El Salvador and to attract considerable and growing international support on this account alone. More importantly, recognition of this fact fed a renewed and mounting opposition within the US Congress to the direction and content of the administration's policies in Central America, to which Reagan was eventually forced to respond decisively. In February 1983 he despatched Jeane Kirkpatrick on a fact-finding mission to the region from which she returned with the message that, if the war in El Salvador continued along its present path, then defeat for the US cause was inevitable. She therefore recommended a large-scale political and military effort to reverse this development, the concomitant of which was that within the administration itself the president should take direct control of Central American policy. Over the next few months moves were made to effect this, leading eventually to the dismissal of Thomas Enders, not for being 'soft' on Central America but allegedly for being 'soft' on Congress.

If El Salvador was the main focus of foreign policy in the early months of the Reagan administration, Nicaragua was not far behind in importance. Following the victory of the FSLN in July 1979, Carter had adopted a policy of coexistence with the Nicaraguan government which even included a small element of economic assistance. On taking office Reagan immediately suspended this and signalled a change towards the politics of hostility. Central to this was the policy decision taken in November 1981 to mount a campaign to destabilise Nicaragua, in which the leading edge would be constituted by the provision of covert support to anti-Sandinista forces (known as 'contras') operating militarily against Nicaragua from bases in Honduras. Initial recruitment was only for some 500 'contras' whose purpose was to 'interdict' flows of arms from Nicaragua to El Salvador, yet by the early part of 1983 numbers had risen to 7,000 of which some 5,000 had entered Nicaragua, changing the nature of the operation, as an inside informant put it, 'from one of harassment to one of trying to overthrow the Sandinistas'.[19] Directing this was the US ambassador to Honduras, John Negroponte, using CIA funds in flat contravention of a decision taken by the US Congress not to provide appropriations 'for the purpose of overthrowing the government of Nicaragua or provoking a military exchange between Nicaragua and Honduras'. Unsurprisingly, when they learnt of this, Congress reacted angrily, to which Reagan responded with the unusual measure of arranging a joint session on 27 April 1983 during which he defended his administration's policy towards Central America. In this speech, which was televised, he reaffirmed existing prognosis and policy:

> I say to you that tonight there can be no question: the national security of all the Americas is at stake in Central America. If we cannot defend ourselves there, we cannot expect to prevail elsewhere. Our credibility would collapse, our alliances would crumble, and the safety of our homeland would be in jeopardy.

He also made the additional pledge that US forces would not be committed directly to the conflict — 'Let me say to those who invoke the memory of Vietnam: There is no thought of sending American combat troops to Central America. They are not needed, indeed they have not been requested there.'[20] This declaration won him a measure of support in the country, but can be considered more cosmetic than definitive, since then, which has been towards asserting the military option as

The self-evident truth of this can be seen in the thrust of US policy since them, which has been towards asserting the military option as paramount, with all that this necessarily entails as regards increased US military commitment. A prominent example of this was the despatch in mid-1983 of two US navy carrier task forces to the Pacific and Caribbean coasts of Nicaragua and the start of six months of military exercises by US and Honduran troops on the frontier with Nicaragua. Backing up this intimidatory action has been renewed tough rhetoric from within the Reagan administration. Fred Ikle, Under Secretary of Defense for Policy, in a speech cleared by the National Security Council, called in September 1983 for nothing less than victory in El Salvador. 'We do not seek a military stalemate', he said, 'we seek victory for the forces of democracy.' In respect of Nicaragua, he spoke in similar vein: 'We must prevent consolidation of a Sandinista regime in Nicaragua that would become an arsenal for insurgency.'[21] Correspondingly, the Contadora initiative (a search for a negotiated solution to the conflict in the region being pursued jointly by Mexico, Panama, Venezuela and Colombia and enjoying the support of the UN Security Council and a number of Commonwealth Caribbean and West European governments) has been officially dismissed as irrelevant and privately condemned from within the administration as a 'diplomatic stupidity'.[22] Faced with such intransigence Nicaragua understandably expects the worst — the real prospect sooner or later of military attack by US forces.

Reagan and Cuba

As the Reagan administration believes that insurgency in Central America is the direct product of Cuban conspiracy, it has sought from its earliest days in government to 'justify' this fact and to punish Cuba accordingly. Its opening gambit in this strategy was the release in February 1981 of a widely-publicised State Department white paper, entitled 'Communist Interference in El Salvador', which purported to show that 'the insurgency in El Salvador has been progressively transformed into a textbook case of indirect armed aggression by Communist powers through Cuba'.[23] In support of this claim a number of captured documents were published, with a view to proving that Cuba, with Nicaraguan assistance, was the conduit for channelling arms from the Soviet Union, Vietnam, Ethiopia and various Arab countries to the insurgent forces. Unhappily for the administration, however, the white paper soon became a source of embarrassment as the documentation within it was shown to be false in parts and the conclusions consequently open to serious question. As the *Wall Street Journal* put it, 'a close reading of the white paper indicates ... that its authors probably were making a determined effort to create a "selling" document, no matter how slim the background material.'[24] Nevertheless, the administration was not to be deterred and in December 1981 a new document emerged from the State Department. It was entitled 'Cuba's Renewed Support for Violence in Latin America' and made the same types of claims as earlier, but in a wider hemispheric context and with particular attention to Central America and the Caribbean. Again it was argued that 'Cuba's policies abroad are linked to its relationship to the Soviet Union' and that 'by intervening on behalf of armed struggle in Latin America, Cuba injects East-West dimensions into local conflicts'.[25] Again it was stated that Cuba had mounted a major campaign to promote insurgence. Once more too, both its handling of the 'facts' and its interpretation of them were questioned by observers. However, by now it was clear that establishing the 'truth' about Cuba was not an essential part of the administration's policies; punishing Cuba was.

The Reagan administration has therefore imposed new sanctions on Cuba, including a tightening of the economic blockade, and has lobbied vigorously, and with some success, to re-isolate Cuba diplomatically within Latin America. It has also spurned negotiations on a number of occasions, even though its senior official in Cuba, Wayne Smith (chief of the US interests section in Havana, 1979-82), was reporting in favour of such an option being explored.[26] He eventually resigned in July 1982 precisely because it was not being seriously considered. In fact, the Reagan administration appears to have interpreted all moves by Cuba to initiate negotiations as a vindication of its own 'get tough' policy, and correspondingly to have increased its pressure against the Cuban regime. In 1982 it stepped up the propaganda war by taking it directly to Cuba with the establishment of an anti-Castro radio station in the Florida Keys, Radio Marti. The same year also saw the staging of large-scale US naval exercises in the Caribbean under the code-name 'Ocean Venture 82'. This involved some 45,000 troops, 60 naval vessels and 350 aircraft and preceded an announcement that the Key West naval base at the southern tip of Florida was to be re-opened for promoting military activity in the region. The co-ordination of such actions could not but look ominous to Cuba. Prior to Reagan's election an influential right-wing 'think-tank' had prepared a report on 'A New Inter-American Policy for the Eighties'. This stated:

> Havana must be held to account for its policies of aggression against its sister states in the Americas. Among those steps will be the establishment of a Radio Free Cuba, under open US government sponsorship, which will beam objective information to the Cuban people that, among other things, details the costs of Havana's unholy alliance with Moscow. If propaganda fails, a war of national liberation against Castro must be launched.[27]

Only the last part of the prescription now remains unfulfilled.

Reagan and Grenada

The policies of destabilisation and denial already applied by Carter to Grenada were, of course, policies wholly appropriate to the general posture of the Reagan administration towards the Caribbean basin. Accordingly, it was to an intensification of existing measures for dealing with the PRG, rather than to any change of direction, that the incoming US administration looked on taking office.

The destabilisation strategy, as it developed during the early part of the Reagan administration, combined the usual mix of regional and local pressures, particularly in the propaganda field. Editorial comment and news coverage in both the regional and US media continued to be almost uniformly hostile to the revolution and appeared to be increasingly concerted in action. It was noted, for example, that the United States International Communication Agency had hosted a conference for Caribbean editors in May 1981 in which offers of assistance had been extended to the papers concerned if they would collaborate in helping to isolate Grenada by means of adverse publicity. It was also noted that on 20 September 1981, in an unprecedented move for the Commonwealth Caribbean which Bishop said reflected 'an extraordinary level of co-ordinated vulgarity',[28] identical front-page editorials appeared in five Sunday newspapers in Trinidad, Barbados and Jamaica 'calling on Mr. Bishop and his colleagues to give freedom to the people of Grenada'.[29] Against this general background, the appearance of the new *Grenadian Voice* in June 1981 could not but appear to the PRG to be part of a CIA plot. Circumstantial evidence pointing to this was given in a speech by Bishop on 19 June 1981 to the annual Heroes Day Rally. In this he stated that, when recently in Washington, Kenrick Radix, who had become Minister of Legal Affairs in the PRG, had been informed by the head of the Caribbean section of the State Department of the imminent appearance of a new newspaper in Grenada. He also noted that in Grenada the majority of the 26 persons concerned had been associated with previous efforts in this area, notably *The Torchlight*, and were moreover drawn in large part from social categories opposed to the revolution. The juxtaposition of the two, in the context, defined the conclusion. As Bishop put it:

> We have to understand, Comrades, that this plan we are seeing now, the first element of which is this newspaper, is a different plan to all that went before, because this is not the type of plan in which local counters, local opportunists are being used, this is not the kind

of plan where the ganja capitalists who are in the employment of the CIA are being used. To understand this plan fully you have to do a piece of magic in your heads, you have to forget the names of that 26 and instead you write one single word, you write CIA. That is how you are going to understand this plan . . . It is not the Committee of 26. It is the CIA. This is not about freedom of the press, it is about overthrowing the Grenadian revolution.[30]

Accordingly, draconian measures were required. He announced a new law, effective immediately, that no new newspaper was to be published for a year until a media policy was formulated. It was at this point too that he introduced the concept of 'revolutionary manners', of which mention has already been made.

Whether or not this escalation of will and determination was read in Washington as significant is uncertain, but what is known is that soon afterwards, in July 1981, plans drawn up by the CIA for the destabilisation of Grenada and presented to the Senate Intelligence Committee were rejected outright. Thereafter the administration concentrated upon its policy of denial. Whereas under the Carter administration, this policy was pursued inconsequentially, under Reagan it was elaborated and pursued relentlessly. Three areas stood out: economic resources; the question of political recognition; and, in a combination of the two, the launching of a 'mini-Marshall' plan for the region, the Caribbean Basin Initiative (CBI).

The Reagan administration's determination to deny economic aid to Grenada manifested itself in a number of ways throughout 1981. In April the US representative on the IMF successfully argued that a loan of US$19 million be 'held over' despite earlier approval by the IMF's managing director. In June the United States abstained when a US$4 million stand-by credit was approved to assist the Grenada government's fiscal programme over the next twelve months. The same month also saw pressure by the US government in respect of a US$4 million loan to the Caribbean Development Bank (CDB) for distribution among the smaller states of the Eastern Caribbean. In this instance the US government sought to attach the condition that none be distributed to Grenada. Creditably, the CDB was instructed by Commonwealth Caribbean leaders not to accept the loan, although later a number of them did decide that if such an offer was repeated they could not refuse again.

By far the most important attempted act of denial in 1981 was, however, the political pressure brought against the EEC. The basis of this was a move by Grenada to mount a co-financing conference in conjunction with the EEC Commission to raise the US$30 million needed to complete the new international airport. When the US government learnt of this it lobbied intensively in European capitals, drawing critical comment from within the EEC Commission and from the African, Caribbean and Pacific (ACP) countries. When the conference finally met in Brussels in April, the US government could claim some success in limiting the direct participation by certain European governments, but at the same time also had to recognise Grenada's triumph in securing the conference's approval of the project and, more to the point, pledges of aid, including EC$6 million for the airport, from the EEC itself.

On both the day Reagan was elected and the day he was inaugurated, the PRG sent messages expressing a desire for friendly relations between the two countries. The first was only formally acknowledged and the second never answered at all, nor was a third letter sent in August 1981, so confirming that Carter's policy of diplomatic isolation would continue. Thus Milan Bish, when appointed as the new US ambassador to Barbados and the Eastern Caribbean, was pointedly not accredited to Grenada. British policy in almost every respect followed suit. Economic aid was denied and the British government sought to ignore Grenada. The Minister of State at the Foreign Office, Nicholas Ridley, was quoted as saying that 'Grenada is in the process of establishing a kind of society of which the British government disapproves, irrespective of whether the people of Grenada want it or not',[31] whilst the following year his successor, Richard Luce, refused to visit Grenada during a tour of the Eastern Caribbean on the grounds that 'there is no democracy there'. Similar arguments were heard elsewhere in Latin America and the Caribbean at the behest of the US government.

The Caribbean Basin Initiative was announced by President Reagan on 24 February 1982. Its origins lay, in part, in lobbying in Washington by Commonwealth Caribbean leaders such as Edward Seaga of Jamaica and Eugenia Charles of Dominica and, in part, in arguments presented by the 'new right' for the development of policies which would more effectively combat Cuban influence by combining security assistance and economic aid. Both the selective and cross-cutting purposes underlying the initiative quickly became apparent. In respect of 'aid', for example, it was noted that political and military criteria took precedence over 'need'. Thus in Central America, El Salvador was to be the most favoured country and Honduras the least, whilst in the

Commonwealth Caribbean the same places were occupied by Jamaica and the Eastern Caribbean respectively. The plan was also presented in a way specifically designed to exclude Nicaragua and Grenada, particularly in its emphasis on private sector development strategies as most appropriate to the needs of the region. Finally, it was argued that it offered too little (and too late). The offer of one-way free trade was seen as hollow given that some 87 per cent of Caribbean basin exports already entered the US market duty-free, whilst the sums of financial assistance being considered were seen as derisory in the face of studies suggesting the urgent need for external financing over the next five years at more than double the figures the US government was prepared to commit.

Such weaknesses ensured that the CBI was extensively criticised, by 'friends' as well as opponents. In the US Congress the legislation encountered stiff opposition and only reached the statute book in August 1983. Delays of such length had led to questions being asked, even by fervent supporters. In December 1982 Eugenia Charles had stated: 'The Caribbean has been expecting action on this programme since 1981. Our people will say to us, their leaders, that you are jokers and the U.S. is the biggest joker of all . . . The people and government of the U.S. are talkers, not doers.'[32] More to the point, Lynden Pindling of the Bahamas, at the same venue, had queried:

> If Cuba is worth nine million dollars a day to Russia, how much is the Caribbean worth to America? If Russia, for three and a quarter billion dollars a year, underwrites the cost of insurrection and totalitarian aggression in our region, how far would America go to underwrite the preservation of peace and democratic freedom?[33]

These comments did no more than reflect the congruence of the CBI with the Reagan administration's vision of the region as a theatre of East-West conflict. Reagan himself had made this plain in his visit to the region over Easter 1982. He repeated his administration's frequent charge that Cuba was making a 'large-scale attempt to undermine democracy throughout the Americas, financed by its master across the sea', and directly related this to Grenada, of which he said:

> El Salvador isn't the only country that's being threatened with Marxism . . . all of us are concerned with the overturn of Westminster parliamentary democracy in Grenada. That country now

bears the Soviet and Cuban trademark, which means that it will attempt to spread the virus among its neighbours.[34]

Images of the Caribbean islands as 'splashing dominoes' were clearly uppermost in Reagan's mind and constituted the reality of the CBI as far as the Grenadian leadership were concerned. As Bishop put it at the time:

> this plan is meant only to deal with narrow military, security and strategic considerations of the U.S.A., and is not genuinely concerned with the economic and social development of the people of this region . . . the CBI plan reflects the chauvinism and Ugly Americanism of Reagan, in the vulgar way in which he has completely ignored and discarded the views of Caribbean countries, as to what kind of plan they wished to see. The concern of his plan is with his warmongering 'national security' interests . . . his Basin plan has turned out to be the con game of this century.[35]

The final, and ultimately determinant aspect of the Reagan administration's policy, was military. This, of course, was not new, but in emphasis and scale of commitment it introduced a qualitatively new dimension to policy. Grenada was quite simply seen as a threat and contingency plans for invasion were laid in Reagan's first year in office. Notable here was a large military exercise code-named 'Ocean Venture 81', which took place off Puerto Rico in August 1981 and included over 120,000 troops, 250 warships and 1,000 aircraft. Worrying as this was for the whole of the Caribbean, there was within it a separate training exercise code-named 'Operation Amber' which was seen as a direct provocation of Grenada – by design and intent. In a statement issued to foreign governments, international organisations and prominent political personalities, Bishop spelled out his fears:

> The exercise on the island of Vieques off the coast of Puerto Rico is a practice run for a direct invasion of Grenada by U.S. troops.
> 1. The country subject to invasion in the manoeuvre is code named Amber and the Amberines which clearly refer to Grenada and its sister islands in the Grenadines.
> 2. An amphibious landing of forces took place on the south-eastern tip of Vieques. There is in fact an area on the southern tip of Grenada called Amber which is in close proximity to a security zone and the site of the new international airport.

3. Vieques like Grenada has a mountainous terrain. A combat unit of 'rangers', specially trained for warfare in such rugged conditions was used in the manoeuvres.

4. As part of the manoeuvre the 75th ranger batallion was flown from the Norton Air Base in California non stop to Vieques, covering approximately the same distance needed to attack Grenada.

5. The reasons for invasion of the islands are similar to the propaganda themes used consistently by the Reagan administration against Grenada. These are (a) to take power from the Amber government, which is described as 'unfriendly'; (b) to station troops in the island until an election is called; (c) to install a government favourable to Washington's brand of democracy.

6. Rear Admiral of the Caribbean contingency joint task force, R.P. Mckenzie, emphasised the importance that his Government places on 'protecting Atlantic sea lanes along which travel 62% of United States imported oil, 65% of the bauxite and other strategic imports'.

7. Mckenzie describes Nicaragua, Cuba and Grenada as 'practically one country' and referred to the situation as a 'political-military problem'.

8. Mckenzie stated that the objective of the exercise was to 'reinforce in the eyes and minds of those watching our military commitment around the world – to give an example of one facet of the U.S. capability to respond in the Caribbean basin'.[36]

Needless to say, the US government denied that it was an invasion rehearsal, stating that it was a training exercise for 'a variety of eventualities' such as had been conducted in past years 'under various titles'.[37]

Accordingly, further exercises followed at the end of 1981 and throughout 1982 although, given the effective publicity the PRG had mounted around 'Operation Amber', none was so overtly political. Nevertheless, Bishop continued both to warn Grenadians to be vigilant and to press the theme of US aggression before international audiences. Typical were his remarks to an audience of Caribbean journalists in April 1982.

> Like an overgrown child at his bathtime, President Reagan is about to drop into what he believes is his bathtub, his fleet of toy battleships and aircraft carriers filled to the brim with plastic planes and clockwork marines. Such huge military manoeuvres, so perilously close to our shores . . . only demonstrate one more time the

proximity of war and the blasé, imperial and Monroe doctrine-like attitude of the United States to our region and waters.[38]

The essential truth of this analysis was shown once more in March 1983 when military exercises again singled out Grenada as a target. A total of 77 US and allied warships assembled off Grenada, some using Barbados as their base and some approaching within six miles of Point Salines. As they did so, President Reagan decried those who denigrated the importance he attached to Grenada because its best-known export was nutmeg. He declared: 'People who make these arguments haven't taken a good look at a map lately . . . it is not nutmeg that is at stake in the Caribbean and Central America, it is the United States national security.'[39] Maurice Bishop, in India attending the Non-Aligned Summit, was forced to cut short his visit and on his return to declare a full-scale alert. He dismissed Reagan's claims of Soviet and Cuban military installations as 'a pack of lies'[40] and, by way of reply, announced that Grenada's intelligence services knew of an impending attack organised by CIA-supported exiles using a neighbouring island as a base.

None of this counted in Washington. On 25 March Reagan returned to the attack showing aerial photographs of the Point Salines international airport and alleging that no country of Grenada's size needed such a facility unless it was for sinister purposes. Oblivious to Grenadian arguments that the building of the airport was critical for the development of its economy, the US government case against had been first outlined by Thomas Enders to the Senate Foreign Relations Committee in December 1981. The runway was far too long for the modest level of traffic to and from Grenada; it would be a potential Soviet military base threatening the Venezuelan and Trinidadian oil fields and the oil shipping routes which passed through the deep water Grenada Channel separating Grenada from Tobago; or alternatively 'all types of Soviet aircraft' could use it 'to land and refuel', particularly on the Cuba–Angola route. Indeed, such was the importance attached to it by the State Department that the possibility of Soviet Mig-23 and Mig-25 aircraft being based there was cited as a major reason why the Senate should ratify the sale of F-16 aircraft to Venezuela.[41]

The PRG countered the propaganda by pointing out that Barbados and Guyana had originally been used as staging points for Cuban troop carriers to Africa and that the runway length of 9,800 ft was comparable to other runways in the region such as Antigua, St Lucia and Trinidad, all at around 9,000 ft, and Curaçao, Barbados and Guadeloupe, all in excess of 11,000 ft.[42] It also reminded the United States that there were being built no military facilities, such as underground fuel tanks and bomb-proof shelters; that the runway was in a completely indefensible position, with the control tower on a hill; and that British, European and US companies, as well as Cubans, were involved in its construction. The non-military character of the project was subsequently confirmed by Plessey, the British company concerned, to whom the British government had extended export credit guarantees for the airport contract. It is hard to believe, given existing British policy, that the Thatcher government would have been prepared to do this had it harboured any real doubt as to the airport's prime purpose.

Nevertheless, the US government persisted in its claims. Only three days later, Ludlow Flower, chargé d'affaires at the US embassy in Barbados, referred to a 'Point Salines – Calivigny – Egmont complex' in south-west Grenada, which he said 'was becoming a separate entity' and 'could be thought of as a stationary aircraft carrier'.[43] The focus was different, but the perspective was the same and was emblematic of the general geopolitical approach of the Reagan administration. As such, it is hard not to share the view of one authority on US security issues, Michael T. Klare, who observed that it was surprising that the administration 'did not move *sooner* to carry out its strategic design'[44] of invading Grenada. In his view, by mid-1983, only the appropriate pretext was missing.

Notes and References

1. J. Plank, 'The Caribbean: Intervention, When and How', *Foreign Affairs*, vol. 44, no. 1 (1965).
2. Figures cited in R. Sim and J. Anderson, 'The Caribbean Strategic Vacuum', *Conflict Studies*, no. 121 (1980), p. 3.
3. Figures include Mexico but exclude Bermuda, Puerto Rico and the Netherlands Antilles. Calculated from R.F. Ramsaran, 'Issues in Commonwealth Caribbean-United States Relations' in A.J. Payne and P.K. Sutton (eds.), *Dependency under Challenge: the Political Economy of the Commonwealth Caribbean* (Manchester University Press, Manchester, 1984), Table 7.4.
4. R. Pastor, 'Sinking in the Caribbean Basin', *Foreign Affairs*, vol. 60, no. 5 (1982).
5. J. Bartlow Martin, *U.S. Policy in the Caribbean* (Westview Press, Boulder, Colorado for the Twentieth Century Fund, 1978), pp. 250-1.
6. P.C. Habib, 'Address by the U.S. Ambassador-at-large to the Miami Conference on the Caribbean, 28 November 1979' in United States Department of State, *U.S. Relations with the Caribbean and Central America* (Bureau of Public Affairs, Washington, 1979), p. 2.
7. Cited in J. Pearce *Under the Eagle: U.S. Intervention in Central America and the Caribbean* (Latin American Bureau, London, 1981), p. 237.

8. F. Castro, 'Interview with C.B.S., September 30, 1979' in M. Taber (ed.), *Fidel Castro Speeches*, vol. 1 (Pathfinder Press, New York, 1981), p. 265.
9. *New York Times*, 30 November 1980 cited in Pearce, *Under the Eagle*, p. 153.
10. 'In Nobody's Backyard', National Broadcast by Maurice Bishop on RFG on 13 April, 1979 in M. Bishop, *Selected Speeches, 1979-81* (Casa de las Americas, Havana, 1982), p. 9.
11. *Caribbean Insight*, July 1979.
12. Letter from Neil Marten, Minister of State for Overseas Development and Aid, cited in ibid., February 1981.
13. 'Organise to Fight Destabilization', National Broadcast on RFG on May 8, 1979 in Bishop, *Selected Speeches 1979-81*.
14. *Caribbean Contact*, November 1980.
15. 'Address to the First Conference of Journalists from the Caribbean Area', 17 April, 1982, in C. Searle, *Grenada: the Struggle against Destabilization* (Writers and Readers, London, 1983), p. 156.
16. J. Kirkpatrick, 'U.S. Security and Latin America', *Commentary*, vol. 71, no. 1 (1981), p. 29.
17. N.D. Sanchez, 'The Communist Threat', *Foreign Policy*, no. 52 (1983), pp. 48-9.
18. National Security Council Document, 'U.S. Policy in Central America and Cuba through F.Y. '84. Summary Paper: April 1982', reprinted in El Salvador Solidarity Campaign, *El Salvador News Bulletin No. 20*, May-June 1983, p. 6.
19. *New York Times*, 3 April 1983, cited in L. Whitehead, 'Explaining Washington's Central American Policies', *Journal of Latin American Studies*, vol. 15, part 2 (1983), p. 341.
20. R. Reagan, 'The Problems in Central America', Address delivered to a Joint Session of Congress, 17 April 1983, in *Vital Speeches of the Day*, vol. XLIX (1983), pp. 450-4.
21. Cited in *Latin America Regional Report: Mexico and Central America*, 23 September 1983.
22. Comment attributed to Lawrence Motley, the successor to Enders as Under Secretary of State for Inter-American Affairs, cited in El Salvador Solidarity Campaign, *El Salvador News Bulletin No. 21*, Autumn 1983, p. 2.
23. Cited in Pearce, *Under the Eagle*, p. 240.
24. *Wall Street Journal*, 8 June 1981, in ibid., p. 243.
25. Appendix 14 to the Minutes of Evidence, House of Commons, *Fifth Report from The Foreign Affairs Committee, Session 1981-82*, p. 312.
26. W. Smith, 'Dateline Havana: Myopic Diplomacy', *Foreign Policy*, no. 48 (1982).
27. Cited in *NACLA Report*, July/August 1981, p. 30.
28. Interview with M. Bishop in Searle, *Grenada*, p. 129.
29. The editorial appeared in the *Guardian* and *The Express* (Trinidad); *The Advocate* and *The Sun* (Barbados); and the *Daily Gleaner* (Jamaica).
30. 'Freedom of the Press versus CIA Destabilisation' in M. Bishop, *Forward Ever! Three Years of the Grenadian Revolution* (Pathfinder Press, Sydney, 1982), p. 184.
31. *Caribbean Contact*, March 1981.
32. *Latin America Regional Report: Caribbean*, RC-83-01, 21 January 1983.
33. Ibid.
34. *Caribbean Contact*, May 1982.
35. 'Three Years of the Grenada Revolution' in Bishop, *Forward Ever!*, pp. 275-6.
36. 'U.S. Preparing to Invade Grenada', Statement by Maurice Bishop, Prime

Minister of Grenada, reported in full in El Salvador Solidarity Campaign, *El Salvador News Bulletin*, no. 10, September 1981.

37. *Caribbean Insight*, October 1981.

38. M. Bishop, *Address to the First Conference of Journalists from the Caribbean Area*, 17 April 1982 (People's Revolutionary Government, Grenada, mimeo), p. 12.

39. Speech on 10 March 1983 to the National Association of Manufacturers, cited in *Caribbean Contact*, April 1983.

40. *Latin America Regional Report: Caribbean*, RC-83-03, 31 March 1983.

41. *A State of Danger in the Caribbean*, Testimony given by Assistant Secretary of State for Inter-American Affairs Thomas Enders, Washington D.C., 14 December 1981 (Government Printing Office, Washington D.C., mimeo). See also *Aviation Week and Space Technology*, 21 December 1980, pp. 19-20.

42. Figures cited in Embassy of Grenada, *Proceedings of Aid Donors Meeting Held in Brussels at ACP House on 14-15 April 1981. International Airport Project – Grenada*, Appendix 1.

43. *Latin America Regional Report: Caribbean*, RC-83-04, 13 May 1983.

44. Michael Klare, 'The Reagan Doctrine', *New Statesman*, 4 November 1983. Klare's emphasis.

4 CUBA AND THE CARIBBEAN

Cuban foreign policy has been designed both to defend and advance the revolution at home and to promote national liberation abroad. As with its domestic policy, it has been a blend of pragmatism and idealism, of nationalism and socialism, the combinations of which have varied over time, delineating specific phases of development. In this, broadly speaking, the 1960s must be distinguished from the 1970s, the early part of the 1970s from the later part of the decade, and both from the situation as it unfolded into the early 1980s.

During the 1960s Cuban foreign policy was distinguished by its emphasis on policies of nationalism and revolutionary idealism. It was, above all, defensive in character although in order to safeguard the revolution at home it required the paradox of an offensive abroad, especially in the mid-1960s. During this period Cuba actively supported and fomented revolution in Third World countries and particularly in Latin America. In order to further those goals it established first the Tricontinental Congress of Africa, Asia and Latin America in 1966 and then the Organisation of Latin American Solidarity in 1967. The latter body, in particular, was invested with Castro's considerable authority and the call made for the creation of 'two, three, many Vietnams' in Latin America. However, the death in Bolivia in 1967 of the architect of that policy, Che Guevara, as well as differences at the same time with Latin American communist parties and the Soviet Union over the emphasis on guerrilla warfare as the main path of advance in the region, led to second thoughts and a subsequent change of direction first really evident in 1970.

In that year Castro conceded that other paths to revolution were possible and even desirable and demonstrated his convictions on this point in an extended visit to Chile in 1971, during which he endorsed Allende's electoral road to socialism as authentic and deserving of support. This new pragmatism abroad coincided, as many have noted, with a new realism at home and a concern with establishing the foundations of socialism in Cuba. Attention was paid to developing the Cuban Communist Party, previously neglected, and to establishing the conditions for economic growth which in the later 1960s, under the period designated as 'the revolutionary offensive', had been negative. Central to the realisation of these goals were improved relations with the Soviet

Union. These were achieved in 1972 when in July Cuba was accepted into Comecon and in late December a five-point economic agreement was negotiated with the Soviet Union in which Cuba was granted substantial trade and aid concessions. Just over a year later, in January 1974, Brezhnev was to visit Cuba to cement the ties of friendship. In the joint communiqué issued at the end of the visit both countries declared a 'total unity' in their ideas and positions in world affairs — a conclusion which has been a constantly reiterated theme of Soviet-Cuban relations from that day to this.

In November 1975 Cuba committed troops to defend Angola against the South African invasion. This act marked an outward turn in Cuban foreign policy which by the end of the decade saw some 50,000 Cubans serving in 37 countries in a variety of tasks — as doctors, nurses, dentists, teachers, construction workers and soldiers. While behind this lay a new confidence in the strength of the Cuban revolution at home, it also corresponded to what Cuba perceived as a shift in the correlation of world forces in favour of socialism and national liberation and against imperialism. Cuba was therefore under less constraint in its actions than previously had been the case and was able to undertake initiatives more directly and with a greater certainty of success. Although Angola and Ethiopia stand out in this respect, Cuba was also engaged in other fields, notably in the Non-Aligned Movement over which Castro secured the chairmanship in 1979, confirming the high prestige in which he was held in the Third World in general and to which an extensive bilateral network of relations had contributed significantly. Cuba also deepened and consolidated its relations with the Soviet Union and other socialist countries in Eastern Europe during this period, especially in economic areas where a greater dependency, co-ordination and integration of economic policy can be recorded. Indeed, according to one report, Cuba 'cost' Moscow during the 1976-9 four-year period alone 'an estimated U.S. $9.6 billion in total economic assistance, most of it outright grants and trade subsidies'.[1] Agreements signed with the Soviet Union in October 1980 and April 1981 continued to underwrite Cuban development expenditure, in fact practically doubling it between 1981 and 1985, as compared to the previous five-year period.

It is, of course, the provision of such levels of assistance that underlies and informs the various 'proxy' theories of Cuban foreign policy, seeing in it no more than subservience to the Soviet Union in its supposed 'global designs'. However, this belies the considerable autonomy Cuba possesses in foreign policy, especially in regions such as Latin

America and the Caribbean, where informed observers are more likely to argue a 'convergence' of Soviet and Cuban interests rather than specific direction by Moscow as such.[2] The same may also be said of its African policy where authoritative accounts again argue that 'collaboration' and 'division of labour' with the Soviet Unon more accurately explain the Cuban presence than any 'proxy theory'.[3] Nevertheless, it is indisputable that Cuba remains closely allied to the Soviet Union and that in the early 1980s this has led to as many difficulties for its foreign policy as it has provided opportunities. In the Non-Aligned Movement, for example, Cuba's attempt to act as 'broker' between the Soviet Union and the Third World received a set-back over the issue of Afghanistan when it identified with the Soviet Union's position in opposition to the view taken by nearly every other state in the Third World. Thereafter, it found its influence within the movement compromised, with Castro's stature in the Third World correspondingly diminished. In Latin America and the Caribbean also, Cuba began encountering problems where but a short while before it had met mainly with success.

However, it is, above all, the intensified conflict with the United States and Reagan's 'Cold War' policy which colours all Cuban foreign policy and which distinguishes the 1980s from the late 1970s. Castro expressed alarm at just such a possibility developing in his speech to the Second Congress of the Communist Party of Cuba held in December 1980 when he stated:

> Reagan's election introduces an element of uncertainty — rather of danger — in U.S.-Cuban relations . . .
> Statements have been made threatening the world, Latin America and Cuba in particular . . .
> Reagan and his advisers speak of a military blockade of Cuba, under any pretext, even if as they assert, the Soviet Union were to carry out an action in any other part of the world. This is a repulsive and cynical thought . . . Cuba believes that for the world it is a historical necessity that normal relations exist among all countries based on mutual respect, on the acknowledgement of the sovereign right of every one and on non-intervention. Cuba considers that the normalisation of its relations with the United States would improve the political climate in Latin America and the Caribbean and would contribute to world detente. Cuba, therefore, is not opposed to finding a solution to its historical differences with the United States, but no one should expect Cuba to change its position or yield in its

principles. Cuba is and will continue being socialist. Cuba is and will continue being a friend of the Soviet Union and of all the socialist states. Cuba is and will continue being an international country. Principles cannot be negotiated.[4]

Cuba and the Caribbean Basin

The four phases of Cuban foreign policy identified above correspond closely to the pattern of Cuban foreign policy in the Caribbean basin. In the 1960s the Cuban government was associated, sometimes directly and sometimes not, with a number of attempts to subvert reactionary governments in the region. In the earliest years these 'adventures' were amateurish and romantic in conception, drawing directly on and attempting to repeat, in what were considered similar circumstances, the successful formula of the Cuban revolutionary war against Batistá. Panama, Haiti, Nicaragua and the Dominican Republic were chosen as the sites for such actions and in every case the venture proved to be utterly unsuccessful. Beginning with Venezuela, however, a more sophisticated approach emerged, in which local forces were more evident and in which revolutionary socialist change, rather than simply a change of political regime, came to be identified as the principal goal of the protagonists. This quickly brought Cuba into direct conflict with the governments concerned and with the Inter-American system at large as constituted by the OAS. On a Venezuelan initiative this body took the decision in July 1964 to impose diplomatic and economic sanctions against Cuba, effectively isolating it from Latin America, except for Mexico which refused to implement this decision. Cuba's response was to step up support for guerrilla activity in the area, particularly in Venezuela, Colombia and Guatemala where established guerrilla movements existed and the chances of success were deemed high. In time, though, the failure of such expectations to be realised and the polemical conflicts which resulted with other revolutionary forces in these countries led to changing assumptions, levels of support, and finally explicit recognition of the inability of armed struggle alone to bring about change. Without necessarily abandoning this strategy, particularly in certain countries of Central America and the Caribbean, where it was recognised that entrenched dictatorship might preclude other paths to power, Cuba sought new openings in which traditional diplomacy was to play the major part.

The most immediately successful instance of this new policy concerned the Commonwealth Caribbean. In 1970 Dr Eric Williams of Trinidad and Tobago, in his capacity as Chairman of the Inter-American Economic and Social Council, called for the reabsorption of Cuba into the OAS, and as if to underline Trinidad's own commitment to that policy, technical exchanges with Cuba were arranged. It was not, however, until 1972 that the decisive breakthrough occurred when, with the return of the Michael Manley government in Jamaica and on the initiative of Forbes Burnham of Guyana, the Seventh Conference of the Heads of Government of the Commonwealth Caribbean jointly agreed to the early establishment of relations with Cuba 'be they economic, political or both'.[5]

This inaugurated a period of Cuban-Commonwealth Caribbean co-operation, particularly with Guyana and Jamaica, where close relations rapidly developed. In 1973 both Manley and Burnham accepted Castro's invitation to travel with him to the Non-Aligned Conference in Algiers and both subsequently paid highly publicised visits to Cuba where they were awarded the José Marti National Order established 'for heads of state and government and leaders of political parties and movements who have distinguished themselves for their international solidarity with the struggle against imperialism, colonialism and neo-colonialism and for their friendship with the Socialist Revolution of Cuba'.[6] Supplementing these connections was the structure of bilateral relations. In the case of Guyana these included, by the end of 1976, commercial agreements relating to the sale of rice, timber and cement and, in the technical assistance area, the training of Guyanese pilots and fishermen in Cuba. Guyana also permitted Cuban transport planes on their way to Angola to refuel in Guyana despite strong US protests. With respect to Jamaica, bilateral relations were especially close. Cuba applauded Manley's moves to establish the International Bauxite Association as a producers' association along the lines of OPEC as consistent with its oft-stated policy of national control of natural resources. It also welcomed Manley's unequivocal support for Cuban involvement in Angola and labelled the Jamaican government as 'progressive'. Considerable Cuban aid, which was both highly visible and aimed directly at the problems of the poor, accompanied the rhetoric. The construction of a secondary school in Spanish Town by a joint Cuban-Jamaican workforce, the assignment of Cuban doctors to the Jamaican health service and the provision of condensed milk from Cuba for sale in Jamaica to low-income groups are just a few examples of assistance given by the end of 1976. There also developed collaboration in the fields of fisheries, agriculture, tourism, transportation and public health, as well as wider commercial relations between the two countries and exchanges of personnel, including the training of young Jamaicans in Cuba in aspects of building and construction. However, these undoubted gains for Cuba were to some degree offset by the only limited relations it was also to establish with Trinidad and Barbados. The latter, in particular, proved difficult, the government of Barbados not only refusing to allow Cuban aircraft to continue to refuel in the country *en route* to Africa but also condemning the Cuban action in Angola as meddling in the internal affairs of that country.

A similar pattern of mixed but nevertheless definite headway is evident elsewhere in the Caribbean basin in this period. In 1972, for example, Cuba demonstrated the new pragmatism of its foreign policy when it sent two medical brigades to Nicaragua to aid victims of the earthquake — a gesture repeated two years later towards Honduras when medical teams and relief assistance were provided to aid the victims of a hurricane. During this period Cuba also demonstrated its withdrawal of support for indiscriminate guerrilla warfare in the region. In 1973, for example, it offered no assistance whatsoever to the ill-fated attempt of Colonel Camaaño, leader of the 1965 uprising in Santo Domingo, to establish a guerrilla force in the Dominican Republic, and towards both Panama and Venezuela efforts were made to reach a new understanding. This resulted, in the case of the former, in a lengthy visit by General Torrijos to Cuba in 1976 and, in the case of the latter, in a gradual normalisation of relations between the two countries. Relations with Mexico also deepened in this period and in 1975 an exchange was made at the highest level when President Echeverría was a visitor to Cuba and Raúl Castro was a guest in Mexico.

The theme at the bilateral level was repeated at the multilateral. In May 1972 Peru introduced a motion in the OAS to allow each nation to resume relations with Cuba if it so wished. It was defeated 7 for, 13 against, with 3 abstentions. The matter was then raised on a number of subsequent occasions, notably in November 1974 when virtually the same motion was again put before the members. This time the vote went 15 for, 3 against, with 6 abstentions (one of which was the United States). Finally in July 1975 the question was again reintroduced, this time passing 19 for (including the US), 3 against, with 2 abstentions.[7] Sanctions, it must be stressed, were not officially lifted by this action, but they too had suffered an erosion throughout the early 1970s and the extent to which Cuba was now accepted as a full member of the Latin American economic community was underlined by its endorsement of and membership in the Latin American Economic System (SELA), a body established in 1975 to negotiate a common Latin American front on economic matters which, specifically and significantly, excluded the United States.

Compared to but five years earlier, the position of Cuba in the Caribbean basin at the end of 1975 was greatly enhanced. It had been achieved almost exclusively through Cuban and Caribbean initiatives and thus demonstrated the plausibility of an autonomy of developments in the region outside the control of either the United States or the Soviet Union. Cuban policy, as it was projected in the region throughout the remainder of the 1970s, was to deepen and consolidate this trend by more of the same patient, pragmatic diplomacy as had achieved it in the first place. Castro emphasised and underlined this in his speech to the First Congress of the Communist Party of Cuba held in December 1975:

> Latin America is not at this moment directly on the eve of overall changes that lead, as in Cuba, to sudden socialist transformations. It is clear that these are not impossible in some of the Latin American countries. But what determines the circumstances in our America is, above all, a general consciousness — not only among its working class and the peoples, but also at key levels of some of its governments — that the conflict of interests between Latin America as a whole and each of our countries separately with the policy of Yankee imperialism, cannot be resolved by way of sell out or conciliation, but requires joint resistance, already under way.[8]

Continued co-operation in policy thus became the key to future progress. None was ruled out, be they a bourgeois class or a bourgeois government, as long as they genuinely sought an independence from the United States.

In the Caribbean basin this meant first and foremost a policy of support for the Manley government. Castro paid a long-expected visit to Jamaica in October 1977 and was followed by the Cuban Minister for Foreign Affairs in February 1978. This was reciprocated in part when Manley visited Havana to attend the Sixth Non-Aligned Conference later in the year and when his Foreign Minister, P.J. Patterson, visited Cuba in April 1979. More technical and commercial agreements followed and, more importantly for Cuba, several areas of common political concern were identified. In the Caribbean basin this included support for Cuba's call for the independence of Puerto Rico, as well as approval of the revolutions in Nicaragua and Grenada. Further afield, and by no means coincidental to this, Manley was to seek closer relations with Eastern Europe and to visit the Soviet Union where a trade agreement was signed. Panama was another country with which relations were further strengthened during this period. Cuba had fully supported Panama in its renegotiation of the Panama Canal Treaties with the United States, emphasising in particular Panamanian sovereignty over the Canal Zone and arguing for the immediate withdrawal of the United States from that area. Cuba also welcomed the more active interest in Third World affairs which Panama was developing at this time and especially praised its active support of the FSLN in Nicaragua. Relations were also consolidated with Mexico, President López Portillo endorsing Cuba's demands for an end to the US embargo and the withdrawal of US forces from the Guantanamo Base when he met Castro in August 1980.

Supplementing these bilateral accords was the continued development of multilateral relations. Cuba remained an active supporter of SELA and was a participant in the Caribbean Group for Co-operation in Economic Development which was formed under World Bank auspices in 1977. It was also a member of the Caribbean Committee of the Economic Commission for Latin America and applauded, as 'objectively necessary', the development of the Caribbean Community and Common Market (CARICOM) and closer integration between all Latin American and Caribbean states. This was to be encouraged without regard to the internal political systems of such states. As Osvaldo Cardenas, head of the Caribbean Section of the Central Committee of the Cuban Communist Party, put it in April 1980:

> Cuba has no designs on the Caribbean. We do not get upset when the U.S.A. and Caribbean countries work to improve their relations. We have never publicly criticised or disagreed with Caribbean governments even when some of them choose to deliberately misrepresent Cuba and make statements that could breed misunderstanding. We take the view that they behave in this manner because of U.S. pressures. But the Caribbean's not a capitalist lake. We do not subscribe to any idea of the Caribbean being in the American sphere of influence. Nor do we regard it as a concession on the part of the U.S. to now say that it does not object to ideological pluralism in this region. The reality is that in practice it has no use for ideological pluralism. Twenty-one years after, the U.S. still cannot come to terms with the Cuban Revolution.[9]

As for Cuba, it was joyfully coming to terms with the fact that it no longer represented the lone example of revolutionary change in the Caribbean basin. The Grenada revolution in March and that in Nicaragua in July 1979 had given it dependable allies and revived the concept of revolutionary militancy as the path to power. 'There is only one road to liberation: that of Cuba, that of Grenada, that of Nicaragua. There is no other formula'[10] was how Castro was to put it in a speech to the Cuban people made just after his visit to Nicaragua in July 1980. At the same time he also took care to point out that there was a distinction to be drawn between the processes of change in Nicaragua and Cuba:

> Nicaragua does not have a socialist system. What it has is a mixed economy. There's even a multi-party system. There's the Sandinista Front and left-wing groups, and why not? — there are also several right-wing parties. Therefore, we can't imagine Nicaragua's situation as exactly like Cuba's . . . we cannot be thinking of a strictly Cuban formula, because that formula is specifically for us. Of course, many of the other formulas have many of the ingredients that ours has, but they'll never be completely alike.[11]

Pragmatism and enthusiasm were thus at the centre of policy with, if anything, an emphasis on the former.

In turn, this dictated a cautious approach and carefully measured assistance. In Nicaragua, in the first year after the revolution, aid was thus almost exclusively medical and educational in character, not military, and corresponded to the 'low-key approach' taken by Cuba during the insurrectionary struggle against Somoza.[12] Likewise, in respect of Grenada, Cuba was 'more wooed than wooing'. In short, Cuba recognised that, if 1979 had seen a decisive shift in its favour in the Caribbean basin, further gains elsewhere should not be jeopardised by over-celebration of this fact. This was made explicit in the 'Resolution on International Policy' adopted by the Second Congress of the Communist Party of Cuba held in December 1980. While this welcomed 'the resounding peoples' victories in Nicaragua and Grenada', it also considered 'other situations in Latin America and the Caribbean to be very important'. Accordingly:

> In the coming years, Cuba will express its continuing solidarity with all patriotic, anti-imperialist governments that have decided to oppose Washington's domination with dignity. Cuba will maintain its strategic guideline of seeking the broadest possible unity for

national independence, progress and democracy in the region. Our party encourages and supports all sovereign actions and attitudes by Latin American and Caribbean governments and political forces protecting their legitimate national interests and promoting more just and equitable economic relations.[13]

If Cuban influence in the Caribbean basin reached a new peak in 1979, in the following year it began a decline which has yet to be arrested. Several factors have contributed to this, but three stand out as of particular importance. The first reflected the beginnings of a reaction against Cuba's close alliance with the Soviet Union. Afghanistan was here the key. The UN General Assembly resolution calling for the withdrawal of Soviet troops was supported by all Caribbean basin countries, including Jamaica and Nicaragua, with only Cuba and Grenada voting against. Cuba subsequently tried to minimise its losses but the damage was done. Proof of this came with the withdrawal of support by non-aligned nations for the election of Cuba, and the subsequent selection of Mexico, as Latin America's representative on the UN Security Council.

The second factor which brought about a fall in Cuba's standing in the region was the election of Reagan to the US presidency shortly after a swing to the right in several elections in the Eastern Caribbean and Jamaica. In the case of the former, Reagan's well-advertised antipathy to the Cuban revolution encouraged those who were alarmed at the drift of events in the region to act on their fears. In March 1981 Colombia severed diplomatic relations with Cuba and in May 1981 Costa Rica followed suit. Relations with Panama also deteriorated following considerable US pressure on the government of Panama to reduce its links with Cuba. In the case of the latter, the elections brought to power governments keen to circumscribe Cuban influence in the Commonwealth Caribbean. Within days of taking office the new Jamaican government of Edward Seaga had asked the Cuban government to recall its ambassador on the grounds of alleged involvement in Jamaica's internal affairs. A year later in October 1981 it severed diplomatic relations completely on the equally dubious grounds of Cuban non-co-operation in the return of three wanted men who were presumed to have taken refuge there.

The final factor contributing to the fall in Cuban prestige concerned developments in Cuba. In April 1980 an incident at the Peruvian embassy led to a massive exodus of Cubans seeking refuge in the United States. The Venezuelan government also became embroiled in the affair, leading to strained relations which came close to breaking point in October 1980 following a decision by a Venezuelan military tribunal to acquit four men accused of blowing up a Cubana Airlines plane off Barbados in 1976. In a move that was perhaps even more damaging, Venezuela also suspended the annual supply of three million barrels of oil that had been initiated in 1978, thereby emphasising Cuba's continuing vulnerability and dependence on this key commodity. It also underlined the difficulties into which the Cuban economy had run at the end of the 1970s, which have continued to limit policy in the early 1980s, particularly in regard to providing the basis for expanded overseas initiatives and assistance.

Cuba has thus only been able to condemn, and certainly in no way even begin to match, the new thrust of US policy in the region as represented by escalating military involvement and the CBI. Indeed, in respect of Central America, its profile has remained relatively low, with the US government being hard pressed to find any firm evidence of significant military assistance by the Cubans to the insurgents in El Salvador, even if Cuba has remained committed to Nicaragua and been generous in its supply of largely non-military assistance to the Sandinista government. Otherwise, and especially in the Commonwealth Caribbean, Cuba found itself increasingly isolated and relegated to the side-lines, committed largely to the support of just one government, Grenada. Consequently, this became something of a test of Cuban intention and design, watched with particular interest by others in the English-speaking Caribbean and, of course, by the United States.

Cuba and Grenada

The close association that was to develop between Cuba and Grenada began within hours of the seizure of power on 13 March 1979. Faced with the very real possibility of a mercenary invasion from Miami organised by Gairy, the PRG requested military assistance from Britain, Canada and the United States. Although Britain and Canada pledged non-intervention, all three refused to give assistance on the grounds that the threat was non-existent. Not so Cuba, which, along with Jamaica and Guyana, had also been approached by the PRG. Thus, exactly one month after the revolution, a Cuban freighter with 1,000 tons of cement for Grenada docked in St George's and reportedly also unloaded a number of wooden cases containing arms. On the same day Bishop, in a national broadcast, angrily rejected the US warning not to develop ties with Cuba, stating that 'the argument of the American ambassador that we would only be entitled to call upon the Cubans to come to our assistance after the mercenaries have landed and commenced the attack' was 'quite ridiculous'.[14]

While such initial assistance was obviously very important, even critical, it was not this alone, or even the promise of more to come, which brought Cuba and Grenada together. There was also the ideological factor. The NJM as a whole, and particularly the leadership, viewed the Cuban revolution very positively, seeing in many aspects of it a 'model' for Grenada to follow. Bishop, especially, was an enthusiastic exponent and in his speeches singled out Cuba time and again for praise. For example, in an address to the sixth summit conference of the Non-Aligned Movement in September 1979, he noted:

> Cuba laid the basis for Grenada, Nicaragua, Vietnam, Cambodia, Laos, Guinea-Bissau, Angola and Mozambique. The example and spirit of the Cuban revolution has therefore had international impact. But, perhaps, most important of all is the fact that it is now the best example of what socialism can do in a small country for health, education, employment, for ending poverty, prostitution and disease. It is now the best example in the world of what a small country under socialism can achieve. This is what socialism is all about.[15]

And six months later, in the extensive first anniversary celebrations, he was quite specifically to affirm:

> The very warm and fraternal relations which our country and people have developed with the brother people of Cuba have been one of the major sources of inspiration for our country and our process. In recognising as we do the tremendous contribution from the very earliest days and continuing today, which the fraternal government and people of Cuba have rendered to the people of Grenada, we must also acknowledge the most important fact about our relations with Cuba; the greatest debt of gratitude owed to the Cubans is that if there had been no Cuban revolution in 1959 there could have been no Grenadian revolution in 1979.[16]

The positive evaluation of Cuba was also cemented in Bishop's case by the warm and intimate relationship he established with Castro. The depth of this, and the very high regard in which Castro held Bishop, were only fully revealed in November 1983 after Bishop's death. Of him, Castro then said: 'It was impossible to imagine any one more noble, modest and unselfish . . . he was a true revolutionary – conscientious and honest . . . He could never have been guilty of being authoritarian, if he had any defect, it was his excessive tolerance and trust.'[17]

With Cuba ready to extend assistance, and Grenada more than willing to receive it, it is not surprising that a considerable programme of joint endeavour soon developed. Following upon the early provision of cement and military supplies to re-equip the People's Revolutionary Army, an embassy was opened in St George's, the first full permanent diplomatic mission to be established in Grenada. Thereafter, the immediate assistance provided by Cuba focused on health and education. From June 1979 a Cuban medical team of twelve doctors was operating in the country and shortly after 38 scholarships for higher education in Cuba were offered to Grenada. This latter programme expanded quickly and in mid-1982 it was reported that over 250 Grenadians were currently studying in Cuba.[18] The Cubans were also closely associated with the development of a fishing industry in Grenada, promising to supply up to 12 vessels to form the nucleus of a modern fishing fleet for the island. Such an expanding programme clearly required formal agreement and in June 1980 a 63-point scientific, economic and technical co-operation agreement was signed between the two countries and a Cuba-Grenada Joint Commission established to monitor progress. At meetings held in Havana in July 1981 a new agreement was discussed which, when concluded in September, involved more substantial levels of aid in a variety of areas, particularly road repair, education and educational equipment, prefabricated housing and agriculture and agro-industries. Commenting on it Coard said:

> I think that the provision of technical assistance in specific areas from Cuba to help in building the economy in different directions, is an extremely important part of this coming year's agreement. The emphasis is in the direction of assisting us through collaboration in pushing our economy forward. This will provide greater income for the farmers in our country, and provide greater employment for the people generally.[19]

He also revealed that he was seeking to increase the number of items bought from Cuba, as well as to arrange for a line of credit with the Central Bank of Cuba. Another bonus of the agreement was the opportunity to purchase staples such as rice, sugar and cement at cheaper prices than could be obtained elsewhere. A further agreement followed in December 1982 and a memorandum of understanding in the following June, outlining proposals for 28 areas of bilateral co-operation in 1984, an increase of four over those of 1983. Highlights were a convention centre and a marine aquarium. Finally, such close co-operation demanded better communication. At the beginning of 1981 Cubana Airlines inaugurated a direct weekly passenger service between Cuba and Grenada. Entry visa requirements for nationals travelling between the two countries were removed at the same time.

Assistance for building the airport was kept separate. According to Bishop, the project was discussed with Castro in Havana in August 1979 and again at the United Nations in October of the same year where agreement was reached.[20] Although from the start it was not envisaged that Cuba could or would supply everything, there is no doubt that the Cuban aid was the critical ingredient. Without it, it is difficult to see how the project could have been initiated. Within months some 250 Cubans were involved in construction and 1,500 tons of steel, 4,000 tons of cement and 1.5 million gallons of fuel had been pledged by the Cuban government in support of their activities.[21] In the event, this level of support proved insufficient, as the PRG failed to raise the necessary finance for its completion from elsewhere. The Cubans were thus drawn in ever deeper. In 1981, for example, they provided some 60 per cent of the funding and as the opening day approached – 13 March 1984 – and the terminal building and approach roads in particular were still unfinished, further extra help was drafted in. By October 1983, Cuban financial assistance for the airport had reached the very substantial figure of US$60 million.

Finally, Cuba supplied considerable military assistance to Grenada. The full extent of this was revealed when the CIA obtained the secret protocols to the PRG's treaties with Cuba, followed by those with the Soviet Union and North Korea, totalling five in all. Besides involving thousands of rifles, machine-guns and small arms, the equipment supplied included mines, armoured cars, coastguard boats, trucks, anti-aircraft guns (albeit secondhand) and searchlights, anti-tank weapons, tons of ammunition, wireless equipment, tents and uniforms. Assistance from the Soviet Union was worth US$25.8 million with US$12 million from North Korea. Cuba also pledged 27 permanent and 12 to 13 temporary military advisers and, with the Soviet Union, agreed to train PRA members in their respective countries. Common to the treaties with all three suppliers was the clause that both parties 'will take all measures . . . to assure the secrecy of the military assistance'; that with Cuba (article 12) additionally stressed the need to keep secret 'the permanency of the military personnel in both states and the character of [their] activities'.[22] Although US accusations of Soviet bloc military support for Grenada were thus correct, it is hard to see from where else the PRG could have got weapons and equipment to defend itself, given the manner in which its early requests for help had been denied by the Western allies. Moreover, the revelations about the military treaties need themselves to be kept in perspective. They did not, for example, support the wilder claims made in Washington that a large-scale Soviet base was being constructed in Grenada with direct implications for US defence.

The 'credibility' of such US allegations rested, of course, not only on arrangements internal to Grenada but also on the very active and radical foreign policy pursued by the PRG throughout its period of office. There were many facets to this, but those which stand out relate to the implementation of the platform of 'principled positions' on foreign policy which the PRG had laid down in its earliest days. These were interpreted in a way which fashioned a foreign policy that consisted, firstly, of a close alliance with Cuba and support for the positions it took up on revolutionary questions in all parts of the world, and, secondly, a resolute attempt to broaden Grenada's diplomatic relations and development links to include all manner of countries not traditionally associated with the Commonwealth Caribbean.

The former brought Grenada directly into conflict with the United States. In conjunction with Cuba, very close relations were established with the revolutionary government in Nicaragua symbolised by the presence of a leading member of the Nicaraguan junta, Daniel Ortega, as a guest of honour at the first anniversary celebrations in St George's on 13 March 1980, reciprocated by the Nicaraguans when Bishop and Castro were the guests of honour at their first anniversary celebrations in Managua the following July. Six months later Bishop made the link explicit and unequivocal when, before the Second Congress of the Cuban Communist Party, he stated:

> We give our solemn pledge that wherever circumstances require we shall unhesitatingly fulfill our internationalist responsibilities. Imperialism must know and understanding that if they touch Cuba, they touch Grenada, and if they touch Nicaragua they touch Grenada.[23]

Support for national liberation struggles elsewhere naturally followed on from this. Grenada was to support Cuba in its calls for independence for Puerto Rico and the remaining British, Dutch, French and American colonies in the region; as well as the demands for Cuban sovereignty to be extended over the Guantanamo naval base and Panamanian sovereignty over the Canal Zone. In Central America it supported the FMLN and FDR in El Salvador and in South America was vigorous in its condemnation of the Pinochet regime in Chile (which had established relations and provided military assistance to Grenada under Gairy). Further afield, in Southern Africa, Grenada extended solidarity to the African National Congress and to the South West African People's Organisation, and also fully supported Polisario by recognising and establishing relations with the Saharawi Arab Democratic Republic. In the Middle East solidarity was extended to the Palestine Liberation Organisation. This was not all one way. In turn, Grenada was able to call on support for its revolution from a wide range of states and organisations abroad. At the First International Conference in Solidarity with Grenada in November 1981, no less than 41 countries from all parts of the world were represented, including Mongolia, Vietnam, North Korea, the Congo Republic and Ethiopia.

Parallel to, and drawing on, such developments was Grenada's diplomatic thrust as a whole. This involved establishing, almost entirely on a non-resident basis, diplomatic relations with many states, but particularly those in the Middle East and Eastern Europe. Both Bishop and Coard were to visit these regions on a number of occasions, invariably carrying large 'shopping baskets' for development assistance. The amounts promised in the end were not inconsiderable and came from countries such as Libya, Iraq, Syria, Bulgaria, Hungary, the German Democratic Republic and the Soviet Union, from whom considerable help in the form of scholarships, agricultural machinery, lines of credit and other such matters was obtained and in which an embassy was eventually to be established. The lesson from this last act, though perfectly logical from the point of view of the PRG, was not to be lost on the Reagan administration. It was seen to be symbolic of Grenada's growing integration with, and dependence on, the socialist bloc, in which Cuba was the catalyst. Indeed, what better proof could there be of this than that Grenada's first resident ambassador to Cuba, Richard Jacobs, was reassigned from his Havana posting to be Grenada's first resident ambassador in Moscow and that a resident Soviet embassy was established in Grenada headed by a former senior KGB official, Colonel Gennedy Sazhenev. However, diplomatic contact and development assistance do not automatically imply direction, especially given the context in which the Soviet Union had greatly expanded its presence throughout Latin America and the Caribbean during the 1970s. The notion of a Grenadian 'proxy' also belies the very considerable efforts made by Bishop to maintain good relations with Western Europe, especially France where he established a warm working relationship with Claude Cheysson, the French Foreign Minister and former EEC Commissioner for Development. In the final analysis, therefore, Grenadian foreign policy was based on considerations no different from those guiding the other Eastern Caribbean states – above all, the imperative of acquiring development assistance in a world of diminishing resources. It differed only in the confidence with which it was prepared to approach non-traditional sources, including the socialist states, and the success with which its efforts were rewarded.

Notes and References

1. E. Gonzalez, 'U.S. Policy: Objectives and Options' in J.I. Dominguez (ed.), *Cuba: Internal and International Affairs* (Sage Publications, Beverly Hills, 1982), p. 211.
2. See, for example, W.R. Duncan, 'Soviet and Cuban Interests in the Caribbean' in R. Millett and W.M. Will, *The Restless Caribbean: Changing Patterns of International Relations* (Praeger, New York, 1979), pp. 132–48.
3. See, for example, W. Grabendorff, 'Cuba's Involvement in Africa: An Interpretation of Objectives, Reactions and Limitations', *Journal of Interamerican Studies and World Affairs*, vol. 22, no. 1 (1980), pp. 3–29.
4. 'Main Report submitted to the 2nd Congress by the First Secretary of the Central Committee of the Communist Party of Cuba, comrade Fidel Castro Ruz' in *Second Congress of the Communist Party of Cuba: Documents and Speeches* (Political Publishers, Havana, 1981), pp. 119–22.
5. *Trinidad Express*, 15 October 1972.
6. *Granma Weekly Review*, 20 April 1975, and 29 June 1975, cited in R.E. Jones, 'Cuba and the English-speaking Caribbean' in C. Blasier and C. Mesa-Lago (eds.), *Cuba in The World* (University of Pittsburgh Press, Pittsburgh, 1979), p. 136.
7. Figures on voting from C. Mesa-Lago, *Cuba in the 1970s: Pragmatism and Institutionalisation* (University of New Mexico Press, Albuquerque, 1978), Table 7.
8. 'Report of the Central Committee of the CPC to the First Congress, presented by Comrade Fidel Castro Ruz, First Secretary of the CPC' in *First Congress of the Communist Party of Cuba: Report Central* (Department of Revolutionary Orientation of the Central Committee of the Communist Party of Cuba, Havana, 1977), p. 327.
9. *Caribbean Contact*, June 1980.
10. F. Castro, 'There is only one road to Liberation: that of Cuba, that of Grenada, that of Nicaragua', Speech given on 26 July, 1980 in M. Taber (ed.), *Fidel Castro Speeches*, vol. 1 (Pathfinder Press, New York, 1981), p. 326.

11. Ibid., pp. 318-21.
12. See W. Leo Grande, 'Cuba and Nicaragua', *Caribbean Review*, vol. 9, no. 1 (1980).
13. 'Resolution on International Policy' in Taber (ed.), *Fidel Castro*, Appendix B.
14. 'In Nobody's Backyard', National Broadcast by Maurice Bishop on RFG on 13 April 1979 in M. Bishop, *Selected Speeches, 1979-81* (Casa de las Americas, Havana, 1982), pp. 12-13.
15. 'Imperialism is not Invincible' in M. Bishop, *Forward Ever! Three Years of the Grenadian Revolution* (Pathfinder Press, Sydney, 1982), p. 94.
16. 'Forward Ever: Against Imperialism and Towards Genuine National Independence and People's Power' in Bishop, *Forward Ever!*, p. 114.
17. 'Funeral address given by Fidel Castro in tribute to the Cubans killed in Grenada', 14 November 1983, printed in full in *Guardian*, 19 November 1983.
18. *Latin America Regional Report: Caribbean*, RC-82-04, 7 May 1982.
19. *Caribbean Insight*, November 1981.
20. See 'Against U.S. Sabotage of the Airport Project', Address to the Nation by Maurice Bishop on 29 March 1981 in Bishop, *Forward Ever!*, p. 162.
21. Figures from *Caribbean Contact*, December 1979.
22. United States Information Service, *Secret Grenada/Communist Bloc Documents Released November 4* (United States Embassy, London, 8 November 1983), p. 8.
23. Quoted in H.S. Gill, 'The Foreign Policy of the Grenada Revolution', *Bulletin of Eastern Caribbean Affairs*, vol. 7, no. 1 (1981), p. 4.

5 THE COMMONWEALTH CARIBBEAN DIMENSION

By virtue of their common experience of British colonialism and their consequent insertion into the English-speaking world, the various states of the Commonwealth Caribbean have always had a particular collective identity within the enormous variety of historical connections, social patterns and cultural traditions that characterise the Caribbean region as a whole. This has been reinforced over the years by a long record of association in a range of regional bodies. From the earliest days British colonial administration was marked by regular attempts to achieve a closer union between its Caribbean possessions, albeit chiefly for reasons of economy. Ultimately, the many years of discussion and debate about the creation of some form of regional union came to fruition when in 1958 the West Indies Federation was established, embracing all the islands of the Commonwealth Caribbean, including Grenada.

However, the experience of the Federation underlined the limits of the region's sense of unity and common destiny, for it fell apart in a series of ignominious internal wrangles after just four years in existence. Residual functional ties between the various ex-Federal states maintained a low level of contact between the islands until in the late 1960s the cold draught of self-government opened the way for the negotiation of a measure of regional economic integration. The Caribbean Free Trade Association (CARIFTA) came into being in 1968 and was converted in 1973 into a more elaborate body, CARICOM, committed to the furtherance of economic integration, the expansion of intra-regional functional co-operation and the co-ordination of regional foreign policy. Membership was comprised of all the states of the Commonwealth Caribbean region: Antigua and Barbuda, Barbados, Belize, Dominica, Grenada, Guyana, Jamaica, Montserrat, St Kitts-Nevis, St Lucia, St Vincent and Trinidad and Tobago.

Although CARICOM has been in existence for more than a decade now, it has not succeeded in fully reconciling the competing centrifugal and centripetal forces which have long been at work in Commonwealth Caribbean affairs. On the one hand, all of the constituent territories of CARICOM, except for Montserrat, are now fully independent states. Their formal sovereignty is not threatened in any way by the nature of the regional integration movement, which remains a traditional inter-state association deliberately designed to avoid any hint of supranationality. On the other hand, there has unquestionably developed between the states of the region a coherent and systematised web of economic and political relationships, which is at the same time underpinned by some sense of common identity. The extent and meaning of the latter is hard to measure. No longer (if ever) strong enough to constitute the basis for a West Indian nation, it can nevertheless promote a feeling of togetherness in the face of adversity and a determination to resist external efforts to divide the region. In short, regional politics in the Commonwealth Caribbean have come to be characterised by a paradox — an overbearing immediate potential for division generated by the emergence of separate sovereignties and sustained by a long history of insular self-consciousness, combined with an underlying propensity for unity based upon an emotional sense of brotherhood. Both aspects of the paradox have to be understood in order to grasp the varied and changing reactions provoked in the region by the Grenadian revolution.

First Reactions to the Revolution

The announcement of the *coup* in Grenada in March 1979 took the Commonwealth Caribbean as much by surprise as it did the rest of the world. Reactions certainly varied. The take-over of the New Jewel Movement was immediately welcomed by the two regional states with the most left-wing governments — Jamaica, where Michael Manley and the People's National Party were seeking to implement democratic socialism, and Guyana, where the regime of Forbes Burnham had established a putative Co-operative Socialist Republic in 1970. Indeed, as Maurice Bishop was subsequently to reveal, they were the very first two states to respond to the revolution's call for assistance and solidarity, offering help even before Cuba.[1] Elsewhere in the region, however, the immediate response was considerably less warm. In Barbados particular concern was expressed about the constitutionality of the New Jewel's assumption of power. The government hastily summoned a meeting of the foreign ministers of independent Commonwealth Caribbean states and proposed that the situation in Grenada be regularised by what was in effect a constitutional sleight of hand. It involved the appointment of Bishop as a minister of government by Gairy's Deputy Prime Minister — Gairy being away — who would then resign. The Governor-General would then appoint Bishop as Prime

Minister, and he would select his cabinet from the other five opposition members of Parliament and two former supporters of Gairy. Whilst this extraordinary manoeuvre was being discussed, Barbados announced that it was only prepared to accord *de facto* recognition to the new regime. Meanwhile, the Trinidad government stated that it was not its practice to make statements of formal recognition; the position it took on the *coup* would become evident in its future relations with Grenada.

This emphasis upon the constitutional question did not conceal the deeper political worries which many Commonwealth Caribbean governments felt about what had occurred in Grenada. As one observer noted at the time, their central concern was 'the fear of being taken to accept the legality of the Grenada revolution which would then serve to legitimise revolutionary activity in their own countries'.[2] In this respect, the response of the small Leeward and Windward Islands in the Eastern Caribbean was the most revealing. At an emergency meeting of the council of ministers of the West Indies Associated States (WIAS), the sub-regional grouping which linked Grenada with Antigua, Dominica, Montserrat, St Kitts-Nevis, St Lucia and St Vincent, the revolution was condemned and a decision taken to refuse the new government recognition. In their panic, they forgot that only two of the six states present, Dominica and St Lucia, then had the international legal status as independent sovereign territories to accord recognition, the others still being Associated States of Britain with their foreign policy conducted by London. The WIAS meeting also proposed the establishment of an Eastern Caribbean police force to stamp out revolutionary insurrection in the other islands, attempted to stop the regional airline landing in Grenada and for a while prevented the Eastern Caribbean Currency Authority issuing EC$3 million of new notes which were due to the government of Grenada. As a body, however, the council of ministers did not seek to promote external intervention to overthrow the Bishop regime, although one of their number, John Compton, the Prime Minister of St Lucia, had reacted to the first news of the revolution by sending a note to the British government demanding that 'something be done immediately'[3] to prevent the stability of the whole area being undermined. This indicated the attitude of the small island leaders at this time. To put it simply, they were terrified lest the Grenada 'virus' began to spread, infecting next their islands and thus bringing about their downfall. It was a crude gut reaction to an event with which the Commonwealth Caribbean was unfamiliar.

In the few months immediately following the Grenada revolution, events served only to add to their unease. In Dominica in June the increasingly oppressive government of Patrick John fell amidst violent protests, calls for a general strike and the formation of a committee of national salvation composed of all opposition elements in the country. A month later in St Lucia Compton's own government was defeated at the polls by a newly radicalised St Lucia Labour Party. Grenada seemed to have inaugurated nothing less than a new era of change in the Eastern Caribbean. This apparent trend was further reinforced when the new leaders of Dominica and St Lucia quickly met with Bishop and other members of the PRG in a 'mini-summit' in Grenada. The resulting 'Declaration of St George's' was assertively left-wing in tone: it set 'popular democracy, respect for the rights of workers, and social and economic justice for the masses' as the main domestic objectives of the participating governments, declared its opposition to imperialism in all its forms, and endorsed 'an independent and non-aligned approach to foreign policy relations with all countries'.[4] Moreover, at the conference, it was reported that placards were displayed reading 'Cato next',[5] a reference to Milton Cato's government in St Vincent, where left-wing forces were gathering their strength. A vocal radical group also existed in Antigua and for a while it was possible to believe that further moves to the left would be effected in these two other islands. As these various developments took place, Commonwealth Caribbean concern about Grenada began to focus much more upon the ideological direction in which the revolution was moving – in particular the developing friendship with Cuba – and the longer-term implications which were contained therein for the rest of the region.

For this, in large part, the PRG itself was responsible. The series of 'principled positions' on foreign policy issues which it adopted in the first few months of the revolution made no concession to the views of other Commonwealth Caribbean governments, with whom it was associated within CARICOM. To be fair, from the moment that it assumed power, the government had reaffirmed Grenada's commitment to CARICOM and its readiness to continue to participate within the WIAS council of ministers. Yet no attempt was made to hide its disaffection for the more conservative governments of the region and its feeling that they had held back the proper development of CARICOM as a vehicle for challenging dependency. The founding manifesto of the New Jewel Movement had expressed the point in these words:

We support completely the political and economic integration of the

Caribbean. But . . . we believe in real and genuine integration of all the peoples of the Caribbean for the benefit of all the people. We support the integration of the economies of the islands under ownership and control of the people of these islands. We oppose the present trend of integrating those economies to make it easier for foreign companies to exploit us . . . We will work towards ensuring that CARICOM becomes a meaningful reality.[6]

Convinced, as Bishop put it in a speech to the Non-Aligned Movement in Havana in September 1979, that 'the balance of forces in the world' was changing and that there was 'being built a new Caribbean – Jamaica, Guyana, a new Grenada, Dominica, St Lucia',[7] the PRG was initially in no mood to seek to allay the anxieties of its neighbours and regional partners.

Just over a year later, however, the Commonwealth Caribbean must have looked rather different to the Grenadian leadership. A series of events combined to isolate the regime. First, the anticipated further radicalisation of small island politics did not ensue. Elections in St Vincent in December 1979 and Antigua in 1980 returned right-wing governments and saw the complete trouncing of those emergent radical parties whose political positions resembled that of the New Jewel Movement. Secondly, the potential for support from reforming governments in Dominica and St Lucia evaporated – in the case of the former in corruption and electoral defeat in July 1980, in the case of the latter in bitter internal argument. Thirdly, relations with Guyana were soured when in June 1980 the PRG bluntly accused the Burnham government of complicity in the murder of the well-known political activist, Dr Walter Rodney. Lastly, and of critical importance, there was the defeat of the Manley government in Jamaica in October 1980. Manley had been the only Commonwealth Caribbean head of government to attend the first anniversary celebration of the revolution in March 1980 and had been an invaluable supporter of Grenada within the region. To make matters worse, the Grenadian government had been unable to establish more than correct relations with Trinidad. This mattered, not only because many Grenadians live in Trinidad and the cultural and economic links between the two islands have long been close, but also because Trinidad, courtesy of oil, was a wealthy country in Commonwealth Caribbean terms and had established an aid programme for the states in the region. Yet repeated Grenadian efforts to open a dialogue were coldly rebuffed. Personal letters from Bishop to Dr Williams went unacknowledged and unanswered, as did other correspondence from PRG ministers to their Trinidadian counterparts. Formal diplomatic relations existed between the two states but, according to Trinidad, no more substantive co-operation could be discussed until elections were held in Grenada.

No doubt feeling increasingly beleaguered within the Commonwealth Caribbean, Bishop's temper finally snapped in the face of a sharply critical attack made on his government by the Barbadian Prime Minister, Tom Adams. Speaking, significantly, immediately after Reagan's election to the US presidency in November 1980, Adams warned that Grenada's failure to hold elections would soon begin to damage the ability of one of the most important regional institutions, the Caribbean Development Bank, to attract funds from other international lending agencies. There followed an exchange quite oblivious of diplomatic niceties, in which Bishop described Adam's call for elections as 'provocative and hostile' and disparagingly referred to him as 'Uncle Tom Adams'. 'Like an expectant dog barking for his supper', Bishop went on, 'he rushes in to please his new master Reagan like all good yard fowls by attacking Grenada.'[8] The row underlined the extent of Grenada's isolation in the region and amply illustrated the ease with which Commonwealth Caribbean divisions could be drawn into the global ideological battle which Reagan had committed his new administration to fight.

Within the region the Adams-Bishop squabble led to the Barbados government withdrawing all diplomatic courtesies normally offered to members of the Grenadian government and produced several instances of intimidation and harassment of PRG ministers as they passed throught the Grantley Adams International Airport in Barbados. In the event, however, the disagreement marked the nadir of the PRG's relations with other Commonwealth Caribbean governments. By the early months of 1981 the latter were beginning to realise, with relief, that the revolution in Grenada was not the harbinger of other similar acts throughout the region. Recent election results had, in fact, pointed in precisely the opposite direction. By the same token, the PRG was alarmed by its increasingly isolated position in the region and was newly motivated by Reagan's election to make friends and establish alliances with fellow Commonwealth Caribbean regimes. In short, the basis was founded for an accommodation.

Towards the Acceptance of Ideological Pluralism

The first signs of a change in the way Grenada was treated in the region came in May and June 1981. The issue in question was the US government's attempt to stipulate that a grant which it was giving to the Caribbean Development Bank to help the least developed countries of the Commonwealth Caribbean should not be disbursed to Grenada. As has already been mentioned, the bank's directors voted unanimously to reject the grant on the grounds that it would contravene that aspect of the bank's charter which prohibited it from interfering 'in the political affairs' or being influenced 'by the political character' of any member-state.[9] Whatever they felt about the particular merits of Grenada's revolution, the region's governments were not prepared to see one of their number discriminated against by an external power. From the US point of view the intervention was badly timed since, after months of negotiation, agreement had just been reached on the structure of a new Organisation of Eastern Caribbean States (OECS), planned, with Grenada's backing, as the means by which to revive subregional co-operation between the old Associated States. The heads of government of these now independent territories signed the treaty at Basseterre in St Kitts on 18 June 1981 and, in one of their first pronouncements, endorsed the stance taken by the directors of the Caribbean Development Bank. So too did the whole of the membership of CARICOM at a foreign ministers' meeting held for the first time in Grenada at the end of the same month. In his opening address to this meeting Bishop again pledged his government's willingness 'to continue to work in a spirit of fraternal and sisterly co-operation for greater Caribbean Community integration'[10] and was rewarded with a final communiqué which 'noted with concern the economic aggression being waged by the United States against Grenada' and condemned any such effort 'to subvert Caribbean regional institutions built up over long years of struggle'.[11]

Similar considerations of regional unity influenced the Commonwealth Caribbean's initial response to the emerging Caribbean Basin Initiative, which from the outset appeared likely to exclude Grenada from the list of potential beneficiaries. Commonwealth Caribbean foreign ministers, meeting in September 1981 to consider the region's collective response, accordingly adopted a set of negotiating guidelines, in which the first and most important point was their insistence that 'participation in the programme should be open to all territories in the region'.[12] The plea was ignored, and once the money was on the table, as it were, the Commonwealth Caribbean split. Following Reagan's flattering reference in his CBI speech to Jamaica as a country that was now 'making freedom work',[13] Seaga was quick to applaud the CBI proposals. He also indicated that he would not object to Grenada's exclusion, since other countries, mainly Cuba itself, would be taking care of its needs.[14] By comparison, the rest of the region was much more dubious about the contents of the CBI, notably its emphasis on investment and trade rather than direct development aid, and was additionally embarrassed by Grenada's obvious exclusion, although, it must be said, not to the extent of choosing to opt out of the CBI in solidarity with Grenada. Nevertheless, the region's rather muted reaction to the US plan was revealing in itself, for, amongst other things, it demonstrated how far the PRG had come in the preceding year in winning the grudging respect of several of its CARICOM colleagues.

It is clear that the United States administration failed to realise this. As a result, the 'working holiday' spent by Reagan in the Commonwealth Caribbean in April 1982 was not a great diplomatic success for the Americans. He travelled first to the favoured territory of Jamaica, where he allowed himself to indulge to the full his anti-communist rhetoric, declaring that Cuba was on the 'road to serfdom' and again applauding Seaga for 'rescuing' Jamaica from a government that was 'virtually under communist control'.[15] In Barbados, however, the same sort of talk did not receive such a warm welcome. Reagan chose to invite the leaders of only Antigua, Dominica, St Kitts-Nevis and St Vincent to meet him there. The prime ministers of Grenada and St Lucia were ostentatiously excluded and the new Trinidadian Prime Minister, George Chambers, who following Dr Williams's death in March 1981 had tried to reopen contacts with the PRG, declined to attend. Yet even the highly pro-Western figures the President did entertain were not impressed to hear him suggest that Grenada would sooner or later try to spread the 'virus' of communism among its neighbours. Eastern Caribbean leaders had themselves thought and spoken in these terms in 1979, but they no longer felt frightened for their own positions and were prepared to work with Bishop within a Commonwealth Caribbean framework. The United States had completely misjudged the softening of attitudes which had taken place towards Grenada in the Eastern Caribbean during 1981. Indeed, the local leaders' rather cool reaction to Reagan's crude anti-communism showed that they had been rather more sophisticated in their acceptance of the reality of ideological pluralism in the Commonwealth Caribbean than had their supposedly more worldly allies in Washington. Although Seaga and, to some extent, Adams had still to be excluded from that judgement, the attitude of the other CARICOM leaders suggested that, at last, they were learning to live with revolutionary Grenada.

The CARICOM Summits

More evidence to this effect was provided by the decisions taken at the CARICOM Heads of Government Conference which took place at Ocho Rios in Jamaica in November 1982. It was the first meeting of the governing body of the Caribbean Community to have been held in seven years and the most contentious issue facing the heads of government was still undoubtedly Grenada. In the weeks before the summit, Adams had returned to the attack by frequently expressing the view that the Community's leaders should consider changing the CARICOM Treaty so as to commit its members to the maintenance of parliamentary democracy and the defence of human rights. His suggestion was immediately supported by Seaga, who was quoted as saying that there had appeared in the Commonwealth Caribbean 'something called people's democracy, and this was the Cuban model which we reject'.[16] Elsewhere in the region, discussions among some of the OECS states (excluding Grenada) and Barbados on the formation of a regional defence force armed with US and British equipment, particularly small naval craft, had finally borne fruit with the signing of a Memorandum of Understanding in Dominica in October 1982. It was specifically aimed at providing mutual support in the event of a threat to 'democracy' and national security, whether from mercenaries or other states, but could conceivably be used, as the Antiguan Prime Minister, Vere Bird, admitted in an unguarded moment, to forestall further 'Grenada-style *coups*'.[17]

Against this background, the CARICOM summit was not without its tense moments. Adams formally proposed an amendment to the Community Treaty which would have committed member states 'to the principle of political liberty and the protection of the fundamental rights and freedoms of the individuals through adherence to the principle of the rule of law and practice of free, fair and regular elections'.[18] Bishop retorted that fundamental human rights should also be deemed to include the right to life, a job, education, good roads, electricity and piped water. The debate was resolved only by means of private dialogues outside formal conference sessions, in which it seems that George Chambers was particularly influential. Chambers reported that Bishop had personally given him an undertaking to hold elections in Grenada, although not necessarily of a Westminster type; added to which, during the conference, Bishop personally ordered the release of some 28 political detainees in a move obviously designed to defuse further criticism of his government's record by Adams and Seaga. In the event, neither leader pushed the point and the conference decided to make no alterations to the CARICOM Treaty, adopting instead a statement on human rights entitled the Declaration of Ocho Rios. It omitted the original Barbadian call for free and fair elections and specifically included the Community's commitment to 'the political, civil, economic, social and cultural rights of the peoples of the region',[19] as well as the concept of ideological pluralism and the right of all states to choose their own path of development.

Within the Commonwealth Caribbean, the agreement was generally interpreted as a victory for Grenada and a defeat for Barbados, Jamaica and, above all, the United States, which many believed to have been the instigator of the whole manoeuvre. It was noted that the idea of trying to force Grenada out of CARICOM emerged only after President Reagan's April visit to the Caribbean and that there was an unusually strong US diplomatic presence in Ocho Rios during the summit. Certainly, this was the view taken by Grenada. In a public speech delivered immediately upon his return from Jamaica, Bishop excoriated Seaga and Adams for their deference to United States imperialism. 'Every morning at breakfast one of them had to go over to the Americans to take the morning instructions, every lunch time one to go down and report how the morning went, and at night another set had to go across and tell them how the rest of the afternoon went and plan strokes for the next morning.'[20] More generally, he claimed that the meeting had been a triumph for Grenadian diplomacy and for his government's decision to try to explain as calmly as possible where Grenada stood on a range of issues of concern to its regional partners. This undoubtedly impressed the conference. By their reasonable approach and their obvious commitment to Caribbean integration, Bishop and his Foreign Minister, Unison Whiteman, succeeded in winning the confidence of a number of other CARICOM leaders and were thus able to capitalise upon the mellowing of hostility to Grenada which was already taking place in the region. In this sense, Ocho Rios was potentially a turning-point.

That feeling was confirmed by subsequent regional gatherings. At a CARICOM Foreign Ministers' meeting in April 1983, Lester Bird,

Antigua's Deputy Prime Minister, whose personal relations with Bishop had long been quite close, openly stated that he saw no evidence to support the US charge that a military base was being built in Grenada. He and others also resented having to take a public stand on the matter which, since it had 'escalated beyond all reason [in Washington] and appears to have become a key element in the President's strategic policies',[21] could either affect their general relations with the US or divide CARICOM. For the moment they seemed to prefer to risk the former rather than the latter.

Certainly, by the time the next full summit met in Trinidad in July 1983, the particular issue of Grenada's place in CARICOM was dead. As far as most of the other heads of government were concerned, Bishop was no longer on probation: instead he took his place at the conference table as a fully legitimate participant. His relations with Seaga remained poor, especially as he strongly opposed a Jamaican proposal to widen the Community to include the Dominican Republic and Haiti. But the Grenadian argument that a further deepening of the existing integration arrangements was a higher priority was accepted by the conference and the widening issue postponed for further discussion at the next meeting. Generally, Grenada's contribution was much appreciated, not least by the other OECS states who spoke as a group on several issues of particular relevance to them. Behind the scenes too, Chambers and Bishop held several private meetings. Bishop, anxious further to improve relations with Trinidad, strongly supported Chambers in the conference in his successful bid for Trinidad to be recognised as the oil supplier of 'first resort' for those CARICOM territories without refineries and the source of any oil needed by territories with these installations. The Trinidadian delegation made it clear that Trinidad did not wish to see 'nations from outside the region, that might be considered a threat to Trinidad's national interest, stepping into the power vacuum created by the US government's isolationist policies towards Grenada'.[22] The two leaders also discussed once more the question of elections in Grenada and agreed finally that the point had been reached when proper diplomatic representation between their countries had again become appropriate.

As the various heads of government returned to their home states at the end of the Trinidad conference, there was thus a real prospect that the Commonwealth Caribbean would in future be able to conduct 'business as usual', reasonably confident at least that the Grenada 'problem', as perceived in 1979, had been contained. It was not that the Grenadian model of development was any more widely espoused in the region or that Grenada's relationship with Cuba was newly acceptable. The politics of hostility had only been replaced by the politics of toleration, based on the acceptance of Grenada as a fact of regional life. In some quarters even this was mainly the product of a developing regard for Bishop himself. This was typical of the Commonwealth Caribbean, where the nature of regional politics has always been substantially influenced by the tenor of the personal relationships between the various island leaders. Nevertheless, the change of mood was significant. As long as good relations were maintained on this level between Grenada and the rest of the region, it meant that whatever external threats the revolution faced from elsewhere, they were not likely to come in the first instance from the Commonwealth Caribbean.

Notes and References

1. M. Bishop, *Forward Ever! Three Years of the Grenadian Revolution* (Pathfinder Press, Sydney, 1982), pp. 111 and 129.
2. R.E. Gonsalves, 'The Importance of the Grenadian Revolution to the Eastern Caribbean', *Bulletin of Eastern Caribbean Affairs*, vol. 5, no. 1 (1979), p. 7.
3. Cited in D.S. DaBreo, *The Grenada Revolution* (Management Advertising and Publicity Services, Castries, 1979), p. 339.
4. 'The Declaration of St George's', *Bulletin of Eastern Caribbean Affairs*, vol. 5, no. 3 (1979), pp. 32–4.
5. *Caribbean Contact*, August 1979.
6. 'The Manifesto of the New Jewel Movement', reproduced in Institute of International Relations, University of the West Indies, *Independence for Grenada: Myth or Reality?* (Institute of International Relations, St Augustine, 1974), p. 154.
7. Bishop, *Forward Ever!*, p. 97.
8. *Latin America Regional Report: Caribbean*, RC-80-10, 5 December 1980.
9. *Agreement Establishing the Caribbean Development Bank*, Kingston, Jamaica, 18 October 1968, Article 35, paragraph 2.
10. Bishop, *Forward Ever!*, p. 195.
11. *Press Release No. 46/1981. Sixth Meeting of the Standing Committee of Ministers of CARICOM responsible for Foreign Affairs* (Caribbean Community Secretariat, Georgetown, 1981).
12. 'Memorandum by the Caribbean Community (CARICOM) Secretariat' (86/81–82/FM) in *Fifth Report of the Foreign Affairs Committee of the House of Commons: Caribbean and Central America*, together with an Appendix; part of the Proceedings of the Committee relating to the Report; and the Minutes of Evidence taken before the Committee with Appendices (HMSO, London, 1982), p. 304.
13. President Reagan, 'The US Caribbean Basin Initiative', speech to the Organisation of American States, St Lucia, 24 February 1982, p. 8.
14. See *Latin America Regional Report: Caribbean*, RC-82-03, 26 March 1982.
15. *Caribbean Contact*, May 1982.

16. *Latin America Regional Report: Caribbean*, RC-82-07, 20 August 1982.
17. *Caribbean Contact*, April 1983.
18. Ibid., December 1982.
19. *Press Release No. 52/1982. Third Conference of the Heads of Government of the Caribbean Community. Attachment II. The Ocho Rios Declaration* (Caribbean Community Secretariat, Georgetown, 1982).
20. M. Bishop, 'Address by Comrade Maurice Bishop to Bloody Sunday Rally, Seamoon, St Andrew's, 21 November 1982' in M. Bishop, *One Caribbean* (Britain/Grenada Friendship Society, London, 1983).
21. *Caribbean Insight*, May 1983.
22. Ibid., August 1983.

PART II

The Invasion and its Aftermath

6 THE INTERNAL STRUGGLE FOR POWER

The four-and-a-half years of the revolution were characterised by a paradox. The enormous strides made in the economic and social spheres were essentially reformist in character within, at most, a loose social democratic and idealist framework. Capitalism and other traditional institutions such as the church were never seriously challenged. On the other hand, there was from relatively early on a gradual determination by the New Jewel Movement leadership to eliminate bourgeois sentiment and construct a party organisation on strict, disciplined Marxist-Leninist lines. The aim was to be the creation of a truly socialist state and, ultimately, a communist society. Ironically, given the constant reiteration by the leadership of the importance of popular participation in all aspects of the revolutionary process, this search never at any time involved a 'hearts and minds' campaign. The debates and arguments were conducted behind securely closed doors by many whose links with the people, their thoughts and aspirations, had become tenuous. Eventually, it was to result in a struggle for power between what may be loosely called the radicals — broadly identified as a group coalescing around the Coards with strong representation in the officer corps of the People's Revolutionary Army — and the pragmatists, led by Bishop. It was to end in bloodshed and tragedy with the execution of Bishop and several of his followers in the Cabinet.

The struggle also become intimately bound up with the practical problems posed by Grenada's small size and limited resource base. The number of cadres was small and the task that they set themselves immense. Unfortunately, although corruption had been expunged, there was widespread inefficiency at all levels, reaching to that of the Central Committee. Decisions on vital everyday matters were either subject to long delays or never taken. Sometimes personal shortcomings, lack of communication and administrative inefficiency were to blame; sometimes it was because decisions had to be taken collectively by the Cabinet with or without the Central Committee in a time-consuming process. Several key members became very overworked and, by early 1983, illness began to take its toll. Despite this, solidarity and other meetings involving complex organisation continued. Significantly, it was those without direct ministerial responsibilities — for example, Ewart Layne, Liam James and Leon Cornwall, all of whom were PRA officers, Ian St Bernard and Tan Bartholomew, supported by other members such as Phyllis Coard, Chris de Riggs and Selwyn Strachan — who tried the hardest to push the party to ever more radical policies. They disregarded the absence of administrative machinery capable of their supervision and control, let alone the matter of public support.

Against this background, reasons had to be found for collective and individual deficiencies, the disappointing pace of social and economic transformation, the persistence of 'petty bourgeois' tendencies in the NJM and the difficulties encountered in the attempt to construct a Marxist-Leninist party structure and system of control. At first, the problems were attributed to slackness in organisation and poor control mechanisms in the party; a lack of personal workplans and low levels of discipline; loose and improper functioning of the Central Committee and Political Bureau; and a lack of knowledge and appreciation of Marxist-Leninist theory by many members. Later, allegations of lack of leadership were added. As time went on, this criticism became specifically aimed at Bishop, finally describing him as 'arrogant' and accusing him of 'onemanism' and 'right opportunism' and of defending the 'class interest' of the local bourgeoisie.

In the struggle over the theoretical direction to be taken by the party, a further important catalyst was US hostility. The various military aid treaties with Cuba, the Soviet Union and North Korea had helped start a chain reaction which, in turn, triggered the formulation of even more radical 'principled positions'. The US manoeuvres of March 1983 and the island-wide alert had created a genuine sense of foreboding and intensified defiance. Notwithstanding this defiance, the cumulative effect of the pressure also led to a deepening sense of insecurity felt by the leadership. Its growing physical isolation, combined with administrative overload, meant increasingly rare contact with the public. As more resources and manpower had to be diverted into defence and security after the March 1983 alert, the influence of the PRA and its officers within the Central Committee accelerated. Newly trained by Cuban and Soviet advisers and politically inspired by their experiences in those countries, PRA officers were often in the forefront of Bishop's critics. A siege atmosphere developed: even more than before, all opposition — or critical comment — relating to PRG policies, whether internally or regionally, was perceived as being, at the very least, CIA inspired. This could only be met by further stressing the regime's revolutionary credentials and a search for more material and moral support from the socialist community. The rigidity of the PRG's principled foreign policy became more accentuated, in sharp contrast to its pragmatism in domestic affairs. But it was counterproductive. As one analyst noted:

> Insistence on the correctness of a position may be psychologically rewarding to a country's leadership but does not necessarily redound to the advantage of a country. But the David Syndrome of responding forcefully to every challenge and error by external Goliaths is a reality of Grenadian policy. It is a position that makes no concession to the concerns of others, friend or foe, and yet demands recognition of one's own concerns.[1]

Just as important, the population became bewildered. The constant rhetoric of the leadership directed against the United States contrasted sharply with perceptions at the grassroots. Remittance income from Grenadian communities in North America, especially New York, was very important. Travel between the two countries by Grenadians also increased by over 30 per cent between 1981 and 1983 due to falling air fares[2] and there were long waiting lists for US visas at the Barbados-based US embassy.

The Struggle for Marxism-Leninism

The catalytic effect of US pressure and the policy of destabilisation was in its encouragement of those in the party who urged the deepening of the revolutionary process. There had existed since 1974 a study group led by Coard within the NJM variously called the Organisation for Research, Education and Liberation (OREL) or the Organisation for Educational Advance and Research (OEAR). It had influenced the discussions and decisions of the Political Bureau and was a focus of those in the higher echelons of the party who considered themselves Marxists and revolutionary socialists. Although formally disbanded in late 1977 on the grounds that there should not be institutional divisions in the party,[3] it continued to be an internal and informal pressure group, with fluctuating membership.

Just as the establishment of the Central Committee followed over six years after the formation of the party, it was not until April 1981 that the party began to introduce principles of Leninist organisation into its structure. The committee resolved on higher standards of personal discipline and 'tighter chairmanship'. There would also be a Party Secretariat. Reviewing the situation the following September, the continuing lack of personal workplans was noted. It was resolved that these had to be prepared and presented for review; the committee would meet monthly and would draft rest schedules for members to help alleviate the overwork problem. In December, dismay was expressed during 30 hours of review at the lack of implementation of these resolutions and the absence of follow-up. Growing communication problems within the party were also highlighted. Five months later, in April 1982, and again in June and July, the committee further considered the strengths and weaknesses of members, 'arrogance throughout the party' and the 'bureaucratic nature' of its work. The 'mood of the masses' and morale of the members was described as 'low'.[4] Further, at the July 1982 meeting, the committee's activities were criticised as 'unco-ordinated' and it was accused of not leading the party. In particular, it 'was not seeking to tackle the most explosive issues of the Church and the land'. Layne led an attack on those 'deadweight' members who 'participated little' in the party's work and who used the committee as a smokescreen for their inactivity.

The committee discussed the general problem at a general meeting of members in September 1982. It was resolved that the party be placed on a firm Leninist footing. As a first step, the membership structure would be adapted to that of the Soviet Communist Party, with full, candidate and applicant grades, to ensure selectivity on the basis of commitment and participation. It also agreed on a 'Line of March'. Six specific tasks were identified to 'lift the party out of the rut'. They were, first and most important, to intensify socialist education to press home to the populace the true nature of the US threat, which 'is the most active and leading class focus in the Revolution today'. More effort was also to be put into building the mass organisations; strengthening the Leninist character of the party; planning for greater economic growth, particularly in the agriculture sector; constructing a well-trained and motivated Militia; and finally, creating an international political climate favourable to the revolution.[5]

Events then took a surprise turn in early October 1982 with the sudden resignation from both the Central Committee and Political Bureau of Bernard Coard. Bishop convened an extraordinary meeting for 12-15 October to consider it. Coard said he had decided to resign the previous April. He was chairman of the Central Committee's main sub-committee, the Organising Committee: 'his authority there had been undermined' and he had not convened a meeting since July as a result. Publicly, his decision was because his presence was 'holding back the development of other comrades in the Committee'.[6] This was true:

his dynamism led to many taking a back seat. He was 'the only hatchetman and critique' [sic]. The 'failure of comrades to speak up freely' was because of his presence. In short, 'everyone was depending on him for everything especially in the area in the economy'. As he was in the forefront of those critical of the party's work and ideological direction, he did not want to be seen to be undermining Bishop's leadership. Nevertheless, everyone should realise that the Political Bureau was not functioning. It had no agenda or recording of decisions and the arguments and struggles were 'emotional conflict situations' that 'sapped his energies'.[7] He could no longer continue. Phyllis Coard, however, remained a member.

Over the three days of the meeting, three 'bases of the crises' were identified. The 'Material Basis' was the 'backward and underdeveloped nature of our society' and the existence of a large 'petty bourgeois influence', which was reflected in the committee's work. The 'Political and Ideological Basis' related to the failure to study Marxist-Leninist ideology and a timidity in 'making principled criticisms'. The 'Organisational Basis' aspect of the crisis was seen in the poor functioning and efficiency of many party organs and prominent members which permitted 'petty bourgeois influences to predominate'. It concluded that the party 'stood at the crossroads'.

> The first route would be the petty bourgeois route which would seek to make Bernard's resignation the issue. This would only lead to temporary relief, but would surely lead to the deterioration of the Party into a social-democratic Party and hence the degeneration of the Revolution. This road would be an easy one to follow given the objectively based backwardness and petty bourgeois nature of the society.
>
> The second route is the Communist route — the road of Leninist standards and functioning. The road of democratic centralism, of selectivity, of criticism and self-criticism and of collective leadership.[8]

Galvanised into action, it decided upon a purge of members who, by a complex format of assessment were declared unsuitable. Kenrick Radix scored the lowest. Accused of 'deep seated individualism' and 'petty bourgeois opportunist attitude to criticism', he was obliged to resign. He did so, accusing the committee of 'left opportunism'. Others strongly criticised were UN ambassador Caldwell Taylor, who showed 'signs of deviation into mysticism', General Secretary of the

Agricultural Workers' Union, Fitzroy Bain, and Unison Whiteman.

After that traumatic development, the committee's December 1982 meeting decided to concentrate efforts on three priority areas, agriculture, industry and the Centre for Popular Education. It was also agreed that the number of rallies and solidarity meetings would be restricted. It was hoped that, together, these measures would ease workloads. However, only in agriculture was any thought given to future policy. Between October 1982 and February 1983, intensive discussions took place both in the committee and in the Political Bureau on the best way to collectivise agriculture and build 'a firm alliance between the working class and the peasantry'.

The main conclusion was that 'the development and modernisation of Agriculture holds the key to winning the peasantry to Socialism and the transformation of the countryside along socialist lines'. Accordingly, there were three consecutive priorities. The first was to make the Grenada Farming Corporation (GFC), the body responsible for the management of state farms, the leading vehicle for the socialist transformation of agriculture. The GFC was to be restructured, assume control of an additional 6,000 acres of idle land and establish 36 farm units in eight semi-autonomous regions. Second, the peasantry was to be 'won gradually to socialism' by tax and other incentives, investment in rural infrastructure, the strengthening of existing 'machinery pools' and other services, the expansion of co-operatives and other forms of co-operation and, above all, through reinforcing the role of the Peasants' and Farmers' Union 'to further build the mass organisation of the farmers as the organ for carrying out the tasks of the Party among the peasantry'.

The final priority was to be the establishment of joint venture companies 'with large estate owners who are willing to produce, remain in production but [who] may be faced with economic crisis or bankruptcy'. Such ventures, it was urged, should be immediately established with 'selected land owners'. The scheme was also to be extended to 'appropriate capitalists' not presently in agriculture but who might be willing to invest in that area. The state would accept a minority interest holding, 'given the managerial inputs the capitalist can make in production at this time'.[9]

The agriculture resolution document was marked 'confidential' in the knowledge that, although the measures proposed were, in the circumstances, practical and sensible and in no way threatened the peasantry with forced collectivisation and other drastic measures, it was a highly sensitive issue given the social composition and values of

Grenadian society. Its pragmatic approach was in sharp contrast to the continuing demanos of the radicals for Marxist-Leninist policies elsewhere in the political and economic system. Inevitably their underlying dissatisfaction surfaced again, in March 1983. The Central Committee received a report which alleged that 'it was close to losing its links with the masses' and that this was holding back 'the important task of party building'. Pressure upon Bishop intensified and the first ever Plenary Session of the NJM was called for 13-19 July 1983.

Full and committee members met together for 54 hours over nearly seven days. By now, the leadership question was becoming more specific: to by now well-worn complaints about the 'continued failure of the Party to transform itself ideologically and organisationally' was added a lack of 'firm leadership on a Leninist path'. Much of the time, however, was spent on analysing specific problems. Concern was expressed at the 'spreading of anti-communism', particularly by the church. The mass organisation and the NISTEP and the CPE were suffering from bureaucratic and leadership inefficiency. Although village militia units had decreased in number those based in workplaces had increased. The economy was deteriorating sharply. There was a 'serious cash flow problem' because of the diversion of funds to the airport project caused by the difficulty in raising aid funds. The problem was compounded by a fall in banana export receipts caused by the steady devaluation of the British pound sterling against the US and hence the EC dollar. It showed not only in deteriorating roads and water and electricity services, but, more importantly, in a fall in morale amongst both party members and the population at large. 'The alliance with the bourgeoisie to create a national economy', one member stated, 'had become more complex and must be re-examined.'[10] It was reported too that public dissatisfaction was beginning to show. Rallies had become poorly attended — two in St George's had to be abandoned due to lack of support — while in Sauteurs party cadres were on one occasion chased down the street by irate villagers who dismissed their propaganda as 'communist'. The problem was acute in St Andrew's parish on the east coast, where anger had been expressed that virtually all new investment — by mid-1983, 90 per cent of which was from the state — was concentrated on the west coast at St George's and Point Salines. There was particular apprehension that, after Pearls airport closed, the imbalance would worsen. As the primary agricultural area, its feeder roads needed regular repair, as did other infrastructure.

After a wide-ranging review of the activities and problems of all the subcommittees — organisation and secretariat, workers, international relations, farmers, teachers, youth, women and propaganda — a series of positive decisions was taken. All had a common focus: the need to restore the revolutionary momentum and deepen the ideological process. For members, 'ideological and character qualities' and 'organisational skills' had to be further developed and entry qualifications made even higher. For the general public, workers' education classes were to be extended to the private sector. To counter 'inconsistent attendance' and 'low involvement' by workers, material incentives were to be awarded to participants in the CPE programmes at each successfully completed level. The work of the CPE was to be 'massively stepped up' and its organisation revamped, since it was admitted that 'the CPE was one of the weakest areas of the workers' work', a failure 'linked to the weakness of the CPE administration centre itself'.[11]

Political education for teachers was especially emphasised. Although 'progressive forces' now controlled the Grenada Teachers' Union, 'the majority of teachers remain backward politically'. There was also the problem of the 'unsatisfactory disposition of students to the Revolution', especially in the secondary schools. They were being affected 'by the growing influence of the Church'. Sports too were 'still being conducted without firm political control and direction' and had 'not taken on a mass character'. Therefore, unsuitable head teachers were to be removed, the NISTEP programme extended to secondary schools, and their students involved more in 'proletarianism' and community work. Political education at all levels, including the primary, was to be stepped up and religious instruction declared optional and restricted in 'hourage'.

Farmers were also to receive more ideological attention. There had been a 'total absence of propaganda' and the Political Bureau and the Central Committee were to supervise closely this work. No action had been taken on the Central Committee resolution on agriculture of the previous February. The national leadership was further blamed for problems in the National Women's Organisation, although no criticism was levelled at Phyllis Coard. Many NWO members harboured 'petty bourgeois' ideas and were 'unaccustomed to working on their own'. This coded reference to inefficiency had 'to be seen in the context of the deep petty bourgeois nature of our party' which was a 'privileged clique'. Both the organisation and the propaganda work of the party 'were in deep crisis'. The state of the Militia was such that people would think that 'imperialism no longer existed'.

In respect of the economy, the committee approved the creation of a Ministry of State Enterprises to further the extension of the state sector. The banking sector was earmarked for state ownership and trade with the socialist community to be expanded. Earlier, in March 1983, a working party of the Central Committee had considered the possible establishment of a State Trading Organisation for supervising and encouraging this area of trade. Its report was received and, although no action was taken, it was expected that the new ministry would assume responsibility. Although put on one side, the report was nevertheless instructive in its recommendations. Grenada's growing balance of payments deficit was attributed to 'entanglement in the world imperialist system' and could be alleviated only by the realignment of foreign trade and greater state direction and control of productive enterprises. Diversification of export products and import controls on food and non-essential consumer items were also recommended. Specifically, state intervention in export control was stressed. One option was nationalisation of the marketing co-operatives, and either the establishment of a State Trading Corporation or their incorporation into the Marketing and National Importing Board. Another option was that the state should limit its activity to a monopoly on exports to socialist markets; an even more watered-down option was that the state should simply set annual export levels to these markets.

The report clearly came down in favour of state monopoly export control and the establishment of a state corporation. It fully appreciated the probable scale of opposition from agents and merchants, and went so far as to anticipate sabotage and other counter-revolutionary acts coming from this sector. 'Concrete steps to positively alter the balance of forces' were essential, particularly through 'political work'. Opposition amongst workers in industries was not expected. 'When it comes to the bottom line [and] when forced to choose between continued employment with the State and unemployment, workers are not likely to opt for unemployment.'[12] Likewise, farmers would be won over by the prospect of reliable marketing of their produce based on the state's financial resources and ability to negotiate bilateral agreements with socialist states on favourable terms. Bulk buying of fertilisers by the state for resale at low prices and the provision of technical support services would be added advantages. Opposition from capitalist shipping lines was expected and so new shipping agreements with socialist states might be necessary.

The overall advantages were thus deemed to be conclusive. The state would be the direct recipient of foreign exchange and would use it for the benefit of all. New and more favourable markets and new services would raise farmers' incomes and so 'undoubtedly raise the prestige of the revolution' among this sector. In this connection the report did not mention that the PRG was forced to turn down an offer by the German Democratic Republic to purchase bananas as the price was less than a quarter of that paid by Britain and the EEC. However, it was concluded that, as a first step, the state should limit its monopoly to socialist export markets before assuming full export control. On that basis, 'reactionary antagonisms' would be lessened and operational and administrative experience gained.

There was, however, the more immediate problem of St Andrew's to consider. 'A major source of counter-revolution', it was characterised by 'a proliferation of petty rumours', 'a continued inflow' and cultivation of marijuana, and the 'hoarding of money' by the rural bourgeoisie. A task force would be based there and 'counter-intelligence, army and police' asked to find personnel to maintain control. More positively, the parish was to be given priority in the industrialisation programme. Carriacou was also to be given greater attention due to potential problems there too.

Finally, and by contrast, an altogether happier report was received on the PRG's international relations. Particular gratification was expressed at the far better relationships enjoyed with CARICOM and OECS states, and Foreign Minister Whiteman was congratulated. Some 80 per cent of his time, he reported later, had been spent on Grenada's relations with Commonwealth Caribbean states, whom he perceived as a bastion against possible US aggression.[13] There was a call to 'move rapidly to firm up relations with the Socialist World', which perhaps reflected a growing concern by the radical group in the committee that Bishop, Whiteman and the pragmatists were working for a *rapprochement* with the Reagan administration and regional leaders such as Seaga and Adams. It was feared that this might compromise revolutionary principles and potentially work against the interests of a democratically centralist Leninist party. International and regional diplomatic activity by Bishop had, in addition, added to his growing stature as an international statesman and prominent spokesman of the Third World. Flowing from this, fears of 'onemanism', especially in the context of foreign affairs, were not to be long in coming.

The Risks and Benefits of Rapprochement

Bishop and Whiteman had realised by late 1982 that the new airport could be economically viable only if the North American tourist market was secured. This would be possible only if proper relations were restored with the United States.[14] There was also a slow realisation by the Central Committee that anti-American sloganising was counter-productive. It therefore agreed with Bishop's suggestion after the March alert that a moratorium would be appropriate. There was also the question of the Caribbean Basin Initiative, which was still on the agenda. Although in public the CBI was denounced, in private the PRG hoped that, in time, its provisions might apply to Grenada. As the July Plenary Session concluded,

> The private sector must be encouraged to explore opportunities in the area of investments by the CBI. However, this area must be closely monitored by the Party to ensure that the capitalists are not provided with an effective new base for covert activity by the USA.[15]

At first, the omens for *rapprochement* appeared poor. In December 1982, Vice-President Bush declared at a Miami conference devoted to business activities in the Caribbean and Latin America that Grenada was 'repressive', 'economically weak' and 'dependent' upon Cuba and the Soviet Union. Grenada's reply was quiet and very diplomatically worded, pointing out the PRG's economic and social achievements which 'compare favourably with those of the American revolution, whose earliest years themselves constituted a glorious period in the history of the United States of America'. It rejected the accusation of repression: 'Grenada has certainly been obliged to be alert and vigilant. Such vigilance cannot reasonably be interpreted as repression.' It ended by offering to despatch a 'high level emissary' to brief the Vice-President; and sent a copy of the World Bank Report.[16] It was received by the State Department, at first without comment, but a few weeks later Secretary of State Shultz sent Bishop a lifeline. Not only was it the first official note from Washington since its warning, in the first few days after the *coup*, against involvement with Cuba, but it was conciliatory in tone. It was despatched via the leader of the US black caucus in Congress, Mervyn Dymally, and indicated that all US embassy personnel in Barbados were to be accredited to Grenada except the ambassador, Milan Bish. Congressman Dymally, Trinidadian-born, also extended an invitation to Bishop to visit Washington. In this he was joined by the influential Afro-American foreign affairs lobby group, Trans-Africa. These moves were all the more remarkable since they coincided with Reagan's most belligerent speeches attacking Grenada.

The visit was finally arranged for 31 May to 10 June 1983. Bishop requested a top-level meeting but was rebuffed: 'not the President, the Vice-President, a secretary or even a fortieth secretary'. He turned down as 'inappropriate' a meeting with the US ambassador to the OAS. However, once in Washington with representatives of the Grenadian private business and tourist sectors, congressional and favourable media pressure led to a 30-minute meeting with National Security Council chief William Clark and Assistant Secretary of State Kenneth Dam, who deputised for Shultz. The announcement of the formation of the constitutional commission was welcomed and, although the meeting was strictly confidential, it is known that the possibility of reducing the Cuban presence, resisting future moves against the private sector and arresting the deepening of relations with the Soviet Union was discussed. For the 2,500 Grenadian and other Caribbean nationals who packed a New York auditorium, Bishop's visit was a triumph. As a local magazine vividly reported:

> Standing before their very eyes was the Luke Skywalker of [Reagan's] March 23rd 'Star Wars' speech. He had come to challenge Darth Vader and the Force was with him. The standing, screaming, stomping ovation must have lasted a full three minutes ... Mohammed had come to the mountain.[17]

On his return to Grenada, Bishop issued instructions that the moratorium on anti-American rhetoric was to continue. Although his request for a US diplomatic mission in St George's was only 'to be considered', it was agreed that a Congressional delegation would visit Grenada the following autumn.

The Central Committee reluctantly agreed to the moratorium but concern was expressed at Bishop's meeting with Dam. The committee had laid down firm guidelines for the visit. It was not the fact that the Dam meeting was unscheduled that was the concern, rather that Bishop had conducted negotiations at a sensitive level without prior reference and without guidance. For his part, Bishop replied that, given the punishing schedule and the distances involved, consultation had been impossible in practice. The resentment of some members of the committee worsened when it was later learnt that Bishop had held a private meeting with George Chambers during the CARICOM summit in Port of Spain in early July and had apparently agreed to consider a sharply accelerated programme for elections.[18] According to the press reports, Bishop was also encouraged to release more detainees and capitalise on his Washington discussions by sharply reducing the Cuban and

Soviet presence in Grenada once the airport was opened. He and Whiteman thus returned from Trinidad to discover that rumours of the content of the discussions had preceded them. They were again put on the defensive, but, since the fears of a 'sell-out' could not be substantiated and because Bishop's international stature and popularity with the Grenadian people was beyond doubt, the matter was not mentioned or direct criticism made of the Prime Minister at the July Plenary. However, personal criticism was to surface during the next month, first in private and then in September in the Central Committee as a whole.

'Onemanism' and Joint Leadership

Tension began to build up at an emergency meeting of the Central Committee called on 26 August to consider a report by Leon 'Bogo' Cornwall, ambassador to Cuba and PRA major. Speaking on behalf of 'senior party comrades', he expressed concern at the committee's performance and the lack of action over resolutions agreed at the July Plenary. Bartholomew reported complaints by Cuban and other workers over housing and administrative agreements which prevented them from doing a proper job. He also strongly criticised the 'neglect' of the Militia. Its low morale was being matched by that of the army. Right-wing elements controlled the police, and the police had little respect for the party. Austin confirmed widespread dissatisfaction and demoralisation in the army, which he attributed to poor pay and conditions. Liam James stressed that 'we are seeing the beginning of the disintegration of the party' and DeRiggs made clear that 'the heart of the crisis is the Central Committee'. James also claimed that committee members were timid and feared being labelled revisionist. 'They must be ready to criticise', he urged. It was eventually resolved to meet for a special plenary meeting in mid-September. In his summing up, Bishop conceded that 'there is reasonable basis to share the concern that many key decisions of the party, if not the majority, have been made informally outside the higher organs'.[19] He asked everybody to consult members and 'rap with key sections of the masses', study the history of the Communist Party of the Soviet Union and reflect upon the strengths and weaknesses of each individual committee member.

The stage was set for confrontation. Many thought that the September meeting would follow the pattern of the others and generally review the situation. No prior agenda was circulated — an unprecedented omission — and two days before the meeting began, all those overseas were ordered home. During the period between the last meeting and the special plenary, the radical group met privately. Opinions differ as to whether Coard was present. Although not a committee member, his influence was still very considerable given his pivotal role as Finance Minister and deputy to Bishop. In the end, all were present except Austin, returning from North Korea, and St Bernard, who was ill. The radicals took the initiative from the start by refusing to accept Bishop's agenda as 'it missed the point'. An alternative agenda was proposed and accepted. It was to analyse the present state of the party and revolution; to assess the work of the Central Committee; and to chart the way forward.

Layne opened the discussion by reiterating much of what had been said in earlier meetings. Despondency and dissatisfaction among the public was high and 'the revolution now faces the greatest danger since 1979'. The party's international reputation 'is being affected'. The morale of party members was 'very dread' and the committee was too formalistic and on a path of 'right opportunism'. As Grenadian society was overwhelmingly petit bourgeois, it was all the more necessary to create a vanguard Marxist-Leninist party to lead the way to revolutionary change. John 'Chalky' Ventour, another young committee member, asserted that 'the party is facing disintegration' with many comrades being overworked and 'showing signs of resignation'. The Militia was 'non-existent' and he noted the popular support given to the US position on the Korean plane incident the previous fortnight. 'The people', he said, 'are getting their lines from the Voice of America.' Cornwall agreed: 'the honeymoon of the revolution was over' and the committee must formulate a 'perspective on how the revolution must develop'.[20] Bartholomew complained of 'timidity' of leadership and the 'arrogance' of the disciplinary committee. The mass organisations were poorly led; the NYO, he said, stood for 'Not Yet Organised'. Phyllis Coard interjected by saying that 'party comrades display a harsh attitude to the masses, who are demoralised because of the party's failure to manners the situation'. Strachan questioned 'whether we want to build socialism or just chant slogans?'

Bishop intervened to try to regain control of the meeting. He was 'struck by the levels of thought and preparation of Comrades as evident in their various contributions.' Although many of the conclusions appeared to him to be 'rather premature', they were largely correct. He admitted that the main problem was the Central Committee. Its bureaucratic formalism in its dealings with the masses contrasted with the *ad hoc* approach taken to its work. He noted:

Visits to work places have disappeared, increasing non-attendance at zonal councils and parish meetings, visits to communities to meet people at an informal level, decrease in the number of discussions and meetings with people in all areas of work, failure to participate in public activities. Village meetings have disappeared.[21]

Louison agreed with this 'clear lack of contact' with the masses: in the meantime 'the middle class types have been coming to the revolution for jobs'. But the overall situation was not as bad as had been painted. 'Some Comrades', he remarked, 'give a panicky impression in the way they make their points.' Whiteman's point was that the committee spent too much time on small issues instead of 'fundamental issues' like the church, for which no party policy existed. He suggested a lower-level second leadership structure 'to read and summarise reports' to leave the overburdened leadership time for strategic decisions. As the first day's session came to an end, Bishop tried again to draw conclusions which were not too unfavourable to him. The 'deep crisis' in the party and revolution was due to the functioning of the committee and was compounded by 'the weakness of the material base', such as unrepaired roads, electrical stoppages and 'retrenchment' of employment. Only vague solutions were offered, centring upon the establishment of 'meaningful channels of communication' and action based on 'Marxist-Leninist criteria' to guide 'the work in the future'.

His critics returned to the attack the next morning by proposing their own conclusions to the preceding discussion. For the first time, Bishop was directly and personally criticised. James considered that the 'fundamental problem is the quality of leadership of the Central Committee and the party provided by Comrade Maurice Bishop'. His charisma was not enough: what was required was 'a Leninist level of organisation and discipline', a 'great depth in ideological clarity' and 'brilliance in strategy and tactics'. Bishop had none of the qualities needed to fulfil these tasks 'at this time'. Layne, Cornwall and Ventour agreed: the party could not be put onto a Marxist-Leninist footing under Bishop's leadership. DeRiggs warned, however, that while there was a need to reorganise the leadership, 'the removal of any Comrade on the Central Committee will not help the situation'. Bartholomew was thankful that, at last, comrades were no longer 'hesitant' to make criticisms about Bishop's 'vacillation'. For all these contributions, the hardest attack came from Phyllis Coard. She criticised 'the idealism, the voluntarism and the failure to face up to hard decisions' by certain committee members. Bishop was 'disorganised very often', avoided responsibility for mistakes and was 'hostile to criticism'. He had opposed both the closure of *The Torchlight* — which was decided in his absence overseas — and the prosecution of the 'Gang of 26'. *Sotto voce* comments in the meeting also alleged that he had been against the seizure of power on 13 March 1979.[22] Fortunately, she said, Comrade Strachan had taken 'the full responsibility to hold the party together' and 'must be complimented for the proletarian qualities which he has displayed'.

Bishop's supporters tried vainly to come to his rescue. Bain, while agreeing with the criticisms, warned of 'over-hasty decisions'. Louison said that the quality of leadership was 'not the only problem'. Whiteman echoed him. 'We have to be careful', he warned, 'that we don't shift too much from the Central Committee collectively.' When Bishop himself entered the discussion, he thanked comrades for their 'frankness in their criticisms'. He was disappointed that they had not been raised earlier and appreciated members' concern for the need for 'corrected strategy and tactics'. However, he had 'several problems over the years, especially with the style that entails consensus and unity at all costs, which can result in blunting class struggle'. He concluded by asking for time 'to think of his own role' and again recommended that members 'develop and maintain links with the masses' and, within the committee, 'develop mechanisms for accountability'.[23]

The attack resumed. 'We need to find the root of the contradiction', said Layne, paving the way for James who then surprised the pragmatists and pro-Bishop supporters by suddenly proposing joint leadership to be shared between Bishop and Coard. Bishop would 'direct work among the masses, focus on production and propaganda', be responsible for the work of the 'organs of popular democracy' and the mass organisations, Militia mobilisation and regional and international work. Coard, in turn, would be responsible for party organisation, ideological development of party members, and party strategy and tactics. Bishop would preside over the Central Committee and Coard that of both the Organising Committee and Political Bureau. Both of these would meet weekly. DeRiggs followed this with a proposal to replace Austin as PRA Commander by Layne, with Cornwall being chief of political and academic work in all the armed forces, including the police.

There followed a concert of approval on the respective qualities of Bishop and Coard. Coard, said Layne, 'had given ideological and organisational leadership and had elaborated strategy and tactics even outside the Central Committee'. Others agreed. But there was criticism.

Louison, although he welcomed the prospect of Coard's return to the committee, thought the proposal had no 'theoretical basis'. What was wanted was 'collective mannerising' by the committee to ensure that Bishop could build up the qualities required. Whiteman thought it would be better if Coard was given 'specific functions' as Deputy Leader. Bain was sceptical and had 'difficulty in conceptualising' how it would work in practice. However, they were lone voices. The only criticism which carried the day related to Austin's position, which remained intact. It was agreed, though, that the army was in a 'state of rut and demoralisation', suffering from 'ideological drift' and literally hungry due to low food supplies. Whiteman proposed a salary increase.

Bishop's reply was cautious. Noting comrades' 'ideological growth', he stressed that he never had a problem sharing power or accepting criticisms. He had worked well with Coard from schooldays and had always defended him even when, from 1977, Coard had been accused of aggressiveness and 'wanting to grab power'. But he was concerned about the 'operationalisation' of the proposal in terms of strategy and tactics; he certainly wanted to hear Coard's point of view. 'We will have to decide', he went on, 'how we will articulate this to the party and masses.'[24] The image of the leadership was affected and the world would see it as a power struggle and a vote of no confidence in him. James replied that Bishop would still be Prime Minister and Commander in Chief and sign all Central Committee documents. He was at pains to emphasise that Coard would not decide strategy and tactics 'all by himself' and the committee would have to ratify all his proposals. In fact, anger was directed more at Louison than Bishop as Louison became emotional in his continuing criticism.

Layne summed up the debate. There was a theoretical basis for joint leadership and it was 'creative'. He went on: 'the form of leadership is scientifically decided, based on the situation we face. We have used the example of the Soviet Army where the concept of Political Commissar and Military Leadership had developed and worked'.[25] The matter then passed to the vote. James's proposal on joint leadership received nine votes. Two abstained, Bishop and Austin, and two, Louison and Whiteman, voted against. It was also agreed not to inform the people for the time being. Bishop was now in a corner. He opposed a move to invite Coard to the meeting as he wanted time to reflect personally on the issue. He still found the 'practicalities' of the resolution to be 'unclear'. He wondered about his own role and hinted that he would gradually become more of a figurehead. It was reluctantly agreed by the radicals that the meeting would adjourn and reconvene the next day with Coard present. Bishop would be absent since he and Whiteman had to attend the independence celebrations in St Kitts-Nevis.

The next afternoon, Saturday 17 September, Strachan explained the position of the committee to Coard and outlined the proposed operationalisation of the resolution, consistent with Leninist principles. DeRiggs asserted that the decision was made 'from a standpoint of love and deep respect for the Comrade Leader' and defended Bishop's request for time to reflect as it represented a 'moral crisis' for him. Layne, however, made it clear that frankness was essential and warned that Bishop's reservations would 'intimidate Comrades and harm their Leninist advancement in the party'. Coard's reply was positive. He agreed with all the criticisms of Bishop's leadership and the operation of the Central Committee. The party needed 'a fundamental package of measures' to survive. Although he had never undermined Bishop's leadership, he admitted 'petit bourgeois conduct' as he did not 'manners the Comrade Leader years ago'. He would, none the less, accept joint leadership 'to save the party and revolution'. But the practicalities of the concept must satisfy Bishop and a 'timeframe' be established for informing the masses and starting 'the work internally and hitting the ground scientifically and organisationally'. He did not mention it, but he had had a private meeting with Bishop on the matter immediately prior to Bishop's departure.

After the intervening weekend, the Central Committee under Coard's chairmanship went to work with zest. In an intensive series of meetings held over the following two weeks, it agreed on a series of measures to solve the problems. Coard presented a number of proposals. In order to rebuild the party's image amongst the masses, they included more political education, the allocation of 'small but achievable' tasks for individual members, the utilisation of the talents of non-party people, more efficient and widespread distribution of party publications and a restructured Party Secretariat to ensure 'everything is implemented . . . on a more professional footing'. The masses should be involved in the selection and promotion of party members. The NJM needed both cadres and militants: the former were to be the organisers and leaders, while the latter would fight for the party in the workplace or community.[26] All must be subject to regular assessment, Layne insisted, and a comprehensive personal filing system established. Every member of the Central Committee would be obliged to study Marxism-Leninism 'very seriously' and learn from the experience in party building in other socialist countries. There would be an examination every two years. To help the process, a party school would be established. Selected teachers would be sent to the Soviet Union for in-depth training for between three and five years. All members, whatever their rank, had to 'kill all arrogance' in their relations with the masses. 'Open warmth and selflessness' had to be displayed, although members were warned 'to sink but not drown themselves' in the masses. Of equal importance was the need to restructure the party on Leninist principles. The duties and responsibilities of every party organ were discussed and procedures established. The quantity of mass organisation and Parish and Zonal Council meetings was to be sacrificed in favour of quality. Meetings were to be well prepared and held at regular intervals, with a reporting system between and across levels.

There was no disagreement in principle to these proposals. Ventour particularly wanted the party 'to take sanctions against comrades who show hostility to criticism'. Strachan welcomed the fact that, 'for the first time', the party realised that 'party building is a science'. Coard stressed the need for party planning. 'The party', he said, 'must emulate the state and ensure that it has has an overall national plan, and sectoral and geographical plans based upon this overall national plan.'[27] Planning, others emphasised, went hand in hand with supervision and control. Strict 'prioritisation' of tasks was necessary; the party had been guilty of 'unbelievable idealism' since new tasks had been constantly added to those already being carried out by party members, without any consideration of manpower resources in the party or individual abilities. Similarly, the work to be done by 'internationalist workers' from socialist countries would be carefully planned to gain maximum benefits.

Although recognition was given to the importance of the National Council of Delegates — the forum where delegates from mass organisations and Parish and Zonal Councils met at least annually to discuss specific matters such as the budget — Coard was anxious both to decentralise the work of the party and its institutions further, and to redirect it. The first task was to establish branches at the workplace, whether manufacturing, commercial, estate or governmental. 'For our entire history our party has operated on the territorial principle. Then, after the Revolution, on the sectional principle. This was correct because we had a very high unemployment problem and needed to reach people where they live.'[28] Now was the moment to change. Not only would the establishment of workplace branches result in increased production, but it would assist the mobilisation of workers for the Militia, help improve management and industrial organisation, strengthen trade unionism and ensure that 'the working-class composition of the Party is strengthened'. The 10,000 workers in workplaces of less than ten needed to be organised on a class basis and, through the trade unions, mobilised for the revolution.

Simultaneously, party work in the villages had to be strengthened. Fitzroy Bain recalled the principle of the 'inner and outer circle' of members and supporters respectively. There were about 5,000 in the countryside in the outer circle. They had been organised before the revolution by NJM party support groups. But these had all but disappeared due to the growth of village branches of the mass organisations and village-based Zonal Councils. Besides the administrative and other shortcomings of these institutions, there was the problem of multiple membership at the village level, which begged the question of 'how many leaders a village has'. Coard urged close attention to the peasantry and their 'class interest'.

[Before the Revolution] we did most of our work with the peasantry and very little with the working class. It is since the Revolution that we are working with the working class and all this has implications for our structures. However, we have never organised the peasantry as peasantry but as village dwellers.[29]

Despite the fact that the Zonal Councils were party institutions, no committee member had attended one for 18 months: it was no wonder that the party was losing ground to the church in the rural areas. Coard argued that a restoration of pre-revolution village public meetings, as suggested by Whiteman, was not the answer. Rather, reforms of the Zonal Councils were needed, the role of the party in them should be reasserted and their place in the structure of people's democracy recognised in the forthcoming constitution. There was, Coard insisted, 'insufficient confidence in the masses', which explained a previous hesitancy in strengthening the councils and the mass organisations. This had to be rejected and consideration given in future to the creation of new institutions of people's power to replace older structures as and when it was justified on scientific and material bases. In the meantime, the structure and organisation of Parish Councils needed revamping. It was agreed that each of the seven councils, to be elected by parish party members, would be identified as party institutions. Each would be chaired by a Central Committee member who would live in the parish.

With the party in firm control of Parish and Zonal Councils and the mass organisations, the risk was that non-party members would find it difficult to be properly represented. The answer lay in the Village Co-ordinating Bureaus. Their role as the link between the village Zonal Council and the local branches of the mass organisations was to be reinforced and their functions broadened. The meeting agreed with Phyllis Coard that

> the Bureaus should be bodies that the entire membership should relate to, whether they support the Party or not, and anyone who wanted to can become a member. This will help incorporate the stronger elements in the village into the nucleus of local government. [They] will have no party function. The village council will also evolve into a state body to monitor, supervise, control, and to ensure the implementation of the revolution and state as it affects the village and community. They also must have no party function but the Party should function inside them, to supervise and guide them.[30]

As before, they could 'manners' bureaucrats as well as undertake 'house to house' mobilisation. It was expected that, in time, the bureaus would evolve into executive bodies 'with committees and commissions to do the work in all areas, for example, water, health and housing'. There was one note of caution. The party had to ensure that 'the bourgeois be kept from these bodies because they will seek control'. Ignoring the commitment previously made to open access, Coard said that this would be handled by invitations issued by parish chiefs, based upon a percentage 'giving the majority to the working class'.

There remained two other matters. Propaganda had never been approached by the party 'as a science'. Phyllis Coard was anxious to see it scientifically developed, spreading 'from the inner core to outwards', linked to the 'mass work' and better co-ordinated and directed by the party.

> We need to see propaganda not as flinging things at the masses but to deepen day by day the understanding of the working people in terms of long term and short term goals. Deepening the understanding of the working people has to be done little by little with repetition . . . placed in different areas [to] have a cumulative effect . . . and with a variety of forms.[31]

The Centre for Popular Education obviously had a role to play in this and Strachan's suggestion that it be more village based was adopted. Lastly, there was the question of membership. Some 1,400 party militants were required, but they would have to meet more stringent entry rules proposed by Coard, comply with minimum work schedules and be regularly assessed. The selection of cadres needed, however, further study.[32]

The committee was under no illusions about the extent of the task to which it had committed itself. But its morale was high and Coard, in whom enormous confidence was placed, assured the members that what was proposed was attainable.

> The standards we are aiming for are out of harmony with the level of development of the productive forces of our country but because of the existence of world socialism and the links that are developing with world socialism, this is possible.[33]

It was further encouraged by the successful outcome of a packed general meeting of full members held on Sunday 25 September, which punctuated the committee's series of discussions. Bishop has returned from St Kitts-Nevis late on 22 September. He had been asked to attend the plenary meeting early the next morning, but declined on the grounds of tiredness and the continuing need to reflect. He arrived for a scheduled meeting on the following day, Saturday, but this had been cancelled as documentation for it had not been fully prepared and was not to be ready until the day after.

When they met, the members had been circulated with the Central Committee minutes of the meetings of October 1982 and the crucial meeting of 14-17 September. A report on the background and decision was also distributed. Uncompromising in its terms and language, 'crisis', 'opportunism', 'demoralisation' and 'quality of leadership' peppered the text. It concluded that the

> model of Joint Leadership is an attempt to bring a creative and scientific solution to the leadership question in our concrete circumstances and most fundamentally . . . it is the formal recognition of the leadership of our party for the first ten years . . . up to one year ago.[34]

Bishop refused to attend the meeting, again for the reason that he needed time to consider the concept. Because of this, Coard felt it inappropriate for him to attend 'since this may inhibit free and frank discussion'. He would, however, come if requested. The meetng was virtually unanimous in demanding the presence of both. Layne reported that no message from Bishop had been received and that he was continuing to fulfil the duties of Prime Minister: 'this', he said, 'could only be seen as contempt for the Central Committee, contempt for democratic centralism'. If Bishop's 'road of opportunism' was chosen, he warned, committee members, as 'aspiring communists and Leninists', would have to resign from the committee on principle.[35]

A vote of 46 against one called for Bishop's presence. Coard was also contacted and arrived quickly. In response, Bishop sent a message saying that he still wanted time 'to formulate his position', but reminding members that he had accepted joint leadership in March 1973 when joint co-ordinating secretaries, he and Whiteman, were appointed to lead the then emergent party. Eventually, he arrived. Explaining that he was 'relatively confused and emotional', his main concern was that as the masses in the Caribbean tended to 'build up a personality cult around an individual', their perception of the crisis as a power struggle had to be considered. To his mind it appeared as such, for he questioned 'the real meaning' of the committee's decision. If the qualities needed to carry the party forward were the ones that he lacked, 'I am suspicious that Comrades have concluded that the party must be transformed into a Marxist-Leninist party and I am the wrong person to be leader.' This was 'unprincipled' and he demanded to know 'the genuine substantial preference of the Comrades'.[36] James thought this 'emotional' and made plain that Central Committee decisions were binding on all. Layne was blunt. Quoting Lenin's dictum that 'open criticism of its own defects is not a sign of the weakness but of the great strength of a Marxist party', he went on to accuse Bishop of thinking there was 'a plot and conspiracy to remove him' but that for 'tactical reasons', the committee was only 'going half-way for the time being'. This was, he declaimed, 'gross contempt for the intelligence of the Central Committee. For him to feel that under every chair, under every window there is a conspiracy going on is nothing but contempt.'[37] Whiteman, however, spoke up in support of Bishop, reiterating his argument that 'wherever a leader is missing qualities, collective and not joint leadership solves the problem'. Fitzroy Bain warned that 'left opportunism' could replace 'right opportunism' and urged that members who had genuine disagreements should not be victimised. He also accused some members of 'caucusing' against Bishop, which could 'mash up the revolution'. But, as in earlier meetings, comments were overwhelmingly supportive of the committee's position and in favour of 'resoluteness' and 'firmness'. Gahagan and Redhead, both PRA officers, were 'shocked' at Bishop's position; 'no-one', added Ventour, 'is president for life'. As for a conspiracy, one member wryly remarked that if there was one, it was a conspiracy to build the party and the revolution!

Finally, Coard and Bishop summed up. Coard remarked upon the 'qualitative difference' of Central Committee meetings since he became chairman on 19 September. The same applied to the membership whose words were sincere and showed 'a genuine commitment to struggle for socialism and lay the basis for the eventual building of communism'. He would work with Bishop, he said, for the party, the revolution and the Grenadian working class. To great applause, Bishop then embraced the co-leader. Since the meeting had endorsed the committee's analysis, 'this has satisfied my concern . . . [and] . . . I sincerely accept the criticism and will fulfil the decision in practice'. He pledged 'to erode his petit bourgeois traits' and promised that the past was now behind him. Like Coard, 'his whole life' was for the party and revolution. The meeting ended on a highly emotional note with the singing of the *Internationale*. The crisis, it was thought, was over and the revolution saved. Indeed, Trevor Munroe, a close friend of both Bishop and Coard and chairman of the Workers' Party of Jamaica, arrived that day to advise on the operation of the new policy 'according to revolutionary principles'.

The Showdown

Very soon afterwards, Bishop left for Czechoslovakia and Hungary on an economic aid mission, accompanied by Louison and Whiteman. His security guards were led by his faithful bodyguard, Cletus St Paul. On arrival in Budapest, Bishop confided in St Paul. The crisis was a 'power struggle' for 'no state had joint leadership'.[38] He agreed with Whiteman's contention that collective leadership with himself as *primus inter pares* was both practical and proper. Louison also told Grenadian students in Hungary that the joint leadership issue was 'not settled' and 'still under discussion'.[39] The party returned via Cuba where they were delayed for 24 hours. Bishop had a long meeting with Fidel Castro in Cienfuegos, but Castro later firmly denied that Bishop even mentioned, let alone discussed, the problem.[40]

On the day before they had been scheduled to arrive back in Grenada, Thursday 6 October, St Paul rang a member of the committee from Cuba to say that Bishop had not accepted joint leadership and hinted darkly that 'blood will flow'. This was reported and taken to mean that Bishop was plotting the deaths of the leaders of the radicals. The Coards left home the following morning, 7 October, expecting Bishop to arrive later that evening as arranged. They stayed the night at the home of the father of Rupert Roopnarine of the Working Peoples' Alliance of Guyana who was working as an economic adviser in Grenada. Others took similar precautions.

When Bishop arrived on Saturday 8 October, only Strachan was at the airport to meet him. Bishop confirmed that he wanted the issue put back onto the agenda as 'certain points had to be reviewed'. In the course of a four-hour discussion both at Pearls and back in St George's, Bishop refused to say what the points were, but insisted upon collective, and not joint, leadership. He would, he said, discuss the matter at the next scheduled Central Committee meeting, due the following Wednesday, 12 October. Strachan briefed Bishop on what the party had decided in his absence and Bishop apparently joked about one or two aspects. Coard was then briefed by Strachan, who reported Bishop's mood as 'sarcastic'; Louison, however, later suggested that Strachan gave a 'distorted and exaggerated' account of the conversation.[41] Another, and very bizarre, interpretation of the meeting was given later by the Antigua Caribbean Liberation Movement (ACLM) in its paper, *Outlet*. In a column written personally by ACLM leader Tim Hector, whose relations with Bishop were close, Strachan was denounced as a CIA agent whose role it was 'to foment the leadership struggle into a clear political division'.[42] If this was indeed true, then Strachan's meeting with Bishop was, in the words of another regional paper, 'an act of a modern Judas'.[43]

The Central Committee met in emergency session on Monday 10 October and flatly refused to reopen the question. Bishop sent St Paul to the meeting to discover the general mood of the members and was told of their deep anger. He, in turn, was feeling increasingly isolated, the Central Committee having decided not to contact or have dealings with him except on their terms, although Austin and Education Minister Jacqueline ('Jackie') Creft, his former mistress, did meet him privately on separate occasions. The silence worried Bishop. He and Jackie Creft wanted to inform the public of the struggle but had no means to do so.

Bishop finally met his adversaries at the Central Committee meeting on Wednesday, as arranged. Tension was high during the four-hour session. He complained that 'attempts were being made to marginalise him'.[44] He had expected Coard to meet him at the airport and spend the next day in talks with him. He asked why his assistant security guard, Errol George, had been mysteriously called to two meetings of the personnel security division in the PRA headquarters at Fort Frederick at 1 a.m. and 7 a.m. that morning 'on a matter regarding the Prime Minister', of which he knew nothing and from which St Paul had been excluded. As regards the critical issue, he had been in a state of 'high emotion' at the members' meeting on 25 September and, on further reflection, was not in favour of joint leadership. His perception was that it was a means by which Coard and the committee would ease him out of power.[45] The meeting again delivered its verdict. By a vote of nine to three, it affirmed that joint leadership was essential.

During the meeting, there was another development elsewhere. A rumour that four of the committee – the Coards, Strachan and Cornwall – were planning to kill Bishop was spreading. It was to be of critical importance. Austin ordered an immediate investigation, and in the early afternoon security guard George made a sworn statement that he and St Paul were responsible but had acted under Bishop's instructions. They had to draw up a list of names of 'trustworthy' supporters who would be told of the plot: they were to be asked 'to notify the masses' if Bishop was physically threatened or killed. George stated that 'he could not bring himself to repeat the lies' and had reported them instead to the security forces.[46] He said that St Paul's advice to Bishop had been 'to kill them or arrest them' but that Bishop had refused as he still preferred negotiations. St Paul was then arrested and eventually despatched to Richmond Hill prison. The rumour did, however, reach the streets, mainly due to the efforts of Bishop's mother, 'Ma Bish'. To Bishop, it was the only way that he could let the general public know that something was amiss. On hearing it, some of Bishop's supporters in his constituency, St David's, raided the parish militia armoury and took weapons to defend him. Although disarmed – 'Brat' Bullen, the leader, was shot dead – and denounced as 'known criminals' and 'Gairyites', it proved to be an accurate indicator of what was to come.

While the investigation was proceeding, the PRA made clear its position on the political crisis. After a long meeting, it resolved that 'never would we allow cultism, egoism, the unreasonable and unprincipled desires of one man to be imposed on our Party'.

> Therefore we call on the Central Committee and the entire party to expel from the Party's ranks all elements who do not submit to,

uphold and implement in practice the decision of the Central Committee and party membership. The People's Revolutionary Armed Forces Branch of NJM awaits the decision and orders of the Central Committee![47]

Only one voice dissented, that of Chief of Staff Major Einstein Louison, one of George Louison's brothers. He was promptly dismissed.

The next day, Thursday 13 October, Bishop was summoned to a party members' meeting called at 10 p.m. to account for the rumour. In a 45-minute speech, he denied any involvement and 'could not account for St Paul's actions'. George then repeated his statement. Bishop declined the right of reply which, earlier, he had requested. He remained silent when called upon to speak. The general opinion was that his lack of denial confirmed George's allegations and that he was responsible. Members denounced him: he had 'disgraced the party', he was 'beyond redemption', he should be 'arrested and court-martialled'. But demands for his expulsion from the party were resisted by the Central Committee. Instead, it was resolved that he be put under house arrest and his telephone disconnected. This last step was for his own protection from 'counter-revolutionaries' while further investigations proceeded. Coard, who remained totally silent during the meeting, was very angry afterwards. 'Blow them up', he allegedly said, 'before they do it to us.'[48]

The Masses Take Charge

Deadlock followed Bishop's house arrest. Not only was he convinced that he was to be poisoned and so refused food, but he also refused to negotiate. With all the Cabinet now involved in the crisis, government gradually slowed down. In these circumstances, the decision of the September meeting not to inform the masses of the crisis could not be sustained for long. Radix, although no longer a member of the Central Committee, heard of the conflict and was the first to break the silence when he told civil servants in his department the next day, Friday 14 October. Coming on top of the rumour of the plot to kill Bishop, the news spread rapidly. It was greeted at first with a mixture of disbelief and amazement. But, with the PRA on full alert, tension was mixed with fear and foreboding. An indication of public anger was shown with the physical manhandling of Strachan when he went that afternoon to the offices of the *Free West Indian* in the centre of St

George's and announced that Coard was, in effect, Prime Minister. Reported to the world press by Alister Hughes, the incident was immediately denied by the Ministry of Information. But it may have helped prompt Coard's resignation later that day on the grounds that he had no personal ambition to be Prime Minister. Phyllis Coard also resigned.

Encouraged by the signs of public support for Bishop, his allies in the government and the party began to organise themselves. Whiteman, for example, had rushed back from New York, where he had been attending the UN General Assembly, as soon as he learnt of Bishop's arrest. When he transferred aircraft at Barbados, he had a message from|Adams asking if there was anything that he could do. Although reported as saying that he would 'take his chances',[49] he, in fact, sent no reply and arrived back to witness a demonstration in St George's market square on Saturday 15 October organised by Radix. More than 300 heard Radix denounce Coard as a man 'obsessed with power'. He told them, and a group of businessmen, that 'they should seek out Coard' if they wanted Bishop free. As a result, he too was arrested in the early hours of the next day and detained in Richmond Hill. Sensing perhaps that they were in danger of losing control of events, the commmittee authorised Austin to broadcast a long statement on the situation on that Sunday. He called for calm because 'the NJM is making every effort to settle this problem within our party'. He expressed regret that the public had not been informed earlier. By this time too, all heads of Grenada's diplomatic missions abroad, except those in Havana and Moscow, had declared for Bishop, and the people were growing more restive. On Tuesday 18 October the schools closed, with both teachers and pupils going on strike. Schoolchildren from St Andrew's swarmed on to Pearls airport shouting 'No Bishop, no school' and one flight was delayed.

In fact, Bishop's supporters were trying to hold the people back from coming out on to the streets because, behind the scenes, Louison was actively attempting to negotiate on Bishop's behalf with Coard. Coard recognised his popular support and told other committee members that, despite their opposition to Louison, they should recognise this quality. Talks thus took place between the two groups through the week-end of 15-16 October and continued on the Monday. Mediation was also again pursued. Munroe was unable to come but Roopnarine and Michael Als of the tiny Trinidad and Tobago People's Popular Movement volunteered. Als saw Bishop on the morning of 18 October. He recalled that 'he was smoking incessantly and appeared to be in a state of mental agitation'. He gave Bishop compromise proposals. He would remain as Prime Minister and should address the nation on lines agreed with the Central Committee, calling for calm and saying that a settlement was in sight. He should meet Coard, thrash out their differences and see if Cuba could act as a mediator. In these circumstances, his behaviour since his return would be overlooked and the threat of expulsion from the party lifted. Bishop agreed to the broadcast so long as Whiteman and Louison could help him draft it. He would also speak to Coard: 'Boy', he said, 'dem men tough as hell and I just as tough, we go see.'[50] Later that day, a four-member delegation from the committee met him and made it clear that he also had to accept responsibility for the crisis and accept the party decision on joint leadership. Bishop promised them, as he had Als, that he would give his final answer the next morning. By this time, he was not alone. The day before, Jackie Creft had come to visit him and was told by the PRA guards that if she entered the house, she would also be under house arrest. She accepted these terms.

While these negotiations were proceeding, the battle lines were being drawn up. At a full meeting of NJM members on 18 October the position of the Central Committee was outlined. Although the minutes of this meeting were apparently destroyed in the later fighting, eyewitness accounts described the atmosphere as 'very tense at first and then easier, as it was explained'.[51] By this time, Whiteman and Louison had come to the conclusion that the Central Committee was playing for time. On the afternoon of Tuesday 18 October, along with Minister of Tourism, Lyden Ramdhanny, and Minister of Housing, Norris Bain, they resigned their government posts and, by their own admission, started mobilising people. Louison was soon arrested, but Whiteman successfully made himself available to radio journalists from Barbados, Trinidad and Martinique, as well as Radio Antilles, the private regional station in Montserrat. Since all of them were audible in Grenada, he was able to make plain his opposition to the Central Committee and give his version of events, thereby bypassing the by now very strict control over information broadcast by Radio Free Grenada. Painted slogans appeared, 'Coard means Oppression', and 'No Bishop, No Work, No Revo!'

Early the following morning, Wednesday 19 October, a huge crowd of up to 15,000 assembled in the market square. All shops and offices were closed, their employees on strike. One observer said it was as if 'an underground telegraph system had worked all over the island . . . trucks and buses poured in from everywhere . . . it was much more crowded than Carnival'.[52] At about 9 a.m., some 3,000 to 4,000 people, mainly schoolchildren, broke away and, led by Whiteman and some businessmen, marched up the steep streets to Bishop's house. They wanted him to speak at the square, the traditional meeting place. The PRA guard was quickly reinforced to over 100 but ordered not to fire into the crowd. The Central Committee was meeting in Coard's house, adjoining that of Bishop, but several members were actually in Bishop's large front courtyard waiting for his decision. The troops fired into the air but the gates were forced open. The guards in the house had earlier been ordered to tie up Bishop and Creft in separate rooms and strip both to their underclothes. The crowd found them in this state: both were weak and Bishop was crying. One witness reported: 'He couldn't speak and all he was saying was "The masses. The masses. The masses". It was all he was saying. Tears wash down his face.'[53] It was 10.35 a.m.

Both were taken by truck downhill into the town. They were expected to go to the market square to address the huge crowd, but Bishop wanted to go to Fort Rupert to use the army transmitter to broadcast to the people. He also wanted medical treatment from the nearby hospital. As the crowd reached the fort, cramming the steep narrow access road to capacity, the PRA guards did not fire and gave up their weapons on Bishop's orders. The magazines were emptied. The crowd did, however, beat some women soldiers who resisted. Bishop was carried on shoulders to the upper floor of the two-storey communications block on the first level of the fort. After acknowledging the cheers of the crowd, he announced that Hudson Austin was replaced as Commander of the PRA by Einstein Louison. By this time, Fitzroy Bain and Vincent Noel, another trade union leader, were present and Norris Bain summoned from the market square, accompanied by his wife.

Noel then asked who in the crowd were trained Militia. He and Einstein Louison began distributing weapons, whereupon several PRA soldiers shed their uniforms and said that they wanted no part 'in such madness'. Bishop, accompanied by a doctor and a nurse, telephoned the Fort Frederick army headquarters some two miles away, situated on a prominent hill overlooking the capital. By this time, the Central Committee had left Coard's house and had met up at Fort Frederick with senior officers of the PRA in a large tent. Together, they let it be known that they were willing to negotiate the issue with Bishop with or without the ministers who had resigned. After discussion, four officers were eventually despatched, led by Captain Stroude and Lt Lester Redhead. In the meantime, Bishop attempted without success to make telephone calls to neighbouring islands using a temporary army landline. He also ordered a public address system but it did not arrive in time. He and his party were in the building for nearly two hours, with some 30 to 40 people crammed in a room. The four officers arrived and, with disarmed troops, inspected the situation. Whiteman and Noel made it plain that there was nothing to negotiate about. Merle Hodge, a Trinidadian who worked in Grenada during the revolution, was present throughout and reflected afterwards:

> With the whole country coming down to town to support Maurice, you wouldn't think that it would enter anybody's head to try and take power in the face of all that. Because you'd be fighting the whole nation. Jackie said to me the other side had the radio station. She talked about the possibility of the army sending a detachment so she said to me that when we go outside, we should make sure that the people stay around, because then they wouldn't shoot. Maurice was just kinda smoking and pacing...[54]

The Massacre

Just before 1 p.m., two Russian-built armoured cars and an armoured troop carrier arrived from Fort Frederick, commanded by Major Cornwall. At first, some of the crowd were under the impression that Cornwall and the troops were going to join them but their belligerent attitude soon made them change their minds. Opinions differ as to who began the shooting: those in the town below heard 'the crackle of AKs at first, not the noise of shells'. Several in the crowd had Soviet AK47 rifles, as did the PRA. What is not in doubt is that at Noel's bidding, many more armed themselves after overpowering the armoury guard. Shots were then fired at the building from the armoured cars, including at least one shell. The defenders returned the fire. Although Bishop ordered the shooting to stop, two PRA soldiers were killed as Noel, backed by Whiteman, shouted 'No Compromise, No Negotiation!' from the balcony. Two hand grenades were thrown at the crowd by the troops, followed by a dense hail of bullets. As Merle Hodge again remembered, 'there was a discussion among Maurice and some of the fellas to the effect that what we had to do was go out and say we surrender, that anything else would be suicide.'[55] The building was then surrounded and Noel was killed in the mêlée, his legs shot off. A car was overturned, adding to the confusion. Another soldier was killed and another mortally wounded but not before the civilian death toll mounted alarmingly. Many fled to the higher level, their exit down the approach road blocked by the armoured cars. On the eighteenth-century battlements of the old slave fort, they had to choose between jumping over the edge — a 50 to 90 foot drop — or being machine-gunned.

A red flare was then seen to be fired in the air from Fort Frederick across the bay. The communications building was cleared except for the politicians, Bishop, Whiteman, Creft and Norris and Fitzroy Bain. Major Layne and Captain Abdullah shouted that they were under arrest and instructed them, their hands above their heads, to go through a passageway into the second level courtyard, at the same time ordering the remnants of the frightened public away. Bishop was pulled aside and told that he was to die. One PRA eye-witness reported that 'he gave a deep sigh, folded his arms, and turned silently to face his killers, who shot him in the head'.[56] Redhead was in charge of the execution squad and allegedly was the one who executed Bishop, using his revolver. When it was the turn of the others, another eye-witness heard the conversation. Against a wall marked with the slogan, 'Towards A Higher Discipline in the PRA', Jacqueline Creft screamed, 'Comrades, you mean you're going to shoot us? To kill us?' Redhead's alleged reply was to the point. 'You f— bitch', he shouted, 'who are you calling comrades? You're one of those who was going to let the imperialists in.'[57]

The executions were over by 1.10 p.m. A white flare was fired into the air from Fort Rupert. The whole ghastly episode had taken just over ten minutes in its entirety. The crowd had vanished: all that were left were the walking wounded who, assisted by friends, tried to make their way down the hill to a rapidly emptying St George's. The exact number of deaths that took place around the fort will probably never be known, but the general consensus among observers was that it was over 100. One soldier counted 60 bodies outside the fort's walls alone.[58] Bishop's body was unrecognisable as his head had been shattered; the others were mutilated by machine-gun fire.

The Revolutionary Military Council

The massacre at the fort meant that the situation was now a military one. Thus at 3 p.m. that afternoon, General Austin announced the formation of a 16-man Revolutionary Military Council which would rule 'until normality is restored'. The PRG was dissolved and all Cabinet ministers dismissed. However, continuity was assured since five of the

16 were also members of the NJM Central Committee — Austin, James, Layne, Bartholomew and St Bernard. Austin later broadcast to a tense and shocked population. He announced Bishop's death, but said he had been killed in shooting initiated by his supporters. As for the future, he made clear the intention of the RMC to 'govern with absolute strictness'. Anyone who sought to demonstrate or disturb the peace would be shot. A four-day curfew was imposed as from 9 p.m. that night to 6 a.m. the following Monday. 'No-one is to leave their house. Anyone violating this curfew will be shot on sight. All schools are closed and all workplaces . . . until further notice.' The PRA is, he stressed, 'totally united' and ready 'to protect and defend our country against any attack by imperialism'. A military invasion was possible — which would result in 'deaths of thousands of our people' — and he pleaded for unity.[59]

This was a forlorn hope. With much of the telephone system immobilised and Radio Free Grenada broadcasting only music, rumours multiplied. Indeed, some of the RMC's actions over the next four days exacerbated them. As one Washington analyst put it, 'the politics of hysteria have taken over Grenada. As [the RMC] see it, they have no alternative but to kill all of those who might try and take over from them. In the eyes of General Austin, it's a simple matter of self preservation.'[60] Justified in terms of a fear that the 'hostile bourgeois press' whose 'interests were not of Grenada' would 'manipulate the crisis', the news blackout helped create a regional and hemispheric atmosphere of suspicion, speculation and anger, and did little for the image of the RMC, domestically or internationally. Foreign journalists were expelled or prevented from entering Grenada when they arrived at Pearls airport. All telex and communications facilities were denied.

Not surprisingly in the circumstances, the foreign press turned to US and other hostile external sources who readily interpreted the military take-over and executions as being Cuban-inspired. Bishop, the press said, had been removed by Cuba and Russia as he stood in their way. Coard's personal ambition, pro-Moscow sympathies and plotting was behind it all. A typical example was that of the British populist tabloid newspaper, the *Daily Express*. The 'Russian and Cuban-backed coup', it screamed, 'has turned Grenada into Moscow's base.' Bishop, 'who stood in the Kremlin's way', had been 'liquidated' because Grenada's position was very strategic to the Soviet Union, being 'so close to the oil shipping lines from nearby Venezuela'. To the United States, it was 'an island Afghanistan'. Coard was 'Moscow's man' and would now permit 'the Kremlin to do whatever it wants though its Cuban clients'.[61] In similar vein, in the tabloid *New York Post*, the RMC were 'communist scum' and 'Andropov's angels' led by 'a man [Coard] who would sell his mother for a nickel and his country for a dime of Red money'.[62] These and similar stories seeped into Grenada through radio broadcasts from neighbouring islands. Shocked and dazed, Grenadians could easily believe them.

In fact, Cuba had reacted to the news of the killings and the RMC take-over in a very hostile fashion. In a statement issued on the day after, it condemned what had occurred in no uncertain terms:

> No doctrine, no principle, no opinion calling itself revolutionary, and no internal split can justify such atrocious acts as the physical elimination of Bishop and the prominent group of honest and dignified leaders who died yesterday. The death of Bishop and his comrades must be explained and if they were executed in cold blood those responsible must be punished as an example.[63]

Cuba's political relations with the new leadership of Grenada would have to be 'subjected to a profound and serious analysis'. This veiled threat added to the pressure on the Austin regime as it struggled to restore normality. The curfew was lifted for four hours on Friday 21 October to enable people to obtain food. The shops opened but not the market. All inter-island boat traffic had ceased and passenger flights into Pearls airport had been very strictly controlled. However, the curfew was lifted for employees in essential services who were issued with passes and travelled under escort. In the country, peasants and others could obtain water from neighbourhood standpipes and could feed those of their animals close to their house. In some instances, PRA patrols helped them, anxious to restore good relations. But mothers of newly-born babies had to fend for themselves and those who died at home were left unburied.

Under cover of the curfew, troops removed the bodies from Fort Rupert. They were taken, in the first instance, to the large PRA training and operations camp at Calivigny, about four miles east of Point Salines. There, Bishop's body was thoroughly cremated. However, those of Whiteman, Creft, Fitzroy Bain and Norris Bain were inefficiently burnt in a shallow pit using used tyres and only thinly covered over. Later, it was possible to identify possibly the body of Jacqueline Creft as the bottom of her jeans had not been destroyed. Subsequent information obtained from soldiers suggested that most of the other bodies were disposed of by dumping them into the sea off Point Salines, where the current is particularly strong.[64]

Inevitably, amongst the people resentment turned to deep anger, apprehension to fear. The closure of the churches was particularly felt. News of further arrests came. Hughes, Einstein Louison, prominent businessmen and others identified as 'counter-revolutionaries' were despatched to Richmond Hill and the Ministry of Information had to work strenuously to counter allegations by neighbouring radio stations that they had been executed. By 21 October, the prison was overflowing and conditions deteriorated. Hardly any food was delivered due to administrative confusion. George Louison and Radix had been removed the previous day to a dungeon at Fort Frederick. St Bernard told them that they were to be executed and a 'shot while in crossfire' story concocted. However, saner counsels were prevailing, and they were left alone, but without food or water. After two days, on Saturday, the two dissidents were fed, but by this time Radix, a diabetic, was in a coma. After much argument, he was taken to hospital and Louison transferred back to the prison.

In fact, several of the RMC were very quickly conscious of the possible consequences of the massacre and fully realised the extent of public hostility. On the day following the appalling chain of events, the Council met to consider three pressing needs: to explain the position, as it saw it, to the people; to prepare economic survival plans in the face of the anticipated OECS and CARICOM trade, fuel and transport embargo; and to stave off the growing threat of external military intervention by making contact with neighbouring and other countries. Restoration of good relations with Cuba was regarded as essential after its fierce statement. Intensive discussions for over 24 hours finally resulted in a decision to create a 'broad based' civilian government within two weeks, a process that would commence with the deliberate co-option of businessmen, bank managers and hoteliers in order to restore confidence both domestically and internationally. In addition, all workplaces were to reopen on Monday 24 October.

The 'Political Department' of the RMC, headed by James and Stroude, was charged with public relations. The first statement was issued to the army on Thursday 20 October and detailed the heroism of those who had defended the revolution at Fort Rupert, especially those who had died. No mention was made of Bishop's death.

> Comrades, the masses had no intention to cause bloodshed and in their confusion they were led by Maurice Bishop and his petty

bourgeois and bourgeois friends as cannon fodder to cause bloodshed ... [They] had deserted the working class and working people of Grenada. He instead pushed them in front to cause trouble and bloodshed in the country.[65]

This attempt to boost morale was bolstered by a 15 per cent salary increase, so raising a private's pay from EC$200 to EC$230 per month.

The second statement was broadcast by RMC Chairman General Austin on the same day. Bishop was to blame because he led the crowd into a military camp rather than to the market square. He alleged that 'Noel and his group' fired first, which necessitated a restoration of order by the army. Further, 'it is now known that it was the intention of Maurice Bishop to have all the officers present at Fort Rupert executed almost immediately'. He asserted that allegations that Bishop was murdered, rather than shot in 'the heat of the moment' in the crowd, were 'a lot of lies'. Also, talk of a power struggle in Grenada put out by 'exploiters of the Caribbean masses', such as Adams and Eugenia Charles, was nonsense.[66] Another statement the following day announced the planned formation of the civilian government and admitted that 17 civilians had been killed, although adding that 'it was never the intention of the armed forces of the people to shed the blood of the people'. The grand total of dead was thus officially put at only 24, including the soldiers whom the Grenadian people were urged 'to emulate'.[67]

On the economic front, Nazim Burke, the former permanent secretary in the Ministry of Finance who had taken over as minister when Coard resigned on 14 October, drew up an Emergency Economic Programme. Coard himself assisted although he was by now very much in the background. It recommended an Emergency Economic Commission headed by a 'Political Leader/Minister' who 'would give guidance to the Commission and convey its views to the Government'. The Commission would be responsible for the overall direction of the economy and would supervise any controls deemed necessary. Each area of the economy was to have a co-ordinator. It was to be primarily concerned with the state sector and would maintain a 'low profile'. Managers of state enterprises and senior bureaucrats would be given responsibilities and report to Commission members, 'but would be given only limited information'. All requests by the Commission were to be given top priority. As for the private sector, only 'appropriate briefings' would be given.[68] A lower level of management was also established in a smaller council. Chaired by Nazim Burke, there were to be nine members, two of whom, including Roopnarine, were co-opted 'internationalist' workers, responsible for money and banking and foreign exchange respectively.

Once established, the Commission and Council drew up detailed task and work programmes aimed at conserving food and fuel supplies, including rationing – ration cards were designed and ready for printing – and the restoration of international transport and postal services. The PRA, however, was to have priority in all supplies. Treaty obligations were to be observed, but dismay was expressed at the extent to which Grenada was dependent upon the multinational Cable and Wireless Company, both in St George's and elsewhere in the region, for its international telecommunications. 'The attitude of radio operators' had to be assessed, as some might sabotage equipment. Should any international organisation of which Grenada was a member move towards taking sanctions, 'as a priority we must get in touch with ... and insist on our right to be informed of any meeting and to be heard'. Further, the Commissioner for International and Regional Organisations, Merle Collins, was ordered to 'identify countries on whom we can hope to depend in the coming period. As soon as is possible we must contact them. At whatever stage our emergency programme has reached, we must inform them of our needs and seek assistance.'[69] As the proposed measures meant serious disruption to the everyday lives of many people, 'clear guidelines for public education and propaganda programmes' were further called for. A programme 'of bringing various areas of private property under Martial Law', especially 'key enterprises' such as petrol stations, would have to be justified. Also, since the fruit and vegetable trade with Trinidad was suspended, 'farmers who lose need to be dealt with', and a policy towards the hucksters – the small traders – 'has to be worked out'. A Council on Employment was to be established and no worker was to be laid off without it being reported. Finally, an Economic Monitoring Emergency Desk began work in the Ministry of Finance, to which all co-ordinators were linked by telephone.

While this activity went on at the functional level, the RMC tried to get overseas support. Prime Minister Milton Cato of St Vincent sent a message to Austin on 21 October asking for a meeting. After some delay, Austin agreed but was too late as Cato had left the next day for the CARICOM meeting in Port of Spain. Another message suggested Carriacou as the site but went unanswered in St Vincent as the first US warship arrived in Kingstown harbour. As for Cuba, the RMC was sharply critical of Castro's response. It deplored 'the deep personal

142 The Internal Struggle for Power

friendship between Fidel and Maurice which has caused the Cuban leadership to take a personal and not a class approach to the developments in Grenada'. It was clear that Castro knew nothing of Bishop's 'dishonesty' and that his position had now created 'an atmosphere for speedy imperialist intervention'. It was therefore resolved to ask for military assistance and to work for 'the best relations' based upon the 'principle of proletarian internationalism'.[70]

As regards the United States, the RMC took swift action. In particular, the students at the St George's University were visited by Austin who gave his assurance that they would not be harmed and that anyone who wanted to leave could do so. The same commitment was then given to all foreign nationals, as it was planned to open Pearls airport the next day. A highly conciliatory message was also sent to the US embassy in Barbados. It read in part:

> We are for peace, friendship and for maintaining the historically established ties between our countries and hope they would grow and strengthen . . . The RMC has no desire to rule the country . . . a fully constituted broad based civilian government is [being] established . . . expressing the interests of all social classes and strata in our country. [It] will pursue a mixed economy and will encourage . . . foreign investment . . . The RMC of Grenada takes this opportunity to reassure the honourable . . . USA of its . . . highest regards.[71]

Similar messages of good intent were sent to the British High Commission also in Bridgetown.

On Monday 24 October, shops and offices reopened and an air of normality was at last restored. The airport was opened, closed and then opened again as a result of poor communication within the RMC. PRA armed patrols were withdrawn from the streets and discreetly confined to strategic locations. Schools were still ordered to remain closed and the curfew was reimposed from 8 p.m. to 5 a.m., but there was every prospect that these measures would soon also be rescinded. Some 20 minutes after the first overnight curfew ended, the invasion began.

A Verdict

Of all the possible hypotheses to account for the crisis, four can be readily identified: first, and the most popular, that it stemmed from a carefully planned conspiracy by the ambitious Coards to seize power and fashion a Marxist-Leninist state; second, that it was planned by radical PRA officers and their allies who used Coard for their own purposes; third, that it was a struggle for power on a personal basis between Coard and Bishop; and fourth, that it was a struggle for the control and direction of the revolution in a deteriorating economic situation which, because of the specific circumstances of Grenada, inevitably involved strong personality clashes.

The case for the first rests upon a conspiratorial interpretation of events and preconceived notions of Soviet-Cuban pressure upon a willing Coard. The evidence is circumstantial for the former and non-existent for the latter. Coard was undoubtedly ambitious, as was his wife; there is no doubt of their radicalism and they both enjoyed power. But throughout the revolution, Coard realised the need for public support and mobilisation. He was also aware that he lacked charismatic leadership qualities, so admired by an impressionist and psychologically dependent society. His pragmatic economic policies, and those he influenced such as the plan for agriculture, contrasted sharply with his internal party rhetoric. His method of operating – careful planning and an acute political 'sixth sense', especially in meetings – made it easy for those who feared him and his formidable intelligence to assume conspiracy. Nor was he in anybody's pocket. For this reason, the second hypothesis is far-fetched: he would never have let himself by used by anybody, least of all by assertive but naive, young army officers. Austin, on the other hand, was in all probability manipulated by them, bearing in mind his limited political consciousness and humdrum personality.

The third may be dismissed as too simplistic as the two leaders were not only highly intelligent and politically active, but stood for identifiable, although not necessarily opposed, policies. It is this factor which suggests that the fourth hypothesis is the most plausible. There had always been rivalry between Bishop and Coard – inevitable given their personalities and backgrounds – but no evidence exists of it being destructive, except in the final days. Indeed, it was for a long while highly creative. Their differences lay in their approach to work, methods of operating and priorities. It is likely that it was this that would have fulfilled Bishop's fears of being gradually ousted from effective leadership under the joint arrangement proposed. After all, Coard would have had control of the important subcommittees of the Central Committee and had the powerful army behind him. Bishop would have been left as a public relations front-man and a popular mobiliser. But this was an absolute requisite of the revolution, given the nature of the society and Grenada's geopolitical situation in the Western hemisphere, and Coard knew that he could never assume sole leadership control because of Bishop's charisma and international standing. The rivalry would have caused a constant haemorrhage in the party and revolution in the years ahead, even if the crisis had been papered over in October. The revolution was thus lost the moment the joint leadership proposal was advanced and approved.

In the circumstances of Caribbean politics, where personalism has for long been a dominating characteristic, it was impossible to prevent the crisis being presented as one between personalities, try as the committee members did to make it one only of principle. As one party member put it,

> There is no middle of the road. This is not a personality question until people made it so. It is a question of principle. Principles are principles. That is what I was taught and we owe it to the Grenadian working class to say so.[72]

Both Bishop and Coard were sucked into a situation which neither could ultimately control. That situation derived from a particular characteristic of the revolution, the fundamental nature of the New Jewel Movement. It had begun as a discussion group and, in a sense, never stopped being one. Policies and positions were always arrived at collectively and the structure and operation of party institutions were designed to involve as many as possible and to guard against 'onemanism'. Bishop had certainly let things slip as regards party organisation and decision-making. That was not surprising, given his range of responsibilities, the poor administrative services, the shortcomings of others and a severe lack of resources; he was therefore, an easy scapegoat. The NJM had led a popular revolution, one in thought as well as deed. The struggle against psychological dependency and the creation of a new spirit of national identity and patriotism rested on the breaking of imperial moulds of thought. In that context, whether or not Coard was considered to be more, or less, radical in his positions than Bishop is of less relevance than their respective willingness to work within the political system which they had helped to create. Radicalised with each turn of the screw by the United States, the party could not afford any signs of weakness in its leaders. If it did, the revolution as a whole would be at stake.

The problem was that it left the masses far behind in its struggle for Marxism-Leninism. Although the material base of the revolution was suffering due to a combination of world recession, falling commodity prices and the diversion of investment funds to the new airport, the difficulties on the ground as described by the radicals and ideological militants in the Central Committee were consistently and grossly exaggerated. Paradoxically, despite Bishop's undoubted popularity and *rapport* with the people, it is doubtful whether even he realised the extent of the credibility gap that had opened up between the party's aspirations and the consciousness of the masses.

Notes and References

1. H.S. Gill, 'The Foreign Policy of the Grenadian Revolution', *Bulletin of Eastern Caribbean Affairs*, vol. 7, no. 1 (1981), p. 3.
2. International Air Transport Association, *Traffic Trends, 1980-1983* (Geneva, mimeo, 1984).
3. Information from interview, G. Louison, November 1983.
4. *Minutes of the Extraordinary Meeting of the Central Committee of the NJM from Tuesday 12th-Friday 15th October, 1982* (St George's, mimeo), p. 2.
5. *Minutes of the General Meeting of NJM Members, Sunday 12th-Monday 13 September 1982* (St George's, mimeo), p. 6.
6. *New Jewel*, 7 October 1982.
7. *Extraordinary Meeting of the Central Committee, NJM, 14-16 September 1983* (St George's, mimeo), pp. 43-4.
8. *Minutes of the Central Committee Meeting*, October 1982, p. 3.
9. *Central Committee Resolution on Agriculture* (St George's, mimeo, n.d.), pp. 1-2.
10. Handwritten comment, *Central Committee Report on First Plenary Session*, 13-19 July 1983 (St George's, mimeo), p. 2.
11. *Report on First Plenary Session*, p. 11.
12. *On the Possible Establishment of a State Trading Corporation for Effecting Grenada's Trade With the Socialist Countries* (St George's, mimeo, n.d.), p. 6.
13. Information from interview, U. Whiteman, September 1983.
14. Ibid.
15. *Report on First Plenary Session*, p. 9.
16. *Caribbean Insight*, February 1983.
17. *Everybody's Magazine* (New York), June/July 1983, p. 41.
18. *Trinidad Guardian*, 6 July 1983.
19. *Minutes of Emergency Meeting of NJM Central Committee Dated 26th August 1983* (St George's, mimeo), p. 5.
20. *Extraodinary Meeting of the Central Committee NJM, 14-16 September 1983* (St George's, mimeo), p. 4.
21. Ibid., p. 10.
22. Interview with G. Louison.
23. *Extraordinary Meeting*, pp. 18-19.
24. Ibid., p. 29.

25. Ibid., p. 33.
26. *Fifth Sitting of Central Committee Plenary, Monday, September 19th, 1983* (St George's, mimeo), p. 3.
27. *Sixth Sitting of Central Committee Plenary, Tuesday, September 20th, 1983* (St George's, mimeo), p. 9.
28. *Seventh Sitting of Central Committee Plenary, Wednesday, September 21st, 1983* (St George's, mimeo), p. 12.
29. *Eighth Sitting of Central Committee Plenary, Thursday, 22nd September, 1983* (St George's, mimeo), p. 15.
30. *Sitting of Central Committee 28.9.83* (St George's, mimeo), p. 6.
31. *Central Committee Plenary, Friday Sept. 23rd, 1983* (St George's, mimeo), p. 4.
32. *Central Committee Meeting*, 30.9.83 (St George's, mimeo), pp. 9-10.
33. *Central Committee Plenary*, 23 September 1983, p. 4.
34. *Why Meeting?*, Central Committee Report, 25 September 1983 (St George's, mimeo), p. 11.
35. *Extraordinary General Meeting of Full Members, Sunday 25th September 1983* (St George's, mimeo), p. 7.
36. Ibid., p. 14.
37. Ibid., p. 19.
38. Information from interview with Cletus St Paul reported by Dr E. Messenger, Grenville, November 1983.
39. S. Strachan, *Report of the Political Bureau and Central Committee held on Oct. 12th* (St George's, handwritten), p. 1.
40. *Declaration of the Party and Revolutionary Government of Cuba Regarding the Events in Grenada* (Havana, 20 October 1983), p. 1.
41. Interview with G. Louison.
42. *Outlet* (Antigua), 28 October 1983.
43. *The Bomb* (Trinidad), 31 October 1983.
44. *Report of the Central Committee Meeting*, 12 October 1983, p. 6.
45. Interview with Cletus St Paul.
46. Transcript of Radio Free Grenada news items, 18 October 1983.
47. *Resolution of the People's Revolutionary Armed Forces Branch of the New Jewel Movement* (St George's, mimeo), p. 2.
48. Information from interviews with NJM members, December 1983.
49. *Observer*, 23 October 1983.
50. *Guardian*, 11 November 1983.
51. Information from interviews.
52. Information from interviews.
53. *Guardian*, 8 November 1983.
54. Merle Hodge, quoted in *Guardian*, 11 November 1983.
55. Ibid.
56. *The Times*, 5 November 1983.
57. Information from interview, November 1983.
58. *The Times*, 5 November 1983.
59. Transcript of Radio Free Grenada, 19 October 1983.
60. L. Birns, Council on Hemispheric Affairs, Washington, reported in *New York Times*, 21 October 1983.
61. *Daily Express*, 22 October 1983.
62. *New York Post*, 23 October 1983.
63. *Granma*, 30 October 1983.
64. *Latin America Regional Report: The Caribbean*, RC-83-10, 9 December 1983.
65. 'Their Heroism is an Example for us', *Bulletin from the Main Political Department, Revolutionary Military Council*, 20 October 1983.

66. Transcript, Radio Free Grenada, 20 October 1983.
67. Transcript, Radio Free Grenada, 21 October 1983.
68. *Emergency Economic Programme: Economic Report No. 1* (St George's, mimeo, 22 October 1983), pp. 2-5.
69. *Emergency Economic Programme*, section 6(4), p. 6.
70. *On Cuba's Response to the Issue*, 21/10/83 (St George's, handwritten report), pp. 1-3.
71. Transcript, Radio Free Grenada, 23 October 1983.
72. *Report of the Central Committee Meeting*, 12 October 1983, p. 5.

7 THE US INVASION

It is not possible to say what knowledge the United States government had of the developing internal struggle for power in Grenada prior to the moment when the conflict emerged into the open with the news of Bishop's house arrest. Estimates of the efficacy of US intelligence vary widely. What is now a matter of fact is that within two weeks of that event a US military invasion of the island had been launched. Indeed, from the earliest moment it seems that plans for an invasion, already drawn up and tested on Vieques two years previously, were being considered by the US government and the political ground being prepared in the Caribbean.

The Preparation Stage

According to the Barbadian Prime Minister, Tom Adams, the initial move in the planning of an invasion came from the United States. He had come to the conclusion, he said, that whatever differences had existed in the past, Bishop deserved the support of Commonwealth Caribbean governments in the particular circumstances of his arrest, which had first been made public on 13 October. Adams claimed that he was seeking opinions as to whether Bishop could be got out of the hands of his enemies when, on Saturday 15 October, 'an official of the Ministry of Defence and Security reported to me that he had been tentatively approached by a US official about the prospect of rescuing Mr Bishop from his captors and had been made an offer of transport'.[1] The US State Department denied this and claimed that, by contrast, it had been approached by unnamed Caribbean governments that same weekend. Both sides, however, agree that informal discussions continued over the intervening few days before the murder of Bishop and the other ministers on 19 October.

Following this grave development US attention was focused on Grenada at a more senior level. The Secretary of State, George Shultz, met to discuss the situation with some of his staff on the night of the killings, Wednesday 19 October, and the following day joined with members of the National Security Council in a special 'situation group' meeting at the White House convened, at Reagan's request, by Vice-

President Bush to consider potential US responses. The group decided immediately to divert a naval task force, headed by the aircraft carrier *Independence*, which was on its way to the Lebanon carrying marines scheduled to replace those already on duty in Beirut. Instead the ships headed for Grenada in what was, according to Shultz's statement at the time, 'a precautionary measure'[2] designed to enable the US government to rescue, if necessary, the thousand or so Americans on Grenada, who included the some 700 students at the St George's University School of Medicine. Nevertheless, in military terms, the move also gave the United States the option of invasion which several influential figures in the State Department in Washington were already favouring.

Proponents of invasion realised that they needed to make political as well as military preparations. Crucial in this connection was the attitude of the leaders of the six territories other than Grenada which belonged to the OECS. They met in Barbados on the Friday after Bishop's murder and were joined for all or most of their discussions by Adams and Edward Seaga, the Jamaican Prime Minister, neither of whose countries were members of the OECS grouping. Also present, according to several accounts, was the US ambassador to Barbados, Milan Bish. There can be no doubt that the leaders of the other small Eastern Caribbean states were greatly shocked by what had happened in Grenada over the previous few days. They felt that such brutal behaviour was as unprecedented in the Commonwealth Caribbean as it was unacceptable. Angrily led by John Compton, the Prime Minister of St Lucia once more, following his re-election to office in May 1982, they looked around for ways of avenging Bishop's death. How much they were guided in their search for an appropriate response by United States participation and advice is a matter of conjecture, but it is not unreasonable to assume, in the light of known US attitudes, that this was a significant factor. For the leaders ultimately took the momentous decision to ask the United States to lead and organise a joint US–Commonwealth Caribbean invasion of Grenada.

Thus began the busiest weekend of Reagan's presidency. He had flown to the Augusta National Golf Club in Georgia late on Friday 21 October, ostensibly for two days of relaxation playing golf. However, Shultz and the President's new National Security Adviser, Robert McFarlane, were also present. According to US accounts, Shultz was awakened at 2.45 a.m. on the Saturday to be told of the (officially unexpected) arrival of a telegram from Barbados, informing the administration of the OECS request. Shultz and McFarlane reported the the news to Bush in Washington and he consulted with other members of the National Security Council before reporting back that the advice he was receiving was to move quickly forward with the invasion plan. At 5.15 a.m. Reagan himself was briefed and consulted further with Bush and his Secretary of Defense, Caspar Weinberger. At 9 a.m. in Washington Bush convened a meeting of top officials, including Weinberger and General Vessey, chairman of the Joint Chiefs of Staff, in which Reagan himself joined for a few minutes by speakerphone. According to one anonymous participant, 'everyone was gung-ho'.[3] Such reservations as were expressed appear, in fact, to have come more from the Pentagon, which was wary of symbolic displays of military power and apparently uncertain of the extent of the opposition that might be expected in Grenada, rather than from White House or State Department staff, who were eager to make the political gesture to the world, especially the Soviet Union, which invasion represented.[4] The latter point of view easily prevailed and it seems that the critical decision of principle to prepare militarily for an invasion was taken at this Saturday meeting.

Knowing that a sudden return to Washington would fuel speculation, Reagan and Shultz deliberately continued to play golf at Augusta, until interrupted by the bizarre news that a drunken gunman demanding to speak with Reagan had taken hostages in the club's golf shop. Although this incident was resolved peacefully, the drama continued because Reagan was again awakened in the middle of the night – at 2.37 a.m. on the morning of Sunday 23 October – to be given the first reports of a suicide bombing of American and French troops in Beirut. From this point onwards the Grenada operation became closely intertwined in Reagan's mind with the atrocities in the Lebanon. He returned to the White House for a round of National Security Council meetings which focused on the implications of this link. Did the disaster in the Lebanon mean that a further loss of life in military action in Grenada was too risky or did it alternatively make the planned invasion all the more imperative as a sign of US determination to stand up in defence of its perceived national interests? There were those present who took the first view, but Reagan, it seems, was not one of them. As one participant explained to a journalist,

> the President felt, whether consciously or unconsciously, that America was being kicked around as it had been when Carter was in charge. And at a moment where, perhaps, further thought should have been given to what he was going to do, as he struggled mainly to cope with Beirut where he could *not* react, it crystallised in

his mind that here [Grenada] he bloody well could react – and would.[5]

Thus the decision to invade was confirmed and the date set for the following Tuesday. It was also decided not to tell US allies, including Biitain, of the administration's intention.

Jamaica, Barbados and the OECS states were similarly bound by the need not to divulge their real intentions. Following their meeting in Barbados on Friday 21 October, they were obliged to proceed to Port of Spain in Trinidad to attend a full CARICOM meeting, which began on the Saturday evening, to consider the Grenada situation. According to reports from inside that meeting, Seaga and the other OECS leaders were particularly quiet, giving no indication of their commitment to an armed US invasion. Adams, in any case, was not present, Barbados being represented by its foreign minister. Other proposals were advanced for a wholly Commonwealth Caribbean solution to the crisis, involving the establishment of a CARICOM fact-finding team, arrangements to ensure the safety of nationals from other countries in Grenada and a call for the speedy creation of a broad-based civilian government of national reconstruction in Grenada. They appeared, what is more, to win general agreement. In a subsequent statement to the Parliament of Trinidad and Tobago, the chairman of the meeting, the Prime Minister of Trinidad, George Chambers, indicated that when the meeting adjourned in the small hours of Sunday morning the only significant disagreement to have emerged, as far as he was concerned, was over what action CARICOM should take if the regime in Grenada refused to treat on the basis of these proposals.[6] On this point some members, although not Trinidad, did, he conceded, express a readiness to use force.

However, when the meeting reconvened later in the morning, only Trinidad, Guyana, the Bahamas and Belize were represented. The other states were apparently meeting together in caucus with the US ambassador to Trinidad, presumably to be told that the Reagan administration had decided to respond positively to their 'invitation', and so arrived at the CARICOM session an hour late. As Chambers himself put it, 'certain heads for the first time stated that there was no consensus on the proposals'.[7] Instead, they wished to direct their attention to two papers which had earlier been circulated, one by Seaga, portentously and in the circumstances ridiculously entitled 'the Protocol of Port of Spain', and the other by the OECS states. The former called for major reforms of the CARICOM Treaty along the lines previously discussed and rejected at the Ocho Rios summit, the latter proposed sanctions to be imposed on Grenada. After discussion, in which Guyana in particular was opposed to these suggestions, a tougher collective line was adopted and a majority of member states took the political decision provisionally to suspend Grenada from CARICOM and to support the proposed OECS sanctions. These were as follows:

1. No official contact with the existing regime.
2. The regime would not be permitted to participate in the deliberations and business of the organisation.
3. Representatives of the regime would not be permitted to participate in or chair caucuses of groupings pertaining to meetings of international agencies and would not be permitted to speak on behalf of the OECS in international agencies.
4. The regime would not be allowed to benefit from the trade, economic and functional co-operation arrangements of the organisation.
5. No new issues of currency will be made to the regime under the East Caribbean Central Bank (ECCB) arrangements.
6. The OECS governments will cease all sea and air communication links with Grenada.[8]

If ever implemented, such a package of measures would have put considerable pressure on the Revolutionary Military Council in Grenada, but, as is now clear, this was not a genuine response on the part of the majority of CARICOM member states present. When revealing these plans to the press, Chambers may have taken them to be an honest reflection of the views of the meeting: what he did not realise was that there were several other heads of government who knew what was being planned in Washington and who were only going through the motions of a collective CARICOM decision as a means of covering up their true allegiance and intention.

The opposition to military intervention expressed by Trinidad, Guyana, the Bahamas and Belize does not appear to have given the United States administration any pause for thought. By this stage, it was not of a mind to be persuaded by any attempt to divert it from its chosen course, not even conciliatory moves on the part of the new military regime in Grenada. It must be remembered that by the weekend after the death of Bishop the RMC was desperately worried by the predicament in which it found itself. It had learnt (presumably from Cuban or Soviet intelligence) of the diversion of the US task force to its waters and had sent the highly conciliatory message to the US embassy in Barbados quoted earlier. It also tried to arouse diplomatic assistance on its behalf, as was revealed when on the night of Sunday 23 October a telex arrived in London at an old Foreign Office number presently occupied by a plastics firm. It was from the RMC and contained two messages: one to the British government asking it to take whatever action it could to forestall invasion, the other a copy of the telex it had sent to the US embassy.[9] As late as the Monday night before the invasion further similar anxious notes were being received in both London and Bridgetown. In another attempt to defuse the situation, the Cuban government, although manifestly not at all sympathetic to the new Grenadian regime, had also sent a message to Washington on 22 October, offering to co-operate in solving whatever difficulties might arise between the United States and Grenada without violence or intervention in that country.[10] All the Grenadian entreaties were ignored by the United States and the Cuban message only received a reply three hours after the landings had actually begun in Grenada.

It was evident, in other words, that by Monday 24 October military matters only were being discussed in Washington. A final technical planning meeting took place that afternoon and at 6 p.m. Reagan signed the order formally putting the invasion plan into action. From the US point of view, the only remaining political hitch to be overcome was an unexpected midnight call to the President from Mrs Thatcher, the British Prime Minister, imploring him to change his mind. Britain's role in the preparation of the invasion had, from the outset, been surrounded by confusion. As far as the governments of Jamaica, Barbados and the OECS states were concerned, Britain had always been fully informed. Adams claimed that he saw the British High Commissioner in Barbados on both Friday and Saturday 21 and 22 October, telling him on the latter occasion of the invasion decision taken by the OECS grouping and delivering what Adams has described as 'a fully formal verbal request for British assistance'.[11] Admittedly, by common consent, it was not until late on the following Monday afternoon that the OECS request was formally relayed to the British government by the High Commissioner for the Eastern Caribbean States in London, but that is regarded in the Caribbean as a technicality. The probability is that the British government knew of these Eastern Caribbean requests, but simply did not take them seriously. It had assumed that the CARICOM decision on the Sunday had overridden the OECS view and was, in any case, firmly being assured by Washington that the United States had no invasion plan. Thus on Monday 24 October the

Foreign Secretary, Sir Geoffrey Howe, answered an opposition question in the House of Commons about US intentions by saying that he had 'no reason to think that American military intervention is likely'.[12] He appears to have been telling the truth. It was not until the Monday evening that messages from the British embassy in Washington alerted the government to the fact that something was afoot and not until 10 p.m. that this was confirmed by the Americans. Hence Mrs Thatcher's call transmitting 'her very considerable doubts'[13] about the proposed action came far too late to have any chance of stopping the invasion. Reagan was obviously uncompromising and all the press accounts say that when she eventually retired for the night Mrs Thatcher was in no doubt that the invasion was going ahead even at that moment.

The Initial Justification

Just after 9 a.m. on Tuesday 25 October, Reagan appeared in the White House briefing room to make the following announcement: 'Early this morning, forces from six Caribbean democracies and the United States began a landing or landings on the island of Grenada in the Eastern Caribbean.'[14] Accompanied by the Prime Minister of Dominica and current chairman of the OECS, Eugenia Charles, he reported that the United States had received an urgent call from the Eastern Caribbean states to assist in a joint effort to restore order and democracy in Grenada and had acceded to their request to become part of a multinational force which included contingents from Antigua, Dominica, St Lucia, St Vincent, Barbados and Jamaica. These last two states were not OECS members but had, he said, been initially approached by the OECS and then had joined with them in unanimously asking the United States to participate. Turning to the justification for what he called 'this decisive action', Reagan gave three reasons:

> First, and of overriding importance, to protect innocent lives, including up to 1000 Americans whose personal safety is, of course, my paramount concern. Second, to forestall further chaos. And, third, to assist in the restoration of conditions of law and order and of governmental institutions to the island of Grenada, where a brutal group of leftist thugs violently seized power ... Let there be no misunderstanding, this collective action has been forced on us by events that have no precedent in the Eastern Caribbean and no

place in any civilized society.[15]

The image he sought to portray, in other words, was one of proper concern for the well-being of citizens for which he was responsible, combined with a neighbourly willingness to help a small group of peaceable, democratic states stamp out a brutal and uncivilised regime in its midst.

In reality, Reagan's reasoning was disingenuous in the extreme. In respect of all three stated justifications, the evidence did not sustain his position. In the first place, it does not appear as if any American lives were threatened by the policies of the Grenadian Revolutionary Military Council. On the contrary, the regime had gone out of its way to inform the Medical School in particular of its good wishes. As we have seen, General Austin and another officer visited the campus to speak to staff and students in an attempt to reassure them of their safety and urge them to stay. In this forum, on its radio and in its communications with the US embassy in Barbados, the RMC made it absolutely clear that arrangements were in the process of being made to enable those non-Grenadians who wanted to leave the island to depart in normal fashion by commercial aircraft. This was certainly the impression formed by the Chancellor of the University, Dr Charles Modica, who kept in close touch with the situation from his New York office via amateur radio operators at the school. On the day after the invasion he said: 'I think that the President's information is very wrong because some of the Americans started to go out yesterday . . . I think the orderly evacuation of the island could have been maintained throughout this week.'[16] The Cuban diplomatic note of 22 October confirmed the absence of immediate danger for foreigners in Grenada; so did the visit of a British diplomat to the island on Sunday 23 October, at least in respect of the safety of British subjects; and so too, more tellingly, did the soundings of the two US diplomats who actually spoke with many of the medical students on the same visit on the Sunday. One of them, Kenneth Kurze, said afterwards: 'We have not recommended that they leave.'[17] Against all this evidence, the US administration could only offer the 'Tehran syndrome', the fear that hostages might have been taken as they were four years earlier in Iran, and, retrospectively, the understandable relief of the American students on returning home once the actual fighting had started. Even if the former anxiety had been well founded, it would have necessitated only a limited evacuation mission.

Secondly, the prospect of further chaos in Grenada which Reagan felt it necessary to forestall was not likely. In fact, after the killings of Bishop and the others on 19 October, the strict curfew had effectively put a stop to further outbreaks of disorder. By the Sunday before the invasion the island was 'calm but tense' in the view of the visiting British Deputy High Commissioner from Barbados.[18] What was concerning the RMC in these few days was not the organisation of further bloodletting, but rather its attempt to recreate the basis for orderly civilian government in Grenada. As was indicated earlier, talks had taken place with businessmen and hoteliers and the principle of a return to civilian rule agreed. So far from portending further chaos, the situation at the time of the invasion was that various prominent individuals were being approached and asked to serve in a new government.

Thirdly, the central claim that the United States had a legitimate motive for seeking to restore governmental institutions to Grenada by virtue of the invitation proffered to it by the 'Caribbean democracies' was itself highly misleading. As the CARICOM meeting showed, not all the Caribbean democracies were involved. Reagan's definition seemed to embrace only the closest allies of the United States in the region, those Commonwealth Caribbean countries with the most rightwing governments. As for the legal, rather than the political, justification of the OECS action, much reference was subsequently made to Article 8 of the OECS treaty as the proper basis for the intervention. The critical part of this article, which concerned the composition and functions of the defence and security committee established within the OCES, read as follows:

> The Defence and Security Committee shall have responsibility for co-ordinating the efforts of Member States for collective defence and the preservation of peace and security against external aggression and for the development of close ties among the Member States of the Organisation on matters of external defence and security, including measures to combat the activities of mercenaries, operating with or without the support of internal or national elements, in the exercise of the inherent right of individual or collective self-defence recognised by Article 51 of the Charter of the United Nations.[19]

Moreover, all the decisions and directives of the committee were required to be unanimous. With its competence limited to these carefully-defined circumstances, the OECS could not possibly have lawfully authorised the US invasion of Grenada. There was no question of mercenary activity or external aggression and, manifestly, no pretence at unanimity with Grenada itself absent. If the OECS states truly believed that the new regime in Grenada created a serious threat to the future peace and stability of the region, the appropriate legal remedy would have been to bring the matter to the attention of the Organisation of American States which possesses the competence to take action under circumstances not tantamount to external aggression.[20]

When the transparency of this particular pretext quickly became apparent, the United States and the OECS tried to rescue the legitimacy of their action by drawing in to the argument the Governor General of Grenada, Sir Paul Scoon. Speaking under some pressure at the United Nations on the day after the invasion, Eugenia Charles claimed that it was Scoon who had first requested OECS assistance in a message which reached the members of the organisation on Friday 21 October as they began their meeting in Barbados. She did not make public the text of the request, indicate in what form it had been made or say what sort of assistance he had asked for. However, other official accounts of Scoon's role cast doubt on this. On Sunday 23 October he spoke with one British and two American diplomats at his residence and gave no indication that the situation demanded military action or that a request to the OECS had been made. Indeed, in an interview later given on BBC television, he said it was only late on the Sunday night that he decided to call for assistance. Significantly, in that same interview, he said: 'What I asked for was not an invasion but help from outside.'[21] US sources also later gave the date of his appeal as 23 October. The confusion further extends to the actual letter Scoon allegedly wrote. The press officer to Tom Adams, the Barbadian Prime Minister, was reported as saying that letters addressed to each country participating in the invasion were taken into Grenada by the invading forces for Scoon's signature.[22] There were apparently two separate batches of identical letters, drafted by someone other than the Governor General and all dated 24 October – the day before the invasion – one set taken in by the Caribbean contingent in the force, the others by US troops. All of this must cast considerable doubt on both the spontaneity and the substance – not to mention the questionable legality – of Scoon's action. In doing so, the last fig-leaf covering up the implausibility and dishonesty of President Reagan's initial justification of the invasion was removed.

The Battle

Operation Urgent Fury, the US battleplan for the invasion of Grenada, began unostentatiously in the earliest hours of 25 October when an elite squad of navy 'seals', trained in special seaborne operations, landed near St George's, with a view to securing control of the Governor General's residence at the earliest possible moment. The main attack came shortly afterwards in two waves. At 5.36 a.m. 400 marines landed at Pearls airport on the north-east side of the island aboard armed helicopters from the US amphibious assault ship *Guam*, which was part of a nine-ship task force supporting the invasion off the coast of Grenada. A single Grenadian-manned anti-aircraft battery fired briefly at the invaders, but the airport was quickly and easily taken. Meanwhile, in the south of the island at the Point Salines airport, some 800 army rangers, flown in from Barbados, landed by parachute just after 6 a.m. According to American accounts they were met by considerable anti-aircraft machine-gun and rifle fire which it is claimed came from the Cubans working at the airport.[23] Thus it was with some difficulty that the runway was cleared of obstacles and the area made safe for the landing of the many US C-130 transport planes that were waiting to bring in more men and equipment.

However, the Cuban government gave a very detailed and very different account of the events following the initial parachute landing by the rangers. In a series of statements it explained that the option of evacuating its personnel following the death of Bishop had been considered but rejected as 'demoralising and dishonourable' since it was by then known that US ships were approaching Grenada. Cuban personnel were instead told to defend themselves 'energetically', but 'only if they came under direct attack'.[24] According to Castro, this was precisely what occurred. In his funeral address in tribute to the Cubans killed in Grenada, he declared:

> The assertion that the Cubans initiated the acts of hostility is false and cynical. The irrefutable truth is that the Cubans were sleeping and their weapons were stored at the time of the air-drop on the runway and around the camps. They had not been distributed. There weren't enough to go around, and they weren't distributed until the landing was already underway and that is when the Cuban personnel went to the places assigned to them for that emergency. Even so, our personnel, now organised and armed, had time to see the US paratroopers regrouping on the runway and the first planes landing. That

was the invader's weakest moment. If the Cubans had fired first, they would have killed or wounded dozens — perhaps hundreds — of US soldiers in those early hours. What is strictly historical and strictly true is that the fighting began when the US troops advanced towards the Cubans in a belligerent way.[25]

It is, of course, impossible to know which version is correct. No side likes to admit it fired first and no journalists were allowed to land with the American forces to offer an independent assessment. Independent sources in Grenada suggest, in fact, that the airport was defended only by two revolutionary army soldiers armed with rifles but that they did succeed in shooting down some of the American parachutists as they descended. This would account for the reference to early US losses on landing. It is also quite plausible that the Cubans initially thought the Americans aimed only to secure the safety of the nearby medical students, in which circumstances they had been ordered by Castro to refrain from interfering.

At any rate, both sides agree that fierce fighting took place for a while in the Point Salines area. Yet it does not appear to have been protracted; stocks of Cuban ammunition were limited and some 600 Cubans were captured within a few hours of the assault and placed under the guard of the 300 Caribbean troops in the invasion force who had been flown in once the airport area was secure. The students at the True Blue campus of the medical school, located right at the inland end of the runway, were quickly secured and flown out early on the Wednesday morning. The other students at the Grand Anse campus, some two miles away, were not, however, reached until approximately 4 p.m. the following day. It is not even clear that the first US forces realised that there was a second campus. When they did advance towards it, they again met stiff resistance from the Grenadian army and from a few retreating Cubans. Only a helicopter landing on the beach enabled them to rescue the remaining 200 students, who were certainly by this time in danger of being injured in the cross-fire. It should be noted that no attempt was made to take them hostage even at this stage in the fighting.

In the meantime, 250 of the marines who had landed at Pearls had re-embarked on the *Guam* and been taken by sea round to the west side of the island, where at Grand Mal Bay just to the north of St George's they landed at approximately 7.30 p.m. with five tanks and thirteen amphibious vehicles. They quickly secured the Texaco oil farm and the Beau Séjour wireless relay station. By early Wednesday morning they had overcome resistance from Grenadian troops protecting the outskirts of St George's and surrounding the Governor General's mansion, and had joined the 'seals' inside. Scoon was quickly carried away by helicopter to the *Guam*. The capital was taken with little fighting. Its defences had been softened up all the previous day by repeated air attacks from US planes flying from USS *Independence* offshore and both Fort Frederick and Richmond Hill prison were found deserted by the marines. On Thursday the main Grenadian army camp at Calivigny Point to the east of Point Salines was taken, after some fighting and heavy US air attacks, by reinforcements from the 82nd Airborne Division. By Friday 28 October all the major military objectives of the US forces had been achieved. According to the US commander, scattered pockets of resistance remained, but the battle for Grenada was essentially over. By then, 6,000 US troops were on the island.

Evaluation of the extent and intensity of the battle is again a matter of differing interpretations. The official US position is that it expected a quick victory but met much more serious resistance than it anticipated, mainly, it suggests, from the Cubans. The vision is of US forces 'inching' their way forward under a constant hail of bullets fired by communist soldiers. Yet a respected British journalist who stayed on in Grenada after the invasion was able later to write:

> A month after the attack, it has become clear that the United States, in the interest of justifying its 'victory', over-reported the amount of Cuban resistance, under-reported the Grenadian resistance, and exaggerated its own military prowess. In fact, only a minority of Cubans and Grenadians, but in roughly equal proportions, put up any opposition.[26]

He even suggested that the US attempt to suppress the fact of Grenadian, as opposed to Cuban, resistance was taken as far as exhuming bodies known to be Grenadian and sending them to Havana with the Cuban dead. The Cubans confirmed this, having revealed that of the 37 bodies returned to them, 13 were Grenadian. The Americans say they killed only three Grenadian soldiers, although they admit that 18 mental patients died when they inadvertently bombed a hospital in St George's from which Grenadian soldiers were firing at their helicopters. Taking, therefore, the official figures from each side (although it must be said several reports consider them an underestimate, especially of Grenadian dead), the military casualties of the invasion were: killed in action: US 18, Cuban 24, Grenadian 16;

wounded: US 113, Cuban 57, Grenadian 280.[27] The Caribbean troops were at no time involved in combat and so did not suffer casualties. In general, the figures suggest that the fighting was limited in scale and yet relatively even in terms of losses. The overwhelming superiority of US numbers was, therefore, in the end what carried the day. The Cubans were few in number, and the Grenadian forces barely 1,500 in total, since the Militia, which was predominantly pro-Bishop in its sympathies, hardly mobilised. The military battle for Grenada would unquestionably have been a lot harder if the internal splits in the government and the murder of Bishop and the other ministers had not destroyed the will to resist of so many former supporters of the revolution.

The Alleged Cuban Take-over

The way in which the US administration chose to present the battle to the American public exposed more fully the real politics that lay behind Reagan's decision to invade. This was the desire to achieve at least one 'victory' in the world-wide anti-communist crusade to which his administration was dedicated. In the context of this world-view, Grenada appeared to offer the perfect opportunity – a small island close to the United States, a bloodstained left-wing regime with Cuban and Soviet connections, and seemingly little risk of serious casualties if intervention was decided upon. Revealingly, in a further television statement to the nation made on 27 October, the third day of the landings, Reagan only briefly reiterated the reasons initially offered to justify the invasion, preferring to shift the main line of argument to the necessity for constant vigilance against the communist threat. 'The events in Lebanon and Grenada', he declared, 'though oceans apart, are closely related.' Not only had Moscow assisted and encouraged the violence in both countries, but it had provided 'direct support through a network of surrogates and terrorists', controlled in the Grenadian case by Cuba. He claimed that the number of Cubans on Grenada, whom he referred to throughout as a military force, was larger than the Americans had anticipated, and further asserted that US troops had discovered 'a complete base with weapons and communications equipment, which makes it clear a Cuban occupation of the island had been planned'. Grenada was no holiday paradise, Reagan went on: it was 'a Soviet-Cuban colony being readied as a major military bastion to export terror and undermine democracy'. Reassuringly, he concluded:

'We got there just in time.'[28] To bolster the President's new justification for invasion the Pentagon immediately released film of a cache of Soviet-made arms found near the Point Salines airport and later made public a series of documents found in Grenada detailing the defence arrangements the Bishop regime had made with Cuba, the Soviet Union and North Korea.

As far as most commentators were concerned, the case was comprehensively proven by Reagan: the Cuban take-over was a fact. However, the various allegations made need to be examined much more sceptically. The number of Cubans working on Grenada may, indeed, have been larger than US intelligence was aware, but it was nowhere near the figure of 1,500-2,000 which unnamed American officials were giving to the press during the first few days of the invasion. On the day of the attack Castro stated that there were exactly 784 Cubans on Grenada, a number which has now been accepted by all sides. Rebutting the suggestion that they constituted a trained battalion of soldiers, he indicated the precise role of every one as follows:

> 636 workers from the Ministry of Construction; 17 from public health; 12 from education; 6 from agriculture; 6 from the State Committee for Cooperation; 5 from fishing; 3 from basic industry; 3 from culture, 2 from domestic trade; 1 from communications; 1 from foreign trade; 1 from the National Institute of Sports, Physical Education and Recreation; 1 from the Central Planning Board; 43 from the Ministry of the Revolutionary Armed Forces (MINFAR), of which 22 were officers and the rest translators and service personnel; 9 from the Ministry of the Interior; 12 comprising the twin crew and guards of a Cuban plane that arrived at Pearls Airport on the day before the invasion; 2 passengers on the plane: Colonel Pedro Tortoló of MINFAR, who travelled to Grenada on a working visit, and Carlos Díaz, an official of the Party Central Committee's America Department; and 18 from the diplomatic mission, including women and children.[29]

The accuracy of this list has not been challenged and indicates that of the 784, only some 25 could be said to have had a specifically military function. The construction workers at the airport were precisely that, as was confirmed by the many foreign journalists who saw them and spoke with them on their return to Havana. Nearly 50 per cent of them were over 40 years old. They were able to fight as effectively as they did because all adult Cuban men have, since the Bay of Pigs invasion of

1961, been given a high degree of military training as potential reserve units. The Cuban statement also demonstrated that there could not have been the 'hundreds' of Cubans hiding in the hills of Grenada a week or more after the invasion which US military briefings repeatedly claimed. Allowing for the 600 or more captured, those killed and those at that stage sheltering in the Cuban mission in St George's, only a very small number were unaccounted for.

As for the other allegations concerning the arms cache and the existence of Soviet-Cuban plans to turn Grenada into a military base, Cuba's refutation was again powerful. In the first place, the stock of captured rifles, which even a *Time* magazine correspondent called 'more of a hodgepodge of wholesale weaponry than a sophisticated armoury',[30] belonged to the Grenadian Militia and had been built up precisely because of the fear in the island of a US invasion. Secondly, the secret documents that fell into US hands referred to a treaty between the Grenadian and Cuban governments to which Castro was quite ready to admit since it involved the provision of only 27 (and possibly later 40) military advisers to Grenada, 22 of which were already there at the time of the invasion. Thirdly, as again Castro himself pointed out in his funeral address, the documents also showed that 'the weapons that the Soviet Union supplied to the government of Grenada for the army and the militia were subject to an article that prohibited their export to third countries, which refutes the idea that Grenada had been turned into an arsenal for supplying weapons to subversive, terrorist organizations'.[31]

Indeed, so far from wanting to turn Grenada into a base, Cuba had resolutely refused several requests from the short-lived Austin regime for it to send troops to Grenada to help resist the anticipated US invasion. One message despatched from Havana to its representatives in Grenada on 22 October read as follows: 'Convey to Austin and Layne the following oral reply to their proposals . . . that sending reinforcements is impossible and unthinkable.'[32] The Cuban workers would defend their positions, if attacked, but no more. As has been demonstrated earlier, the general attitude of the Cuban government to the RMC in Grenada was distinctly cool. It blamed the threat of US invasion upon the serious errors made by sections of the leadership and in the tense days before the invasion sought to maintain scrupulously correct and unprovocative relations with Grenada.

All in all, Reagan's vision of Grenada as a virtual Cuban colony does not stand up to careful examination. The whole farrago of allegations was a political manoeuvre related more to his desire to be seen to have won a significant victory over Moscow than to reality on the island. In the context of its view of the world, the US government manifestly did not like the presence of Cubans in Grenada, but, as Sir Geoffrey Howe indicated in an interview given after Reagan's 27 October broadcast, provided they were there at the invitation of the government concerned, then however misguided that invitation might be thought to be by another government, no invasion could be justified.[33]

The Reaction at Home

Fortunately for President Reagan, most Americans appear not to have reacted in the same way as Sir Geoffrey Howe. It is true that when news of the invasion was first given the tone of much press and congressional comment was more critical than supportive. But it was generally couched in terms of scepticism rather than outrage. For example, the *Washington Post* coolly refused to rejoice, finding the President's initial justification 'hardly adequate reason to invade a small country', but ultimately withheld judgement. 'The burden of proof', it concluded, 'is still on the Reagan administration to justify the immensely grave act of invading a sovereign state.'[34] In similarly equivocal vein the *New York Times* pointed out that no evidence of a threat to American lives or of the collapse of order and authority in Grenada had yet been presented, but was for the moment prepared to give the administration the benefit of the doubt since it was possible that Cuba and the Soviet Union had established a puppet regime in the island. 'If that were clear', it pleaded, 'why was it not proved, or even asserted?'[35] In Congress too the prevailing first reactions were surprise, puzzlement and an unwillingness to speak out whilst American troops were in action. Probably the most hostile comment was made by Senator Daniel Moynihan, a New York Democrat and former US representative at the United Nations, who pointedly asked if the US had the right to 'bring in democracy at the point of a bayonet'.[36]

After this generally uncertain initial reaction Congress never recovered its nerve. The Senate voted 60-24 and the House of Representatives 403-23 to apply the time limits imposed on the use of US troops under the terms of the War Powers resolution. This piece of legislation, passed in the aftermath of Watergate and regarded by all Presidents since as an encroachment on their constitutional power as commander-in-chief, requires that troops be brought home after 60 days unless Congress gives its approval for their continued deployment. In connection with Grenada, rather than reflecting bitter congressional opposition, the votes in favour of the deadline reflected more the routine assertion of congressional privilege *vis-à-vis* the President, combined with the standard post-Vietnam warning to the administration to be wary of open-ended commitments of troops, especially apposite in view of the doubts widely felt in Congress about Reagan's Central American policy. For the most part, the substance of the criticism levied on the Grenada operation in Congress focused on secondary issues: the failures of US intelligence, the restrictions on the reporting of the war and the bombing of the mental hospital. Some potential dissentients felt it necessary to wait until a fact-finding team sent to Grenada by the Speaker of the House of Representatives, Tip O'Neill, reported. However, with the prominent exception of two black Representatives on the mission, the consensus of the majority of the team, when they returned, was that a real potential threat to US interests existed in Grenada. O'Neill himself, who had earlier referred to the invasion as gunboat diplomacy, was forced to issue a statement saying he now felt it to be justified 'under the particular circumstances'.[37]

Politically, the key factor bearing on the situation was that the invasion had proved to be hugely popular amongst the American people, at least in the immediate aftermath of its occurrence. A quick *Newsweek* poll taken by telephone on 26 and 27 October recorded a figure of 53 per cent approving the invasion and an overwhelming 69 per cent believing that the need to protect American citizens in Grenada justified the attack.[38] Two weeks later — after the President had made his second speech, after the fighting was over and after the returning students had been photographed kissing the tarmac on their return to United States territory — the figure approving the invasion, according to a *Washington Post*-ABC News poll, was up to 71 per cent.[39] Reagan was also ahead of the two leading Democratic presidential challengers in the poll for the first time since April. In these circumstances, there was no disposition in Congress to be opposed to the invasion and an increasing unwillingness on the part of the liberal press to be associated with seemingly negative opinions. What had previously been an invasion was now, according to Reagan and conventional wisdom, a rescue mission. The changed stance of the *Washington Post* was the most striking. Even after all the allegations about Cuban infiltration, it had continued to maintain a questioning attitude, but in its editorial on 10 November it effectively gave in. Taking up what it called a 'more settled view', it summarised thus the predominant domestic political reaction in the

166 *The US Invasion*

United States to Reagan's Caribbean adventure: 'We think President Reagan made the right decision in Grenada. He redeemed a truly disturbing situation with an economical use of force.'[40] Reagan was no doubt able to draw considerable satisfaction from this state of affairs. In election years the focus of democratic politicians tends to be very short-term indeed. Yet he must have been aware too that the invasion had created new problems for the United States, not least amongst friends and allies given the much less favourable international reaction which it had generated.

Notes and References

1. *The Times*, 28 October 1983.
2. *Time*, 7 November 1983.
3. Ibid.
4. See the column by Peter Jenkins in the *Guardian*, 14 November 1983.
5. *Sunday Times*, 30 October 1983.
6. Statement by the Honourable the Prime Minister George Chambers to the House of Representatives of the Parliament of Trinidad and Tobago on the Grenada crisis, 26 October 1983.
7. Ibid.
8. Ibid.
9. See *The Times*, 28 October 1983.
10. See *Granma*, 30 October 1983.
11. *Sunday Times*, 30 October 1983.
12. Sir Geoffrey Howe in House of Commons, *Parliamentary Debates (Hansard)*, vol. 47, no. 33, 24 October 1983, col. 30.
13. Mrs Margaret Thatcher in ibid., vol. 47, no. 34, 25 October 1983, col. 140.
14. Statement made by President Reagan on US involvement in Grenada, 25 October 1983 (United States Information Service).
15. Ibid.
16. *Guardian*, 26 October 1983.
17. *International Herald Tribune*, 25 October 1983.
18. Sir Geoffrey Howe in House of Commons, *Parliamentary Debates (Hansard)*, vol. 47, no. 33, 24 October 1983, col. 27.
19. *Treaty establishing the Organisation of Eastern Caribbean States*, Basseterre, St Kitts, 18 June 1981, Article 8, paragraph 4.
20. See the letter to the *Guardian*, 24 November 1983, from Francis A. Boyle, Professor of Law at the University of Illinois and seven other US law professors.
21. Quoted in *New Statesman*, 11 November 1983.
22. See ibid.
23. See the reports in *Time*, 7 November 1983 and *Newsweek*, 7 November 1983.
24. *Granma*, 30 October 1983.
25. 'Funeral Address given by Commander in Chief Fidel Castro, First Secretary of the Central Committee of the Communist Party of Cuba and President of the Council of State and of the Council of Ministers, in tribute to the heroes killed in unequal combat in Grenada by Yankee imperialism, 14 November 1983', reprinted in the *Guardian*, 19 November 1983.

26. Jonathan Steele in the *Guardian*, 25 November 1983.
27. Ibid.
28. Statement made by President Reagan to The Nation, 27 October 1983 (United States Information Service).
29. *Granma*, 6 November 1983.
30. *Time*, 7 November 1983.
31. 'Funeral Address' in the *Guardian*, 19 November 1983.
32. *Granma*, 30 October 1983.
33. Reported in the *Guardian*, 31 October 1983.
34. *Washington Post*, 27 October 1983.
35. *New York Times*, 27 October 1983.
36. *International Herald Tribune*, 27 October 1983.
37. Ibid., 10 November 1983.
38. *Newsweek*, 7 November 1983.
39. *Washington Post*, 10 November 1983.
40. Ibid.

8 INTERNATIONAL REACTION

The military invasion of Grenada inevitably provoked a huge international reaction. Within a week of the invasion 92 governments had made public statements of their position. Of these, the vast majority — no less than 79 — condemned, repudiated or in some way expressed disapproval of the operation.[1] Many of the critics were traditional or current allies of the United States. However, the tone and content of all the various reactions did differ considerably and significantly in detail, which means that a brief summary of the world's immediate response to the invasion is required.

The USSR and Cuba

Predictably, it was the Soviet Union which initially voiced the most scathing denunciation of the US invasion. The official news agency, Tass, branded it 'an act of open international banditry' which 'has exposed before the whole world the US government's true visage — the visage of an aggressor'.[2] The words were deliberately chosen to be reminiscent of the terms in which Washington had condemned the Soviet intervention in Afghanistan four years previously. This was followed the next day by a formal government statement, a device used by Moscow only on rare occasions, which said that Tass was authorised to state that the Soviet Union 'firmly condemns the US aggression against Grenada' and calls upon the invaders to 'clear out immediately'.[3] When later in the week President Reagan specifically drew the Soviet Union into the argument by declaring that Grenada was in effect a Soviet–Cuban colony, Tass replied with a statement arguing that it was in fact the United States which was attempting to impose a kind of *pax americana* on the Third World and especially Central America and the Caribbean. US foreign policy was now based on 'the expansion of US military interference in various regions of the earth'.[4] These remarks also came just before Moscow formally protested to the US government about an injury sustained by one of its embassy staff in Grenada during an American air attack.

By contrast with the aggressive Soviet reaction, the immediate response of the Cuban government to the act of invasion was understandably more restrained. At a press conference held whilst Cuban workers were still fighting in Grenada, Castro called the invasion 'an enormous political mistake that will not benefit the United States at all'.[5] Yet his mood was generally more perplexed than angry. He supposed that the invasion was an attempt to set a precedent, but even in those terms he considered it to be absurd.

> I do not see any rationale for it. What sense was there in intervening in such a tiny country, with the government that was having a hard time simply trying to survive? Not a single US citizen was wounded or hurt; none of their lives was endangered. No big economic interests were involved. It seems to me that this was the application of a philosophy and a policy of force which they are trying to extend all over the world.[6]

In answers to other questions, the Cuban leader reiterated his government's distaste for the events in Grenada which led to Bishop's death and spoke sadly of his unsuccessful efforts to persuade the United States not to use force. Indeed, the whole affair seemed to have shaken Castro and brought home to him the sheer extent of US military power in the Caribbean. Asked to what extent Cuba would be able to support Nicaragua in the face of a similar US attack, he warned strongly against any such action, but indicated that there was little he could do since Cuba lacked the naval and air means to send direct assistance to Nicaragua or any other beleaguered Caribbean territory.

Britain and Western Europe

In Western Europe too the prevailing reaction to the US invasion was critical. From those countries with left of centre governments this was perhaps to be expected. Thus the French government let it be known that President Mitterrand had condemned the intervention in a discussion at a cabinet meeting. 'Right is not divisible', he was quoted as saying, 'international society rests on certain principles, in particular the right of self-determination of peoples, and those principles have the same value everywhere.'[7] The Swedish Prime Minister, Olaf Palme, declared that it was one more example of a big power trampling on the sovereignty of a small country. The Italian leader, Bettino Craxi, called for the immediate withdrawal of US troops from Grenada and urged the United States to pursue a peaceful solution to the problems of the Caribbean basin. The head of the Spanish government, Felipe Gonzalez, indicated his opposition to the use of force in international relations and the Greek government expressed deep concern at the further aggravation of tension in the area which the invasion brought about.

However, a critical stance was also adopted by the conservative Christian Democrat government of West Germany. In a strongly-worded statement to the Bundestag the Foreign Minister, Hans-Dietrich Genscher, expressed regret that the German government had not been consulted before the American decision to send troops into Grenada and declared that, if it had been given the opportunity to do so, it would have advised against intervention. 'We advocate political solutions to conflicts, and not military ones',[8] he said, going on to confirm that he had fully informed the US administration of this viewpoint. The main opposition Social Democratic Party and the Green Party were even more openly hostile to the US action, using it to reinforce their case against the deployment of US cruise missiles in West Germany, the issue that was being most fiercely debated in the country at the time.

In Britain the Thatcher government was even more embarrassed by the invasion than the West German government had been. Its problems were the greater since it had first been given to believe by the Americans that military action was not being considered and then subsequently ignored when it eventually discovered about the invasion plan and counselled against it. Further difficulties were caused by the fact that Grenada was a Commonwealth country whose Queen was also Queen of England. Despite all this, Sir Geoffrey Howe refused actually to condemn the invasion when he formally told the House of Commons of its occurrence. He admitted the existence of British anxieties, but repeatedly fell back on the formula that 'there is room for two views on this matter'.[9] The opposition Labour Party spokesman, Denis Healey, was thus able not only to denounce the American invasion in its own right but also because it represented 'an unpardonable humiliation of an ally'.[10] In an emergency debate the following day Healey further developed his attack on Mrs Thatcher personally and the Conservative government in general for their previous servility to the US President. 'It really is time', he demanded, 'that the Prime Minister got off her knees and joined other allies of the United States, who are deeply concerned about the present trend in American policy.'[11] Yet, even in the face of bitter criticism of this sort, no member of the government could be induced to use the word condemn in regard to the American action. The furthest that Howe would go was to concede that the extent of the consultation between London and Washington about Grenada 'was regrettably less than we would have wished'.[12]

As in West Germany, the Grenada issue was also used by the opposition parties to develop broader arguments about the merits and demerits of close alliance with the United States and the particular matter of the control of the firing of American missiles based in Britain. It did not therefore disappear from the headlines as quickly as in some other parts of Western Europe. After enduring several days of widespread criticism for her failure to make clear the views of her government, it seems that Mrs Thatcher eventually decided to speak out more openly. Questioned in a radio programme she had this to say: 'If you are going to pronounce a new law that wherever there is communism imposed against the will of the people then the US shall enter then we are going to have really terrible wars in the world.' She was, she went on, always delighted when people had the yoke of communism lifted from their shoulders, but 'that does not mean you are entitled to go into every country . . . which is under communist oppression'. When things occurred in other countries which the British government did not like, 'we don't just march in. We try to do it by persuasion.'[13] That was as far as Mrs Thatcher was prepared to go by way of condemnation of the American invasion. It was more than enough to indicate her views and it meant that on Grenada President Reagan had failed to carry with him his closest ally in the western world.

CARICOM

Within the Commonwealth Caribbean itself the invasion produced a strong reaction, especially from those CARICOM territories which were not involved in the operation. In the light of the apparent consensus reached at the CARICOM meeting during the weekend before the invasion they felt slighted and deceived when news of the attack came. In his statement to the Trinidad Parliament, George Chambers revealed that the first official notification he received of the landing came from the US embassy in Port of Spain several hours after it had been effected. He went on:

> I wish to state further that to date [26 October] I have received no notification from any CARICOM member country of any intention to request assistance from the government of the US to intervene militarily in Grenada nor have I been informed by any

CARICOM member country that such a request had in fact been made.[14]

In the circumstances the Trinidad government maintained its original position, declaring that it was 'regrettable that military intervention of this nature has been imported into the Commonwealth Caribbean',[15] especially since the region's heads of government were formally committed by the decisions of their two most recent summits to eschew the use of force in international relations. In a post-invasion statement Guyana's Forbes Burnham reiterated his preference for a peaceful regional solution to the Grenada problem and particularly criticised the involvement of the United States in the affair. The governments of the other two major CARICOM states which were not party to the invasion, Belize and the Bahamas, also expressed their disapproval, as did even more stridently the various progressive parties in the region, including the People's National Party in Jamaica.

Indeed, the extent of the divison of opinion which the invasion generated in the Commonwealth Caribbean was such that even bilateral relations between regional states became strained for a while. Following Chambers's statement Adams publicly called the Trinidadian ambassador to Barbados a liar for denying that he had been informed of the invasion plans and asked that he be withdrawn.[16] The Trinidadian government defended its representative, but replied in kind by telling the Barbadians that it would not be appropriate for the moment for them to send an envoy to Port of Spain. The ban on representation was short-lived, but indicative of the strong feelings generated. Trinidad's and Guyana's relations with Jamaica were also severely strained by the invasion, their feeling being that Seaga had again demonstrated a greater loyalty to the United States than he had to the Commonwealth Caribbean.

The Commonwealth

Several other non-Caribbean Commonwealth countries were also concerned to make known their opposition to the invasion of one of their fellow member states. For example, the Canadian Prime Minister, Pierre Trudeau, speaking in his country's Parliament shortly after the invasion, said he could not understand why the United States had resorted to armed intervention to 'defend' its citizens when, like Canada, it could have secured the permission of the Grenadian authorities to evacuate them. President Reagan's initial justification of the invasion could not, in his view, be sustained. The Indian Prime Minister, Mrs Gandhi, and the leaders of several African Commonwealth states also expressed strong disapproval of the US intervention. By comparison, the initial reaction of the Australian government was non-committal, but its opposition hardened after a Cabinet meeting and a statement was issued, calling for the withdrawal of US troops from Grenada as soon as possible and indicating that, if it had been consulted, it would have argued against invasion. Although another Commonwealth member, New Zealand, was one of the few states that supported the invasion, the Commonwealth Secretary-General, Sonny Ramphal, clearly spoke for the organisation as a whole when he suggested that the attack should occasion disquiet in the Commonwealth. To his mind, the lesson of the events in Grenada was of 'the deep passions and anxieties that are aroused when the contests of super-powers are brought within regions of small developing countries'.[17]

As international demands for the swift withdrawal of US forces grew in the first few days after the invasion, Ramphal saw the opportunity for a Commonwealth role in providing some sort of interim security force which would enable the Americans to leave. He floated the idea and energetically promoted it within the Commonwealth diplomatic community. Canada was ready to commit a contingent of Mounties to a paramilitary force, the British government indicated a reluctance to send British troops to Grenada but said it would 'sympathetically consider'[18] any reasonable proposal to provide police or technical support, and even New Zealand announced that it would be prepared to be involved. For a while Ramphal was able to talk optimistically about having the US troops out of Grenada before the biennial Commonwealth Heads of Government Conference opened in New Delhi approximately a month after the invasion had been launched.

However, by the time the heads of government gathered in India, it had become evident that the plan in its grandest form was unacceptable. It had foundered on the twin obstacles of US opposition and the growing unwillingness of the more radical states of the Commonwealth to become involved in any way with a potential US puppet administration in Grenada. India also took this line, constrained by the delicacy of its position both as chairman of the Commonwealth conference and as chairman of the Non-Aligned Movement. Ramphal was thus able to send only two Commonwealth technocrats to help Sir Paul Scoon form his interim government in Grenada, a far cry from his original proposal. The failure to set up a fully-fledged Commonwealth Security Force removed a lot of the tension from the discussion of Grenada at the New Delhi conference. Some of the African leaders, including in particular Robert Mugabe of Zimbabwe, were outspoken in their condemnation of the Americans and their allies in the Commonwealth Caribbean, but by all accounts Adams, Miss Charles and the others defended their actions vigorously. By this stage nobody wanted a major row at Commonwealth level and the final communiqué achieved a kind of consensus around the notion that 'the emphasis should now be on reconstruction, not recrimination'.[19] The heads of government confirmed their readiness to help Grenada in its recovery from invasion but otherwise confined themselves to stressing the importance of an early re-establishment of the spirit of fraternity and co-operation previously characteristic of relations between the Commonwealth Caribbean countries.

The Organisation of American States

Reaction to the invasion in Latin America was perhaps rather more mixed than in other parts of the world. Although the chairman of the Permanent Council of the OAS, Fernando Salazar Paredes, Bolivia's ambassador to the Organisation, was quick to call the US intervention a clear violation of the OAS charter, an emergency meeting of the Council held in Washington immediately after the invasion ultimately adjourned without the passage of a resolution on the issue. It heard first from Eugenia Charles, who explained and defended the reasons why the Eastern Caribbean states sought US help to eliminate the threat to regional order and security which they discerned had arisen in Grenada, and subsequently from Grenada's ambassador to the OAS, Dessima Williams, who in a tape-recorded plea, prepared in hiding because of a threat to her life, passionately called for the immediate withdrawal of US troops from her homeland. In the ensuing discussion the delegates from Brazil, Mexico, Colombia, Venezuela and Uruguay, the largest and most influential states on the continent, all condemned the invasion, the latter noting that several of the Commonwealth Caribbean countries involved in the intervention had the previous year sided with Britain in the Falklands/Malvinas War thereby showing 'the inconsistency of claims made then in defence of the principle of non-intervention and the self-determination of peoples'.[20] Although the main speakers in the meeting were hostile, they knew that their point of view was not supported by several close allies of the United States in Central

America, notably El Salvador, Guatemala, Honduras and even Costa Rica. With the representatives of Jamaica, Barbados and the OECS countries, these were enough to prejudice the passage of a condemnatory resolution and so the matter was not brought to a vote. Given the fact that the OAS was legally the competent international authority to have dealt with the situation in Grenada, this represented a relative diplomatic success for the United States.

The United Nations

Finally, at the United Nations, the Security Council was called into session during the evening of 25 October, the day of the invasion, following a complaint laid by Nicaragua, which began to fear for the security of its own revolution now that US troops had landed in Grenada. In an angry debate members considered a draft resolution, tabled by Guyana, Nicaragua and Zimbabwe, which declared that the Council

1. deeply deplores the armed intervention in Grenada which openly violates international law and the independence, sovereignty and territorial integrity of that state;
2. deplores the death of innocent civilians as a result of the armed intervention;
3. urges all states to show the strictest respect for the sovereignty, independence and territorial integrity of Grenada;
4. urges that the armed intervention be immediately stopped and that the foreign troops be withdrawn immediately from Grenada;
5. requests the Secretary-General to closely observe the follow-up of the situation in Grenada and to report to the Council within 48 hours of the enforcement of this resolution.[21]

The text was designed to meet with the most favourable response since it avoided the word condemn and did not mention the United States or any of the other invading states by name. In the event, it was passed by eleven votes to one, with three abstentions. Those in favour were the three sponsors of the resolution, plus France, the Netherlands, the Soviet Union, Poland, Malta, Pakistan, China and Jordan. The only vote against was that of the United States, which promptly vetoed the resolution, and the three abstentions were Togo, Zaire and Britain. The British representative stated that his government wished that a different course of action had been taken to invasion, but could not go along with a resolution which did not take adequate account of the honourable concerns which had motivated the United States and its Caribbean partners.

Following the US veto, Nicaragua and Zimbabwe took their resolution to the floor of the General Assembly where, of course, there was no such provision. It was amended by a Belgian resolution to include a clause requesting the holding of free elections in Grenada as rapidly as possible, but then passed by an overwhelming vote of 108 to nine. Although a number of countries abstained, only Israel and El Salvador supported the United States and the six Commonwealth Caribbean countries which took part in the invasion. In the view of most members of the United Nations, the US invasion of Grenada was thus a violation of international law and at least as deplorable as the Soviet intervention in Afghanistan. In fact, the General Assembly's resolution criticising the Grenada action was adopted by a slightly larger margin than the equivalent resolution passed after the invasion of Afghanistan. That itself was perhaps the most significant measure of the international concern generated by the invasion of Grenada. Whatever the level of domestic political satisfaction felt in the United States, there is no doubt that the US response to the Grenada crisis seriously damaged the image of morality in international relations so carefully cultivated by the West in the aftermath of Afghanistan. As a Polish Solidarity leader remarked, 'the US action lowers the common denominator of ethics in international diplomacy to the Soviet level'.[22] In this sense, the invasion of Grenada will have an impact on world politics long after the particular and immediate denunciations of the event are forgotten.

Notes and References

1. See *Granma*, 6 November 1983.
2. *Guardian*, 26 October 1983.
3. Ibid., 27 October 1983.
4. Ibid., 29 October 1983.
5. *Granma*, 6 November 1983.
6. Ibid.
7. *The Times*, 27 October 1983.
8. Statement by Herr Hans-Dietrich Genscher, Foreign Minister, to the Bundestag, 27 October 1983 (Embassy of the Federal Republic of Germany).
9. Sir Geoffrey Howe in House of Commons, *Parliamentary Debates (Hansard)*, vol. 47, no. 34, 25 October 1983, col. 148.
10. Denis Healey in ibid., col. 146.
11. Denis Healey in ibid., vol. 47, no. 35, 26 October 1983, col. 297.

International Reaction 177

12. Sir Geoffrey Howe in ibid., col. 302.
13. *Guardian*, 31 October 1983.
14. Statement by the Honourable the Prime Minister George Chambers to the House of Representatives of the Parliament of Trinidad and Tobago on the Grenada crisis, 26 October 1983.
15. Ibid.
16. *International Herald Tribune*, 1 November 1983.
17. Statement issued by the Commonwealth Secretary-General, Mr Shridath Ramphal, on Developments in Grenada, 25 October 1983 (Commonwealth Secretariat).
18. *Guardian*, 29 October 1983.
19. The Communiqué of the Commonwealth Heads of Government Meeting, mimeo, New Delhi, 1983 (Commonwealth Secretariat).
20. *Granma*, 6 November 1983.
21. *United Nations Weekly News Summary*, 2 November 1983.
22. *Guardian*, 31 October 1983.

9 GRENADA UNDER THE GOVERNOR GENERAL

While governments in different parts of the world took up their stances on the rights and wrongs of the invasion, there were many practical, political and legal difficulties immediately to be faced in Grenada. The Americans knew this as much as the Grenadians. As Major Douglas Frey, chief spokesman for the US forces remarked a month after the invasion, 'the military action was the easy part. Now we have the problems'.[1] Neither he nor his military and diplomatic colleagues nor the Grenadian bureaucratic and commercial elite underestimated the difficulties inherent in attempting to restore constitutionality. They had to reconstruct, perhaps reinvent, a political system that was acceptable both to a society traumatised by dramatic and tragic events and to Washington and its regional allies.

Significantly, popular support and goodwill were clearly on their side. What was an invasion to the outside world and a few in Grenada was a rescue mission to those who had endured the four-day curfew which put the entire nation under house arrest. Indeed, internal support for the military action appeared to be in equal proportion to external condemnation. Although there was no 'reign of terror' in that nobody was killed by the PRA, the brief rule of the Revolutionary Military Council bred fear, insecurity and rumours amongst people used to living in open and closely-knit village environments. For their part, they hardly believed that their popular Prime Minister could have been executed by those who once applauded him and that so many young people could have died and their bodies been disposed of secretly. It is no wonder that in an essentially peasant society, resting on strong religious foundations, even NJM supporters saw the descending paratroopers as saviours. The discovery of arms supplies, although greatly exaggerated in quantity and quality by the US forces and their psychological and propaganda teams, together with the publication of the secret military agreements with the Soviet Union, Cuba and North Korea and the emergency economic and rationing plans of the RMC, served only to intensify the feeling of relief. The emotional, even hysterical, scenes that greeted the release of the political detainees were thus accompanied by widespread slogan- and letter-writing in praise of the US forces and 'Daddy' Reagan and the constant refrain that 'we must never let it happen again'.

The US State Department had for some time previously considered the requirements for a post-invasion political solution. There were seen to be three: an invitation from an authoritative voice in Grenada to mount a 'rescue operation'; a formula ensuring constitutional continuity; and a legal framework to contain future political developments. All appeared capable of achievement because of a little-known facet of the Grenadian revolution. Throughout the period of PRG rule, and in spite of the suspension of the constitution, Grenada had nominally remained a monarchy, with the Governor General representing Her Majesty Queen Elizabeth II in her capacity as Queen of Grenada. The incumbent, Sir Paul Scoon, had been appointed by the Queen on the advice of Gairy in October 1978, following the curt dismissal of the previous Governor General who had opposed his policies. Following Commonwealth convention, Scoon, a Grenadian, was in no sense a representative of the British Government and, in theory, had very limited discretionary powers.

An urbane, dignified but rather indecisive former teacher and senior civil servant — he rose to be Chief Education Officer and Cabinet Secretary in the 1960s and, for a time, occupied the post of Assistant Secretary of the Commonwealth Foundation in London — he had maintained a strictly apolitical and neutral position from the time of his appointment. His constitutional position was confirmed by the PRG in the first few days of revolutionary government by one of the initial People's Laws approved by a Cabinet anxious to assume as much legal legitimacy as possible. In the longer run, the question of Grenada becoming a republic was left to the recommendation of the constitutional commission, although, in fact, its aborted deliberations never touched upon the subject. Scoon's relationship with Bishop was good and, although the NJM Political Bureau occasionally reaffirmed that he could not 'contradict Government's line' and that 'periodic sessions should be held with him so that he would be in line',[2] there are no records of serious disagreement. Indeed, his image was such that he neither featured in the contingency plans drawn up by the RMC nor was he at any time threatened by the regime in the aftermath of Bishop's death.

Ironically, the importance the US forces attached to his abduction and removal to the USS *Guam* was matched by a widespread ignorance, reaching to the highest levels in Washington, as to his constitutional position. He was confused with a British Governor of a colonial territory; one imaginative press reporter, working obviously some distance away, described him as 'a stiff upper lipped Englishman, every inch a

Governor'.[3] Reagan himself seemed to think that Grenada was a colony and invited Scoon to consult London and form a government![4] Once these misunderstandings were cleared up and 'his' appeal for help signed, he was taken back to St George's. He then announced in a broadcast on the now renamed Spice Island Radio on 31 October that, as the sole representative of executive power, he was assuming full legal and constitutional authority and that a state of emergency would be declared. This was effected by Proclamation on 1 November. The emergency provisions enabled him to exercise his executive powers unfettered 'and in his deliberate judgment'; it also legalised the detention of members of the NJM and RMC. In the history of the Commonwealth, and in Commonwealth law, it was a remarkable precedent.

The Legal Imbroglio

For those Commonwealth states which have elected to remain a monarchy, the powers associated with the post of Governor General are severely circumscribed; section 62 of the Grenada Independence Constitution spells out the conventional position, namely that 'in the exercise of his functions the Governor General shall act in accordance with the advice of the Cabinet or a Minister acting under the general authority of the Cabinet'.[5] None the less, he does have residual reserve powers. Although they are narrowly defined, such as in relation to the appointment or removal of the Prime Minister (section 58), his executive authority is not in doubt. Section 57(2) makes this clear, indicating that 'subject to the provisions of this Constitution, the executive authority of Grenada may be exercised on behalf of Her Majesty by the Governor-General either directly or through officers subordinate to him'. More importantly, section 61(2) permits him to use 'his own deliberate judgment' and to exercise this authority should it be 'impracticable to obtain the advice of the Prime Minister owing to his absence or illness'. Normally, of course, he would authorise, upon advice, another minister to perform prime ministerial functions in this situation.

In the situation that faced Scoon there were, of course, no ministers left, the RMC having assumed full executive powers after Bishop's execution. In those extraordinary legal circumstances, the principle of 'necessity' arguably arose. Brought into play only under the most drastic conditions, its foundation is that the safety of the state and the people in a situation of great risk is ultimately the most important consideration. Its legal effect may be summed up by the maxim, 'that which is otherwise not lawful, necessity makes lawful'. As a Chief Justice of Pakistan once remarked in an emergency in 1955, 'at moments like these, public law is not to be found in the books; it lies elsewhere . . . in the events that have happened'.[6] For all that, as a leading authority has noted, 'the necessity must be proportionate to the evil to be averted, and acceptance of the principle [of necessity] does not normally imply total abdication from judicial review or acquiescence in the supercession of the legal order; it is essentially a transient phenomenon'.[7]

There are no clear rules in Commonwealth constitutional law, which is largely made up of 'conventions', concerning the powers of a Governor General of an independent Commonwealth country faced with a *coup d'état*. While it is tempting to argue that the Queen, as Head of State, must be asked for instructions in these circumstances – an act which arguably might or might not detract from the sovereignty of the country in question – there appears to be no obligation to do so. Indeed, as another specialist in constitutional law observed at the time, 'the Governor-General may well be able to do acts in the Queen's name of which she thoroughly disapproves and in respect of which she has no status to act. This but illustrates an unforeseen problem in relation to the anachronistic governor-general system'.[8]

Was there, therefore, a situation in Grenada necessitating a request from the Governor General for military invasion contrary to the will of the effective – but not necessarily popular – government? This is the fundamental legal problem as it implies a very wide interpretation of reserve powers. Ultimately, the answer lay in political judgement rather than legal debate; legal theorists have no option in such circumstances but to accommodate their concepts to the realities of political life. However, a political intervention on such a scale made it likely that Scoon would, in the future, become a football between contending factions. To quote the jurist de Smith, 'this, the most drastic form of royal initiative, [is] a recourse of last resort, an ultimate weapon which is liable to destroy its user'.[9]

However, there is no doubt that it was incumbent upon him to inform the Queen of his intention to request intervention. As has already been made clear, such a message was not given to the British High Commission officials from Barbados who visited him during the short period of RMC rule. His request to the United States, in the complete absence of any consultation with Buckingham Palace, was therefore constitutionally improper, even invalid. In one commentator's view,

If it was made to Dominica, it could only have been for transmission to London: the Dominican Prime Minister, who made much of the alleged request in her speech at the United Nations, was in grave breach of her Commonwealth duties if she in fact redirected it to Washington.[10]

Another legal conundrum was that the removal of the RMC by force did not necessarily mean the complete restoration of the constitution, which had been suspended in its totality by People's Law no. 1, the first act of the PRG. This was not repealed. Instead, the Governor General declared through Proclamation no. 1 that all 'existing laws continue to be in force', except where replaced by those parts of the constitution which were to be reactivated. People's Law no. 2, which had formally established the PRG, was repealed, as was part of People's Law no. 10, which dealt with the declaration and effect of laws under the PRG. One of the restored sections of the constitution was that spelling out the rights and duties of the Governor General. Strictly speaking, this should have been part and parcel of the first proclamation since he derived his authority from it. There was criticism also of the decision to retain many of the PRG's People's Laws. This was done on the advice of Tony Rushford, the original architect of the independence constitution and former legal adviser in the Foreign and Commonwealth Office. He was one of the the two officers sent to give advice to Scoon by the Commonwealth Secretariat in London. It was argued by some that a cleaner break would have been preferable, with the revocation of PRG laws and the re-enactment, by proclamation, of those clearly necessary for the maintenance of peace, order and government.

Proclamation no. 1 also, however, made provision for the appointment of an Advisory Council. It was formally established by Proclamation no. 5 on 15 November. At the same time, the state of emergency and the ban on public meetings was lifted, but provision made for the continuation of preventive detention of those whom 'the Advisory Council is satisfied that it is necessary to do so in the interests of public safety, public order and defence'.[11] The Council was to have a Chairman appointed by Scoon, not more than eleven other members, plus legal adviser Rushford as a non-voting *ex officio* participant. The powers of the Council were, to all intents and purposes, intended to be identical to those of a Cabinet of an elected government. But this was not wholly the case, as article 11 of the Proclamation made clear.

The Advisory Council shall be responsible for the formulation of policy and for the general conduct of the government in Grenada; and accordingly the Governor-General shall act in accordance with the advice of the Council, in the exercise of any power or other function vested in him by or under any law unless that power or function is expressed to be exercisable by the Governor-General acting in his own deliberate judgment or in accordance with the advice or the recommendation of, after consultation with, any other person or authority.

The stage was thus set for a struggle for power between the Governor General and the Advisory Council even while steps were being taken to restore party politics to the island.

Government in Practice

The Advisory Council had an inauspicious start. First, only five of the ten nominated could meet initially. Composed of Grenadians who were not associated with political activities either before or after 1979, several were resident overseas and needed time to reorganise their affairs. They were named as Alister McIntyre, Deputy Secretary-General of UNCTAD in Geneva and, from 1974 to 1977, Secretary-General of CARICOM, earmarked as chairman; civil servants Nicholas Braithwaite (Education, Health and Community Development), Arnold Cruickshank (Agriculture and Industrial Development) and Dr James Pitt (Construction and Housing); university teacher Dr Pat Emmanuel (Foreign Affairs, Tourism and Civil Aviation); management consultant Dr Allan Kirton (Security and the Public Service); teacher Mrs Joan Purcell (Labour and Women's Affairs); onetime cable and wireless manager Raymond Smith (Telecommunications and Public Utilities); and businessmen L. Wilson (Finance, Planning and Trade) and Christopher Williams (No Portfolio). There then followed the news that McIntyre could not assume his post due to ill health, although there was widespread speculation that he had unsuccessfully demanded the full withdrawal of US forces as a condition of appointment.[12] Scoon was then forced to name Braithwaite as chairman. He was the other person, apart from Rushford, who had been despatched by the Commonwealth Secretariat to help and advise the Governor General. A former teacher and senior bureaucrat in the Grenadian Ministry of Education, he had been working on a youth community project in

Guyana when he was summoned. Although respected, his diffident manner and lack of political experience seemed to confirm suspicions that, under his leadership, the Council would not wield effective power.

The problem was clear. The US presence was both overwhelming and omnipresent in nearly every sphere of government. The economy had been badly shaken by all the events and US aid became essential for day-by-day government expenditure. US$3 million was immediately granted as an emergency measure. Many of the workers thrown out of work due to war damage, such as those in the agro-industrial plants, or following the collapse of administration which affected the state farming sector and marketing boards, were given temporary jobs repairing the poor roads. These had already been neglected of late by the PRG because all available funds had been allocated to the airport, but many had then been turned into quagmires by the heavy US military traffic. Also, virtually all security matters were outside the Advisory Council's hands. The local police could do little. Numbering only 180 out of an establishment of 550, few had recently been trained; under the PRG their duties had been largely restricted to traffic control. The 300 policemen of the Caribbean Peace-keeping Force, boosted by US military police, thus took over all the other police work formerly undertaken by the PRA and People's Militia, leaving external security to the US forces.

The US military command interpreted its duties widely. They assumed full responsibility for the interrogation of PRA and Militia members and NJM activists on the grounds that among them were Cubans and other external *agents saboteurs*. They relied heavily, and successfully, on denunciations by local people, but no Cubans were found. Although there were widespread fears that many of the PRA had fled into the bush with their arms, the great majority of the Grenadian forces had simply abandoned their weapons and uniforms and merged as unobtrusively as possible into the community once it was apparent that resistance was useless. Some hid but, one by one, they either surrendered due to lack of food or were rounded up, frightened and dejected. Only a tiny minority took to banditry. The US security thrust was accompanied by posters and broadcasts appealing for information. A sliding scale of money prizes was offered for enemy weapons and personnel. At the top of the list was nearly EC$1,350 for a live Cuban!

It took over a week after the invasion before the US forces captured Bernard and Phyllis Coard, who were in hiding in Mount Parnessis village near St George's, and General Austin. After intensive interrogation on a US warship and, in Coard's case, a severe beating, they were taken to Richmond Hill prison. Filmed by all major North American TV networks, Austin and Bernard Coard were shown blindfolded, stripped to the waist and shackled. Posters aimed at runaway PRA members, announcing 'Your leaders have been captured', were widely defaced as many scratched out the faces of Austin and Coard as a mark of their hatred for those they held responsible for the collapse of the PRG and the subsequent slaughter.

The US forces also organised the expulsion of all Soviet, East European and Libyan diplomats and technical assistance personnel and most of the Cuban embassy. They were all thoroughly searched − only the Soviet ambassador was spared − with the result that the world's press, which had been denied virtually all facilities during the three-day battle itself, widely reported the discovery of two crates of AK47 Soviet rifles in the Soviet embassy's baggage. The large party was flown to Mexico City in a USAF transporter under armed guard. The Cuban workers, on the other hand, were eventually flown, roped together, to Barbados, and thence to Havana under the auspices of the International Red Cross. A skeletal Cuban mission remained after the Cuban workers and other advisers had left, ambassador Julian Torres Rizo initially refusing to leave until all the 784 Cubans on the island had departed. Headed after Rizo's eventual departure by Gaston Diaz, guarded by Barbados police and constantly harried by patrolling US helicopters, the mission tried to retrieve heavy plant and other Cuban property at Point Salines and Pearls airports. However, anything which had not been commandeered by either the US forces or the government had mostly been rendered useless. A small Grenadian mission remained in Cuba, looking after the interests of the 200 Grenadian students there, although it was made clear to them that their passage home was their own responsibility. The 100 or so in the Soviet Union and Eastern Europe were abandoned to look after themselves. By December, the Cuban mission had been reduced to Diaz alone as the US forces removed the radio and telex links so enabling the operator to be declared *persona non grata*.

For captured PRA and Militia personnel, a major interrogation centre was established at Queens Park in St George's. Ironically the scene of many emotional PRG rallies, it was manned by US military intelligence experts. Those suspected of close involvement with the RMC or with organs of the PRG were transferred to a prison camp at Point Salines, built around a recently constructed compound designed for Cuban workers. Prisoners were kept in converted wooden packing cases and closely questioned by CIA and other personnel. Those considered to have played a minor role were issued with a white card. Headed 'Caribbean Security Forces', it read 'The bearer of this pass has been processed through the Caribbean Security Force Refugee Centre [sic] and is cleared to proceed freely and undetained', and was signed 'By Order of the 82nd Airborne Division, G-5'. A green card, however, was issued to those about whom the US security forces harboured suspicions. It read: 'This individual has been released and directed to refrain from anti-government activities. Unless [he does so] he should not be apprehended.' All those processed had to sign an assurance to this effect.

Military activity was paralleled by the diplomatic. Once the airstrip had been secured, an embryonic embassy headed by senior US diplomat Charles Gillespie flew in on 26 October. Taking over a hotel, it rapidly grew in numbers. Together with the military forces, the embassy became closely involved in Grenada's political and economic future as well as the conduct of its everyday affairs. At the highest level, the most significant manifestation of this was the daily meetings between Scoon, Major-General Farris, Commander of the US forces, and ambassador Gillespie who became known in Grenada as 'Sir Paul' Gillespie. Occasionally Lt-Colonel Ormsby, chief of the Jamaican contingent and senior officer of the Caribbean forces, and Rushford were also present. Rarely was Braithwaite invited, giving the lie to Gillespie's publicly expressed hope that Braithwaite would 'probably share the boss's job'.[13] At local level, the lack of effective administration and police led to company commanders becoming arbiters in a myriad of disputes. The general popularity of the US forces added to the embarrassment that many US officials felt. The psychological dependency of many Grenadians, as anxious as the businessmen for the streets to be paved with dollars, led to a fear by Gillepsie that the US would have to act as 'wet nurses'. He said, 'my most important task is to help Grenada in its development', but went on, 'we hope not to turn Grenada into a prodigal son, so that it becomes a disproportionately treated member of the Caribbean.'[14]

His fear was well founded. A three-man team had flown in under the auspices of the Agency for International Development (AID) once the military objectives had been achieved. Headed by a US army major, the others were a reservist major and an emergency and disaster civilian expert. Three programmes were drawn up. The emergency programme was put into effect immediately but those for the short and long term were discussed with President Reagan in a White House presentation on 24 November.[15] The former envisaged a total expenditure of US$30 million, including a payment of US$5 million to the public sector to ease the cash flow problem. A further US$10 million was to replace loans and concessions from the Soviet bloc and radical Arab states while the remainder was to complete the airport and finance a 350-man defence force.

The long-term programme involved a further US$20 million. Included in it were infrastructural development, especially road and water supply improvement, and the stationing of health and educational personnel, including Peace Corps, to replace the expelled Cubans. These investment priorities reflected major policy issues. The Point Salines airport was deemed essential for Grenada's economic needs and regional military security. The 'communist orientated' educational system required 'urgent restructuring'. In the economy, not only were all price and other controls to be lifted, but the state sector in agriculture was to be eliminated. A more liberal code of investment was also planned, and budgetary and balance of payments support established following US pressure upon the IMF to underwrite Grenada's economic recovery. It was noted that the IMF had suspended a stand-by facility of US$14 million agreed in September with Coard, the first instalment of which, US$1.3 million, had been due in November.

In the event, perhaps mindful of Gillespie's warning and left in no doubt of Seaga's claim for increased assistance to ease Jamaica's chronic balance of payments deficit as a recognition of his wholehearted support of US foreign policy in the region, and of similar claims by the other participants in the military action, a total of only US$18.4 million was eventually earmarked for Grenada by the AID. The cost of completion of the airport was not included. However, Plessey recommenced their work from the end of November and it was hoped that the AID headquarters in Washington would reconsider the question of funding. Further largesse was promised with the announcement by Gillespie that henceforth Grenada would be eligible for Caribbean Basin Initiative funds, largely for the private sector.[16] It was also hoped by the United States that the British and Canadian governments would assume a greater burden of the costs of Grenada's reconstruction and ideological reorientation. The visit of the British Deputy Foreign Secretary, Baroness Young, in January 1984 to discuss this possibility was therefore welcomed.

Overall, there was to be close civilian-military collaboration by the US government. 'AID has the money, the military the manpower',

Reagan was told.[17] It was agreed that US combat troops would be withdrawn by 23 December – in fact, they left two weeks earlier – leaving a contingent of 300 army engineers and other specialists, together with a 'psychological operations' programme. It was this aspect that worried the civilian AID expert at the White House briefing. He objected to the heavy propaganda effort mounted by the US Information Service (USIS), but was over-ruled. 'Wake up', said the leader of the group, 'there are people out there who want to kill you. There are National Security questions involved here.' It was explained to Reagan that the USIS was engaged not in propaganda but 'persuasion and salesmanship' due to the need to 're-educate people away from communism'. It was also stressed that foreign investment would flow to Grenada only if there existed sufficient infrastructure. Further, it was agreed with Reagan that private investment would be primarily directed to the tourist industry as there was no worthwhile return in agriculture given the level of world prices for Grenada's traditional products and the price and inefficiency of labour. It was admitted that this would lead to land speculation.

A particular target of the USIS psychological operations specialists – flown in largely from Central and South American posts – were the repressive aspects of the PRG regime. Social and economic advances were played down. Bishop's image was not neglected. Concerned that his charisma had been effective and that he was identified with the positive achievements of the revolution, his Marxist inclinations, personal life and choice of friends were packaged to show him as 'a communist, no better than the RMC in Richmond Hill prison'.[18] Scoon, in a well-publicised broadcast, stopped little short of accusing the PRG of economic mismanagement and corruption. 'Current and capital expenditure' had been at 'unsuitable levels, leading to arrears'; 'financial advances' of some EC$1.5 million to PRG officials had not been correctly accounted for and the salary increase given to the PRA in the dying days of the PRG not properly recorded.[19] This was particularly unconvincing: many of the PRG's harshest critics were prepared to admit its skilful management of the economy, as witness the earlier cited and very favourable World Bank report.

Against this background, however, the Advisory Council – soon popularly named the interim government – had difficulty both in asserting its authority as well as its legitimacy in the eyes of Grenadians. After having been sworn in, Braithwaite voiced their hopes.

We recognise that because we were not voted into office by the people, there are likely to be doubts, suspicion and fears about how we will perform our duties. I would like the people of Grenada to know that [we] were motivated by one consideration into accepting this appointment — that was our interest in the people of Grenada.[20]

But it was not until 1 December that all the members finally met. At the end of a three-day session, from which Rushford, regarded by most of the councillors as patronising and high-handed, was pointedly excluded, they emerged acutely conscious of the limitations imposed on them. To Pat Emmanuel,

> The crucial thing about the Americans now is not the manner of their coming, but the manner of their going. If we want them to go and they start resisting, they will lose their support. Then it will be aggression. The interim government has to reject the impression that it is a puppet. It isn't and I hope the United States doesn't think it is, but unless they leave within six months, it will be hard for us to convince people.[21]

As councillor for foreign affairs, he added that 'we also have to take international public opinion into account on this'.

Notwithstanding the opposition of many to the departure of all or part of the US army, reaction against some of the propaganda excesses of the USIS began to surface by mid-December. Cubans were remembered as hard workers and not bent on making 'slaves' of Grenadians. Letters to the newly re-established *Grenadian Voice*, while supporting the US action, stressed the need to preserve PRG reforms. None the less, when the remaining US combat troops departed, on 12-13 December, there were protests. In a matter of days, a 6,000 signature petition was sent to Scoon calling for a 'closer association' with the United States and for the US military presence on the island to extend for 'at least' five years after which any decision to withdraw 'should be tested by a referendum'.[22] An increase in Caribbean military forces, mainly Jamaican, from 300 to 450 in part compensation was not considered sufficient. Major Frey made it clear, however, that the distinction between combat and non-combat troops was 'fuzzy', since all US forces had, by definition, full military training.

To assist it, the Council appointed advisers, notably the President of the Caribbean Development Bank, William Demas. An immediate problem facing him was the influx of US financial and other entrepreneurs. Presidential officials addressed 100 businessmen in the White

House and stressed investment opportunities in an economy which was 'flat on its back' because of the way that it had been run by Bishop's government.[23] It was also announced by the US Department of Commerce that Overseas Private Investment Corporation (OPIC) insurance protection had been granted to Grenada. The first group of what were expected to be many visiting businessmen arrived in late November. Based in Fort Lauderdale, which proposed a 'twinning' relationship with Grenada and whose mayor accompanied the investors, they and Trinidadian interests planned to build two large hotels in the first instance and opened negotiations with Scoon for substantial land and fiscal concessions. As one put it, 'now that the ideological future is assured, we feel that this is the big take-off'.[24] For its part, however, the Council was concerned that generous concessions might be granted against their advice, given the reality of Washington's influence over Scoon.

There was also little opportunity to diversify aid funds. Britain initially allocated only £750,000 (US$1.1 million), mainly for the training and equipping of the police force, although more was promised. Canadian and EEC assistance was sought but also met with little response. Braithwaite invited the Commonwealth Secretary-General, Sonny Ramphal, to Grenada to discuss the possibility of multilateral Commonwealth aid and to allow him to assess at first hand the mood of the Grenadian people and their attitude to the US-led forces. This was very important since, to the anger of Jamaica and Barbados, the Commonwealth Secretariat in London had insisted that all military personnel had to leave the island before technical or other Commonwealth assistance could be granted. The Secretariat would, in these circumstances, arrange for a multi-member Commonwealth police force to be despatched, to join police personnel already sent by the Caribbean participants in the Caribbean Peace-keeping Force.[25]

Ramphal held extensive talks over two days with Scoon and the Council in January 1984. They were unsuccessful, stalling over his insistence that the 'occupation force' be withdrawn since it would, in his view, have a 'serious influence' on the forthcoming elections. He proposed Trinidadian and Bahamian participation but not that of Guyana, aware that it was Forbes Burnham who was held responsible by many Grenadians for allegedly tipping off the RMC leaders about the imminent arrival of American troops.[26]

It was Rushford who finally laid bare the interim government's growing sense of frustration. He suddenly resigned without notice in early December and left the island, complaining that 'I have never known a situation where a Governor-General appoints himself saviour of his people, calls in foreign armies and then does very little to bring about the restoration of constitutional civil government, which I consider my main task.' He followed this with an astonishingly virulent attack on Scoon. Seeing the situation 'collapsing to anarchy', he described Grenada's government as a 'headless body'. 'The country looks for leadership and it is not forthcoming', he alleged, making clear that his resentment of Scoon's 'condescension and pomposity', which extended to his use of the third person when referring to himself — even in private[27] — was echoed by many Grenadians. However, the force and style of his criticism was counter-productive, as the Council closed ranks in the Governor General's defence.

A longer-term problem was that of elections. While Braithwaite had promised that 'we will not delay by one day the period necessary to take people to the position where they have elected the Government', the question was how long would that period be. Some hoped within a year; others at least two years and a few longer than that. Leslie Pierre, editor of the *Grenadian Voice*, and Alister Hughes were among those wanting more time, while some businessmen wanted no deadline whatever, hoping that the interim government would become semi-permanent. Lloyd Noel was the spokesman of those who recognised the need to have elections 'at some time', but with a permanent US military presence. Not surprisingly, he had taken a leading role in organising the petition to Scoon, pointing to the 'confused minds of young Grenadians'. They, and the other islanders, were not 'politically stabilised to identify true democracy'.[28] Few, however, agreed with his argument that, as Grenada could not afford to pay the running costs of Point Salines airport — estimated at US$6 million per year without interest charges on the many loans incurred and on the US$18 million estimated as essential to complete the project — the United States should have it as a permanent military base, permitting the occasional large civil airliner to land as and when necessary.

None the less, political parties began to emerge and press for voter registration. Scoon announced that this would commence in early 1984, with Barbadian assistance, and promised that a voters' list would be published by May. The election was expected in November.

Filling the Vacuum

When the detainees of the PRG were freed on 26 October, their jailers having abandoned them, they immediately met in Alister Hughes's house and decided that only a united party would be able to combat either, the return of Gairy and a rebirth of the GULP or a resurgent NJM. This was not to be, as the traditional personalist character of Caribbean politics asserted itself. Soon three readily identifiable groups emerged.

First off the mark was the old Grenada National Party. Countering suggestions that it was 'dead and buried', it favoured an early return to constitutional government, mainly in the hope that its emergent rivals would not be able to organise and gain support in the time available. Accordingly, the elderly Blaize notified Scoon in an official statement that 'we pledge ourselves ready and willing to engage in any consultations towards the establishment of Parliamentary Democratic Institutions. And when called upon by the will of the people, we declare ourselves ready, willing and able to lead the Country back to good government.'[29] However, its leadership was last active over a decade previously and its ill-defined and middle-of-the-road policies held out little hope for youth. None of its leaders had been detained by the PRG because 'they did nothing', a fact much stressed by opponents.

Recognising these weaknesses, some former GNP members allied themselves with the Grenada Democratic Movement (GDM). Assuming this name on 28 May 1983, it was formerly the Grenada National Democratic Movement which itself was born out of a loose federation of groups in London and Barbados operating as the Patriotic Alliance of Overseas Based Grenadians. Led by Barbados-based university lecturer Francis Alexis, the fulcrum of its message was a social democratic one: an insistence on constitutional government and national reconciliation through a continuation of much of the PRG's social and economic programmes. Alexis lost no time in offering himself as an 'interim' Prime Minister.[30] However, since most of its activists were unknown to Grenadians, a major identity problem existed. Its rival, the New York-based Grenada Movement for Freedom and Democracy, led by Michael Sylvester, fared even worse in this respect and was largely discounted. It was widely believed that it was heavily funded by the CIA.[31]

A third group centred at first around the ambitious and highly articulate Winston Whyte. His detention in 1980, following an attempt to form a political party in opposition to the NJM, the People's Action Liberation Movement, appeared not to have dimmed his political aspirations. Espousing basically the same policies as the GDM but with a more right-wing flavour and an emphasis on self-help, the party aimed to appeal to the rural vote, anxious to prevent any large-scale movement of support towards Gairy. It rapidly gained the backing of several prominent Grenadian businessmen. However, by early 1984, Whyte himself was showing signs of preferring a business to a political career. Many of his circle thus began to drift away to another party called the New Democratic Party (NDP), newly formed by George Brizan, the Chief Education Officer. Formerly a schoolteacher and then Principal of the Institute of Further Education in St George's, Brizan was associated with the NJM in its earliest days, but, as we have seen, had detached himself after the party moved to the left in the latter part of the 1970s. The NDP is conceived as a party of moderation, keen to develop some of the most positive features of PRG rule in the areas of housing, health and education but without the leftist rhetoric and ideological commitment of the Bishop era. Many in the US diplomatic and AID missions seem likely in the end to favour the NDP.

As for Gairy, it was made obvious by Scoon and the Council that his presence would be unwelcome. From his Washington base, he confidently forecast that 'at least 50 per cent' of the rural population would vote for him, but others calculated a more sober maximum of 20 per cent, assuming that he had financial backing. He accepted that his government had been marked by 'excesses'. These were, however, 'grossly distorted' and the alleged activities of the Mongoose Gang, in particular, were 'a myth created by Communist propaganda'. In fact, they consisted of 'four or five boys' employed by the trade unions 'to kill rabid mongoose and who lacked the intelligence to take on the role of the secret police'! His astounded audience heard him also insist that his interest in, and knowledge of, cosmic phenomena was also 'exaggerated' but none the less recognised by 'scientific circles'. He also called for a continued US military presence in Grenada and the establishment of a British naval base in the island.

Regarding the election, he announced that he would not stand for office but instead fulfil the role of 'elder statesman', honoured by 'over 30 countries'. He insisted, however, that his party, the Grenada United Labour Party, would fight all 15 seats. Moreover, he would seek the return of his sequestrated properties and arrears of salary due to him as Prime Minister from March 1979 to December 1981 when his term of office officially ended. It is very doubtful that such arrears would be paid since the PRG, despite its unconstitutional method of assuming power, was recognised by many states as the legitimate government of Grenada during that period. However, legal opinion in Grenada appeared to believe that an action restoring his properties – hotels and nightclubs – would probably succeed.[32] As for GULP's chances in the election, while there would be no shortage of candidates, mainly drawn from the ranks of dismissed policemen, it was so closely identified with Gairy and had such little organisation outside his office that it is doubtful that it would garner much support if he himself did not stand as a candidate. Notwithstanding the Council's wishes, Gairy returned to Grenada in January 1984, but still disclaims any intention of personally standing for election.

As for the NJM, it was understandably in serious disarray after the invasion. Leaderless and betrayed, the hopes and aspirations of its dwindling number of supporters were rarely expressed, partly for fear of recrimination. The two remaining NJM ministers, Kenrick Radix and George Louison, were amongst the few who dared voice their opinions. While conceding that a civil war between the RMC and the masses had been a 'virtual certainty' if the invasion had not taken place, they insisted that the pro-Bishop forces would have emerged victorious. The threat of bloodshed did not, however, justify 'imperialist attack'. To Louison, 'a country's moral strength and sense of natural being is forged by struggle and violence, such as that seen in the US War of Independence and the Russian Revolution'.[33] However, by early 1984 there were discernible signs that, far from withdrawing to lick its wounds, attempts at reorganisation were beginning, although under no central direction.

A major problem for the NJM was that it was born out of particular circumstances of oppression that no longer existed, and that it was harshly but unavoidably associated with the hated RMC regime. To counter this, the NJM in Grenada — in sharp contrast to the more radical NJM support groups in Britain and North America — joined with the other parties to demand a full trial of surviving RMC leaders, together with the Coards, Strachan and deRiggs. The latter had been arrested on his return from New York in early November after an unsuccessful visit to Grenadian communities both there and in Toronto to drum up support for the RMC. The impending trial froze the actors in the drama into a state of immobility. No Commission of Inquiry was permitted into the events of 19 October for fear of prejudicing its outcome. There was an even greater reluctance to determine the exact number of deaths on that fateful day. It was as if there had been a collective exorcism of the shocking tragedy. Despite numerous pleas from distraught parents for information on missing sons and daughters, nobody would go beyond the RMC figure of 24. Equally striking was a similar reluctance to discover the extent of Grenadian dead and wounded caused by the invasion, other than the 18 mental patients at the Fort Frederick hospital who were killed by USAF shell-fire.

The Future

Clearly, a strong US diplomatic presence will remain in Grenada after the last troops have left, with the undoubted backing of the majority of Grenadians on the island. It is conceivable that a small military force, perhaps in the nature of a coastguard, will also remain. US aid to help fund all or part of the 269 separate development projects identified by the five-man AID team by the end of 1983 — incidentally a team bigger than that based in Zimbabwe — will arrest public dissatisfaction. Indeed, even if it so wished, the United States may never be able to extricate itself from Grenada, given its turbulent history and the realities of economics, geography and military power in the region. But, as Gillespie remarked, 'our presence will diminish as it becomes possible to do so. We hope that in a couple of years we'll be able to treat Grenada in the same way as the others in the Eastern Caribbean.'[34]

Within Grenada and the Grenadines itself, while it is likely that an elected government will continue the reformist economic and social path of the People's Revolutionary Government in response to popular expectations and national needs, the chance to create a new political system has passed. If the New Jewel Movement, with its brand of indigenous socialism, plans once again to rule Grenada, much of its bold programme of 1973 would have to be watered down, at least in the short term. This would be a loss to Grenada and the region: in spite of the more regrettable aspects of the Grenadian revolution such as militarisation, censorship and preventive detention, it did represent a 'total and genuine programme for the masses'. In the words of Louison,

> it was to build popular democracy, to raise political and academic consciousness, identify with the progressive forces such as the Non-Aligned Movement, socialist countries and liberation movements, practise good neighbourliness, plan the economy with balanced development and build Grenada with the clear assurance of the involvement and agreement of the masses.[35]

In short, it was not just another left of centre party of the traditional mould and it is impossible to believe that it ever would become one in the hearts and minds of its most ardent supporters.

The impending trial of the Coard faction and the Revolutionary Military Council leaders will, in these emotional circumstances, be a mixed blessing. It will satisfy a popular demand for justice and yet will reopen deep wounds. Their conviction will undoubtedly help assuage the widespread feeling of horror at the events which the accused allegedly unleashed. An acquittal, on the other hand, could well prolong the sense of bitterness both of those who were directly involved in the slaughter surrounding the *coup* and the subsequent invasion and those who believed their revolution had been betrayed and so lost for ever.

In Whyte's words, 'we must get the people to face the sun in the morning with confidence'.[36] Even so, the trauma of the massacre and the military intervention will never become a mere memory, etched as deeply as it is in people's minds. Elections will help restore normality and the problems thrown up by the strained relationship between Scoon and the Advisory Council, and between the Council and the US security forces, will eventually be forgotten. Grenada will revert to being a small territory of little political significance. Its modernised police force will include paramilitary work among its duties since it is planned that a Grenadian army will never exist again, despite initial American plans to the contrary. But the prospect of deepening dependency upon the rich and powerful of the world is not an appealing one. For the central result of the collapse of the revolution is that the historical heritage of the Caribbean of serving others elsewhere and mimicking their values and assumptions will have reasserted itself, if not forever then at least into the foreseeable future.

Notes and References

1. Information from interview, November 1983.
2. *Minutes of the Political Bureau dated 20th April 1983* (St George's, mimeo), p. 3.
3. *The Times*, 28 October 1983.
4. Ibid., 25 October 1983. See also House of Commons, *Parliamentary Debates (Hansard)*, vol. 47, no. 35, 26 October 1983, col. 323.
5. *Statutory Instrument no. 2155, 1973: The Grenada Constitution Order 1973*. Made 19 December 1973: Coming into Operation 7 February 1974 (HMSO, London, 1973).
6. Justice Muhammed Munir in *Special Reference No 1 of 1955* (1955), I F.C.R., p. 439, cited in S.A. de Smith, *Constitutional and Administrative Law*, 4th edn (Penguin Books, Harmondsworth, 1981), p. 78.

7. de Smith, *Constitutional and Administrative Law*, p. 79.
8. Professor L.H. Leigh in *The Times*, 29 October 1983.
9. de Smith, *Constitutional and Administrative Law*, p. 124.
10. T. Robertson, 'The Repercussions of Sir Paul', *Guardian*, 31 October 1983.
11. Government of Grenada, *Official Gazette*, 15 November 1983: Proclamation no. 5, article 14.
12. *Guardian*, 25 November 1983.
13. *New York Times*, 29 November 1983.
14. *Guardian*, 15 December 1983.
15. *Notes on the Grenadian Aid Strategy* (Washington, DC, mimeo, n.d.), p. 1.
16. *Barbados Advocate*, 19 December 1983.
17. *Notes on the Grenadian Aid Strategy*, p. 2.
18. *Latin America Regional Report: The Caribbean*, RC-83-10, 9 December 1983.
19. *Grenadian Voice*, 10 December 1983.
20. *Daily Telegraph*, 16 November 1983.
21. *Guardian*, 28 November 1983.
22. Ibid., 23 December 1983.
23. *Washington Post*, 7 December 1983.
24. *Latin America Regional Report*, RC-83-10, 9 December 1983.
25. *Guardian*, 4 January 1984.
26. *Daily Telegraph*, 12 January 1984.
27. *The Times*, 7 and 8 December 1983.
28. Information from interview, L. Noel, December 1983.
29. *Statement of the Grenada National Party* (St George's, mimeo, November 1983).
30. *The Nation* (Barbados), 26 October 1983.
31. *New York Times*, 13 November 1983.
32. *Guardian*, 10 January 1984.
33. *Latin America Regional Report*, RC-83-10, 9 December 1983.
34. *Guardian*, 13 December 1983.
35. Information from interview, G. Louison, November 1983.
36. *Latin America Regional Report*, RC-83-10, 9 December 1983.

10 THE INVASION AND CARIBBEAN POLITICS

In the debate in the British House of Commons on the day after the invasion of Grenada, a backbench MP perceptively remarked: 'Small places throw up big principles.'[1] The issues that Grenada raises are potentially very large indeed, with ramifications that go well beyond the immediate vicinity of the Caribbean basin to touch directly on the most sensitive divisions in the world today: those between East and West and North and South. To mention just two related to the former – delineation of agreed spheres of influence and the limits of dissent within intra-alliance relations – and two related to the latter – engagement versus disengagement from the imperialist system and small size as an objective constraint on development – is to signify the scale of questions involved. Yet there is also a sense in which, however large these questions are, the immediate effect has been felt regionally, with the most important consequences concentrated in the Commonwealth Caribbean. Both in the manner of its coming and in the way of its going, the Grenadian revolution has profoundly unsettled the Caribbean region, leaving behind a sense, almost tangible in its intensity, that from now on things will never be quite the same again.

The extent to which the experience in Grenada is, or is not, a turning-point in the region's affairs is the concern of this concluding chapter. It focuses on three broad themes. The first concerns the nature of hegemony in the region – is it now contested or is it not? Has the United States won, in the words of Fidel Castro, no more than 'a pyrrhic victory'? And has the demise of the People's Revolutionary Government in Grenada signalled also the final demise of British power and influence in the region? The second theme relates to the Commonwealth Caribbean as a regional grouping – can it survive the trauma of Grenada as a coherent and distinctive regional unit or is it destined to dissolve into less than the sum of its constituent parts? If so, what is the most likely configuration to emerge given the very different immediate repercussions of the invasion on states in the region? Finally, the third theme focuses on the nature of socialism in the Caribbean. Has the Grenadian revolution contributed anything significant to the theory and practice of socialism in the area? More to the point, have the appropriate lessons been learnt, and is there a future for socialism in the Caribbean in the face of continued US prohibition? In short, was Grenada exception or vanguard?

Hegemony in the Caribbean

The 1970s witnessed the break-up of the traditional model of Caribbean international relations. The view of the region as an unchallenged preserve of the United States with relatively amenable client-state governments, tolerating extra-continental European powers which retained residual sovereignty over increasingly smaller parts of the area, came under mounting attack. Hitherto peripheral state sectors emerged to lay claim to interests in the region, notably Venezuela and Mexico, and from within the Caribbean itself a new assertiveness was evident as a number of countries sought to manage meaningfully, and in some instances even challenge, the neo-colonial structures they inherited at independence.[2] The overall situation as described was thus one of 'fluidity', attracting the designation of 'crisis' from the United States, especially as it saw its influence waning and that of Cuba waxing, almost, it seemed, in direct proportion.

The policies of the Reagan administration have been aimed, above all, at halting this process. The New Jewel revolution in Grenada has, to date, been its principal victim. Yet Grenada did no more than focus these trends, albeit in a more polarised form, and is thus different not in kind but only in degree from other Caribbean states. The light that the experience of Grenada throws upon the policies of Britain in the Caribbean; on those of Cuba and other Latin American states; and, above all, on those of the United States itself, is thus of general significance for the region.

Britain and the Commonwealth Caribbean

British policy in the Commonwealth Caribbean since 1962 has been one of steady political disengagement and diminishing economic interest — such that by the early 1980s there was no compelling reason for it to maintain a close interest in Commonwealth Caribbean affairs. All the more remarkable, then, that at that moment the Foreign Affairs Committee of the House of Commons should choose to address itself to an exhaustive enquiry into 'the British approach to stability, security and development in the Caribbean and Central America'.[3] From November 1981 to October 1982 the Committee deliberated on British policy, publishing in the end a substantial report generally critical of policy towards the region, especially the tendency to subordinate British policy to that of the United States in virtually all matters of substance.

In the Central American region, arguably, sound historical reasons existed for playing second fiddle to Washington. But in respect of the Commonwealth Caribbean these clearly did not apply. Nevertheless, the overwhelming impression conveyed by the evidence of Foreign and Commonwealth Office officials and by the Minister of State directly concerned with the region at the time, Richard Luce, was that British policy, by conscious design or simple inertia, is but an echo of the American.[4] And in so far as this, in itself, remains weakly conceptualised, then so it followed that Britain's position was found wanting. Indeed, so low was its profile that on many occasions expert independent witnesses to the Committee found it difficult to describe, let alone account for, the form British policy took.

In fact, British policy in the Commonwealth Caribbean has been set in an unimaginative and profoundly conservative mould. It has been without guiding principle, other than the above-mentioned uncritical support for US positions, and has in consqeuence been formed pragmatically, largely in response to specific *ad hoc* situations as they have developed in individual countries. The example of Grenada confirms the general pattern. British policy has been identical to that of the United States on almost every issue. When it did diverge, for example over assessment of the airport as primarily a commercial rather than a military venture,[5] little appears to have been done to persuade the US government otherwise. The same may be said of the period immediately preceding the invasion. Although the Foreign Secretary reported to the House of Commons that he had been informed on 22 October both of the OECS decision to intervene and of their request to the US government for assistance in this, the British government did nothing, except to counsel caution only at the very last minute.[6] In this sense what needs to be explained is less Reagan's failure fully to consult Britain, than Britain's failure to support the US position. The Foreign Secretary's refusal to condemn the conduct of the United States was no doubt based upon painful recognition of this fact.

The reaction of the British government to the invasion of Grenada underlines the fact that it is no longer a leader, but a follower, in Commonwealth Caribbean affairs. Action taken by the government since the invasion, and particularly the resumption of substantial aid to Grenada, confirms this. Towards the rest of the Commonwealth Caribbean Britain will continue a low profile policy and in respect of the few remaining dependencies will discharge its residual responsibilities in as unobtrusive a manner as possible. United States hegemony will be supported, not challenged.

All this, however, was very predictable, even before Grenada was invaded. In its report the Foreign Affairs Committee of the House of Commons recommended there was 'ample justification for making an active British contribution to the achievement of stability, security and development in the Caribbean' and firmly expressed its opinion that the view of the region as a theatre of East-West confrontation was 'an unsatisfactory and insufficient policy framework'.[7] While the presence of the United States as the strongest and most immediately interested external power was recognised, it was none the less felt that Britain, with its particular expertise and from its position as close ally, could help the US reach an accommodation with the fundamental changes that have taken place in the Caribbean over the last decade. To do this, it was argued, Britain would have to improve the quality and breadth of its representation and be prepared to affirm its commitment to the area by implementing the recommendations which constituted the final pages of the report.[8] With very few exceptions, it must be noted, none of these were seriously adopted, as was made clear in the government's response tabled in March 1983.[9] This described at length the minutiae of British aid and technical assistance programmes to the area, ignoring entirely the broad geopolitical thrust of the committee's recommendations and its critique of present government policy. There was no discussion of US policy towards the region; no mention of the CBI; and no reply to the committee's major proposal concerning the promotion of *rapprochement* between Cuba and the United States. In other words, there was literally no discussion of the broad strategy which a country like Britain should adopt towards a part of the world like the Caribbean. Instead the government's reply stood only as a series of piecemeal measures advanced in a self-justificatory manner. If a House of Commons Select Committee and the invasion of Grenada cannot bump policy out of this rut, it may be concluded that nothing can or will.

The Latin American Presence and the Commonwealth Caribbean

Among other states with an interest in the affairs of the Commonwealth Caribbean are Mexico and Venezuela. Their presence is relatively new, dating back effectively only to the early 1970s when under energetic and active leadership in the persons of Luis Echeverría in Mexico and Carlos Andrés Pérez in Venezuela they began to develop a web of bilateral linkages with countries in the region. In more recent years the two states have also concerted action in some respects – in the 1980 San José Agreement under which they agreed to supply the net oil consumption of nine Caribbean basin countries on concessionary terms; in 1981 when they met with the United States and Canada in the Bahamas to discuss the co-ordination of aid provision in the region and sought, albeit unsuccessfully, to persaude the US government to take a less rigid approach to the programme which later became the CBI; and, more recently, in the Contadora initiative in respect of Central America. Indeed, the view of Echeverría's successor as President of Mexico, López Portillo, expressed in 1981, was that 'collaboration between Venezuela and Mexico is vital to achieve the stability of the 27 nations in the Caribbean Basin'.[10]

Notwithstanding all this, Mexico's interest in the Commonwealth Caribbean was and still remains insecurely founded. On assuming office in 1976, López Portillo had himself initially signalled a less active commitment than his predecessor to foreign policy concerns, announcing, for example, Mexico's withdrawal from various industrial projects previously agreed with Jamaica. It was, in the event, only a temporary retreat and by 1980 Mexico had reasserted its interest in regional affairs, particularly as they affected Central America and Cuba. Motivating this were both geopolitical considerations and economic factors, the latter grounded in the emergence of Mexico as a major oil-producing nation. It was this aspect which most interested the Commonwealth Caribbean, leading to multilateral initiatives such as the activation of the CARICOM-Mexico Joint Commission which held its inaugural meeting in Barbados in October 1980, and bilateral missions such as the visit by Bishop to Mexico in September 1981. Although this cannot be said to have laid the basis for a particularly close relationship with the PRG, it did result in Mexico agreeing to provide a regular supply of oil to Grenada as well as technical and commercial assistance to a variety of ventures.[11] It also demonstrated Mexico's willingness to make an assessment of the situation radically different from that of the US government. Mexico was able to do this by virtue both of the 'dispensation to dissent' from US policy in Latin America which it has historically enjoyed and its demonstrable economic strength. In so far as this has now become uncertain, so has Mexican policy towards the Commonwealth Caribbean. Whilst Mexico was vigorous in its condemnation of the US invasion of Grenada, its priorities are now with domestic economic matters. At present, it does not enjoy the means, and possibly does not have the will, to contest US hegemony in the region.

The same cannot be said as certainly of Venezuela. Among the Latin American states it is the one that has taken the most consistent interest in the Caribbean. This reflects a considerable change of perspective.

Despite the historic ties with the Caribbean basin manifest in colonial times, for more than a century and a half after independence Venezuela's main concern was with forging a continental destiny. Since the beginning of the 1970s, however, it has claimed a new diplomatic and strategic interest in the evolution of relationships between the countries of the Caribbean basin. Impelling this have been several factors of which undoubtedly the most important has been the fact that Venezuela's important commercial and industrial centres are located on or near its considerable Caribbean coastline and that the Caribbean Sea is now the main avenue through which the country's vital exports of oil and oil-related products flow to the outside world.

Nevertheless, even in this period Venezuelan policy towards the Caribbean passed through different phases. Using the vast new funds at his disposal as a result of the quadrupling of oil prices in 1973, the social democratic *Acción Democrática* government of Pérez was able to win considerable influence in the region, especially in the Commonwealth Caribbean. A procession of leaders were lured to Caracas with a view to negotiating aid agreements, and none returned home empty-handed. Although Dr Williams of Trinidad and Tobago, Venezuela's rival in the Commonwealth Caribbean in the sense of also being an oil producer, was moved to condemn this in 1975 as an attempt 'to recolonise the Caribbean' and 'a threat to the Caribbean Community',[12] his was a lone voice. Pérez was active too in wider Caribbean matters, associating Venezuela both with the FSLN in Nicaragua and the growing call for the reintegration of Cuba into the Latin American system. By contrast, the succeeding Christian Democrat government of Luis Herrera Campins, which took up office in March 1979, set about the conduct of Venezuelan foreign policy in a distinctly more conservative style. Relations with Cuba were allowed to lapse and in El Salvador support was given to the fellow Christian Democrat — and pro-US — government of Napoléon Duarte. In the Commonwealth Caribbean a similar pattern can be detected. For the first two years of the Grenadian revolution, Herrera was sympathetic to the needs of the PRG, receiving Bishop in Caracas, agreeing to the appointment of a resident ambassador in St George's, and promising to supply 10,000 gallons of oil free to the island. But, as Grenada moved closer to Cuba, so Venezuela disengaged and began to adopt policies in the whole region which were interpreted by many as reflecting a new subordination to US policy. The Venezuelan government strongly denied this, arguing that it was more a coincidence of interests and pointing to instances of its criticism of US actions, such as the support given to Britain in the

Falklands/Malvinas conflict. For all that, Washington took comfort from the fact that in regional affairs it had an ally of some importance in the southern Caribbean.

To some extent, the Venezuelan elections of December 1983 may have changed that assessment. They were won by *Acción Democrática* and the new government of Jaime Lusinchi took up office in February 1984, pledged to place the establishment of friendly relations with the Caribbean high on its list of priorities. According to early indications, Lusinchi will first normalise Venezuela's relations with Cuba and then seek to associate Cuba more closely with Latin America. Towards Jamaica and Barbados his government is more likely to favour the main opposition parties, with whom it has some ideological links, rather than the present conservative governments, and in respect of Grenada is unlikely to associate itself closely with US plans or policy. This has been taken by some to foreshadow a return to the independent diplomacy of the Pérez era, but it should not be taken to mean that Venezuela, any more than Mexico, has the desire or the capacity to compete with US influence in the area. Even whilst still President-elect, Lusinchi held a meeting with the US Under Secretary of State for Inter-American Affairs, L. Motley, to discuss, in Lusinchi's own words, 'solutions for the hot Caribbean'.[13] Collaboration is as likely as competition in this endeavour.

Cuba, the United States and the Caribbean Basin

While Britain and the Latin American powers may therefore play greater or lesser roles in future in Caribbean politics, it is the conflict between the United States and Cuba which is decisive. The experience of Grenada in the last four and a half years, if it shows nothing else, must surely confirm this beyond any reasonable doubt. The most important questions raised by the invasion are thus concerned with the nature of this contest. In particular, has it been changed in any significant way by recent events? A full answer to this clearly cannot be given while the events themselves are so close at hand. Nevertheless, the conclusions reached earlier about the nature of Cuban and US policy in the Caribbean basin, when set alongside the invasion and the immediate responses made to it, do indicate that some outcomes are more probable than others.

In respect of Cuba it is clear that the response to the invasion has been one of perplexed and then resigned anger, expressed in terms of measured diplomacy abroad and heightened revolutionary vigilance at home. The latter, of course, stems from the perfectly understandable feeling that, in the minds of US policy-makers, Grenada was a surrogate for Cuba, and that the comparatively easy victory achieved by the United States might arouse expectations that it could be repeated elsewhere. El Salvador, Nicaragua and Cuba itself were the obvious candidates. In these cases, as Castro warned in his 14 November speech, the United States would not find 'the particular circumstances of revolutionaries divided among themselves and divorced from the people that they found in tiny Grenada.' In sharp contrast, he affirmed that, in the case of Cuba, 'our country – as we have already said on other occasions – might be wiped off the face of the earth, but it will never be conquered or subjugated'.[14] In the event that the US government took no heed of such warnings, there was, however, little that Cuba could realistically do to support the others.

Diplomacy since the invasion has recognised this fact. In an interview given in January 1984, Cuba's Vice-Minister of Foreign Relations, Ricardo Alarcón, ruled out the possibility of Cuban military intervention in Central America in spite of increasing US pressures on the region. He stated:

> The Sandinistas do not need that sort of help. The army is well trained, the militia and civil defence well-organised. They have created all the conditions for self-defence and could confront the US efficiently. Our people care a great deal about Nicaragua, but will have to accept that we cannot help Nicaragua. You cannot take it as a wound to the internationalist spirit that you can't go to the aid of all oppressed peoples ...
>
> In the case of El Salvador it is unthinkable that they should ask us for help. Technically, given the nature of the war, it is not feasible. Foreign troops are no use in a guerrilla war – we would have to transport and feed our soldiers. The Salvadorean movement doesn't need extra personnel, given that they have the support of the local population and control important sections of territory. We would simply be a liability. If the US made the mistake of committing its own troops, our response would be political, not military.[15]

Evidence from Central America appears to confirm precisely this. In July 1983 Nicaragua advanced proposals to secure peace in the region by halting arms supplies from wherever to whoever, and Cuba indicated its willingness to stop arms supplies to, and withdraw military advisers from, Central America if the United States would agree to do the same. The Reagan administration chose not to respond. Then in late November and early December the Nicaraguan government announced a series of measures designed to meet what were known as US preconditions for easing pressure on the regime. These included asking the FDR/FMLN to leave Managua and the scaling-down of the Cuban presence. The US reply came on 19 January when Motley accused the Nicaraguan government of being 'deceitful'. He claimed the FDR/FMLN move was purely cosmetic and added: 'We have seen no evidence that any of Cuba's 2,000 military and security advisers have left Nicaragua.'[16] Since Alarcón puts the number of these at less than 200, the gap between the two sides is clearly very wide and diplomacy will need to be very elastic in order to bridge it.

Yet, according to Wayne Smith, the former chief of the US interests section in Havana, this is precisely what will not happen. In an article written just after the Grenada invasion, he argued that the Reagan administration has become 'the prisoner of its own rhetoric', eschewing serious negotiations for fear it would give the impression 'of accommodating aggression'. It therefore 'presses on with its efforts to overthrow the Sandinistas and force a military solution in El Salvador'.[17] His logic is impeccable and the warm reception given by the Reagan administration to the Kissinger report released on 11 January 1984 appears to confirm it. In this Kissinger shares with Reagan the basic assumption that the conflict in Central America is an East-West confrontation stemming from Cuban and Soviet expansion in the area. The case was made that the administration and Congress had hitherto failed to do enough militarily. 'The worst possible policy for El Salvador is to provide just enough aid to keep the war going, but too little to wage it successfully.' Accordingly, emergency military assistance to El Salvador over the next two years was earmarked as a priority. On Nicaragua, the report argued for continuing the military presence as the most effective means of persuading the Sandinistas to change direction and permit 'free elections'. How and who determines these was not considered but clearly it is an important question given the experience of El Salvador in 1982. Finally, in respect of the region as a whole (including Nicaragua if it meets with certain conditions) a US $8 billion medium- and long-term assistance programme over fiscal years 1985-9 was recommended.[18] Although this last aspect, if implemented, does begin to address itself to the real problems of the region, which are rooted in economic underdevelopment and social injustice, in the present context a reasonable doubt must exist as to whether it is anything other than cosmetic.

The same pattern of continuing Cuban diplomacy versus a heightened military profile on the part of the United States appears from recent events to extend to the Commonwealth Caribbean as well. Thus a Cuban trade delegation visited Trinidad in November 1983, despite much adverse publicity surrounding its decision to do so; and Cuban-Guyanese relations are expected to remain cordial with established technical and commercial agreements remaining unchanged. For the United States, however, the invasion of Grenada has conveniently provided an opportunity to achieve one of its long-standing goals in the region. This has been to establish, in collaboration with Britain, a programme to enhance the police, coastguard and security forces of the Eastern Caribbean states. Traditionally, assistance of this kind has been a solely British preserve and the United States entered the field with serious commitment only in the early 1980s. The focus initially was on Barbados, but soon encompassed the other smaller islands of the region, except, of course, Grenada, and bore fruit in October 1982 with the signing of the Memorandum of Understanding on regional security by the governments of Antigua, Barbados, Dominica, St Lucia and St Vincent. Although this new defence force can be interpreted as having anti-subversive or anti-revolutionary implications, it manifestly cannot be seen as a means of defending the Eastern Caribbean against attack by any of the major powers whose armies and navies manoeuvre in the region, unless it has an explicit understanding with one of them.

This is precisely the direction in which events appear now to be moving. A press report in February 1984 claimed that the United States and Barbados were planning to launch a 'mini-Nato' in the Eastern Caribbean financed by a US $15 million appropriation authorised by the Reagan administration a few weeks after Grenada was invaded. Weapons and military instructors have apparently already been sent to persuade political leaders in the area of the need for such a pact. Some will have required no convincing. Tom Adams, for example, has said that his 'feeling is that one regional army rather than a number of national armies would give us an additional safeguard, namely the protection of small governments against their own armed forces'.[19] The reference, of course, is to events in Grenada leading up to and immediately following the death of Maurice Bishop. The rationalisation may be genuine, but such a force, if established, would also effectively prevent a repeat of 13 March 1979 and on past evidence it is exactly this prospect that most exercises the minds of incumbent political leaders in the Eastern Caribbean.

Regional Integration in the Commonwealth Caribbean

On a number of occasions in the recent past commentators have written off the future prospects of regional integration in the Commonwealth Caribbean without the movement ever quite dying away completely. The bells were tolled in 1962 when the West Indies Federation was dissolved, in 1971 when CARIFTA seemed immobilised, in 1975 when some of the region's leaders fell to public squabbling and in 1979 when the *coup* in Grenada appeared to confirm the emergence of an unbridgeable ideological rift within CARICOM. On all these occasions the regional integration movement recovered and, to some extent, prospered — in the latter case, as we have seen, by most member governments of CARICOM coming to realise that they could live and work with the Bishop regime. The events surrounding the fall of Bishop and the subsequent invasion have once again raised serious doubts about the viability of Commonwealth Caribbean integration. The question that has frequently been asked since October 1983 is whether or not CARICOM can survive, let alone articulate a Caribbean voice in the midst of the international conflicts taking place in the region. Central to this is an evaluation of Jamaica's, and more particularly Seaga's, attitude towards regional integration.

The Impact on CARICOM

Undoubtedly the dissension wrought by the invasion has damaged CARICOM. This can be seen in two areas. The first concerns the impact on personal relations between the various heads of government in the Commonwealth Caribbean. It was, after all, not just that the region disagreed about what to do in Grenada once the Revolutionary Military Council had taken over, but that the 'invading states' deliberately connived to conceal their intentions from their remaining CARICOM partners. As the earlier account of events shows, the Port of Spain meeting of CARICOM heads of government took place when several of the participants already knew of, and had indeed contributed to, the decision to invade. In these circumstances the other leaders understandably felt that they had been made to look fools. Chambers's statement on being told of the invasion made no attempt to conceal how personally offended he felt. Subsequent off-the-record remarks by other Trinidadian ministers suggest that they will be very reluctant to work again with Seaga, whom they see as the man mainly responsible for the deception. Forbes Burnham too made some very outspoken comments about his CARICOM colleagues. Seaga, for his part, in a speech to a party rally in November 1983, launched an equally fierce attack on unnamed regional leaders whom he accused of treachery for having leaked to the Grenadians some of the details of the invasion plan. 'In days to come', he told his supporters, 'you may know of whom I speak because it will be very hard for me to sit around a table with them.'[20] All this matters in the Commonwealth Caribbean because the vitality of the regional integration movement has always required the existence of a genuine *rapport* between the heads of government of the major regional territories.[21] Great store has traditionally been set on this 'club' approach, to the extent that it has been institutionalised in the CARICOM treaty which formally recognises the Heads of Government Conference as the highest policy-making body in the whole organisation. In the atmosphere of personal recrimination which has been created by the invasion of Grenada it is hard to see such a gathering of leaders taking place in the near future. There was previously a seven-year gap between 1975 and 1982 when the leaders did not meet, and CARICOM suffered as a consequence. Indeed, it was precisely the holding of two successful summits in November 1982 and July 1983 that was responsible for the greater optimism which many felt about CARICOM up to the moment of the invasion.

The second consequence of the invasion for CARICOM concerns the plausibility of the doctrine of 'ideological pluralism' in the context of regional integration. The concept had first been advanced towards the end of the 1970s in an attempt to reconcile the continuance of the integration movement with the emergence of differing ideological perspectives in the region. As Guyana, Jamaica and then Grenada began to experiment with 'socialist' models of development of one sort or another, there was a fear that this would disrupt the integration process. In response to these worries, the Standing Committee of CARICOM Ministers for Foreign Affairs discussed the matter at a meeting in St Lucia in February 1980, concluding that, since ideological pluralism was 'an irreversible fact of international relations', it should not 'be permitted to constitute a barrier to the strengthening of the mechanism of CARICOM'.[22] This became the official stance of the movement and was faithfully adhered to by the majority of member states, even when challenged as at the Ocho Rios summit in 1982 when Seaga and Adams tried to change the CARICOM treaty to force signatories to comply with the procedures of parliamentary democracy. The resulting Declaration of Ocho Rios, in fact, formally reiterated 'the right of self-determination of all peoples, including the right to choose their own path of social, political and economic development', and insisted that 'there can be no justification for any external interference with the exercise of that right'.[23] In the light of the invasion of Grenada and the role played by some CARICOM states in that event, this commitment can no longer be taken seriously. It has been revealed as a mere device, tolerated by several Commonwealth Caribbean leaders only until they could find an effective way of eliminating the ideological differences which had emerged in the region.

Jamaica and Seaga

Without these two props, CARICOM is in a much more vulnerable position than it has been for a long time. The critical factor will be whether anyone actually wants to destroy it, and here the debate tends to revolve around the role of Seaga. Other Commonwealth Caribbean leaders have known for some time that Seaga has wanted to include in CARICOM other generally pro-American powers in the wider Caribbean region, such as Haiti and the Dominican Republic. In the few weeks after the invasion of Grenada, a number of them came increasingly to suspect that his real aim was to replace CARICOM with a looser organisation embracing non-Commonwealth Caribbean countries but perhaps also excluding any existing member state not willing to accept US leadership in regional affairs. He spoke of the creation of a CARICOM Mark II,[24] arousing the suspicion in Trinidad and Guyana that he was making a threat directed mainly at them. If for the moment nothing more has been heard of this idea, it is clear, to say the least, that for Seaga CARICOM matters are a low priority compared to the question of Jamaica's and the region's dealings with Washington. As and when the two come into conflict, the former must, in his view, not only be subordinated but brought into a position of support for the latter.

This is a point of view which CARICOM will have to learn to live with over the next few years, because Seaga has just been re-elected to office in Jamaica, almost entirely on the basis of reactions to the invasion of Grenada. Aware that his promises to revive the Jamaican economy had not yet been fulfilled and that even his administration had come into conflict with the IMF, Seaga ruthlessly exploited a public opinion poll taken after the overthrow and murder of Bishop which showed a 5 per cent swing to his Jamaica Labour Party (JLP), placing it ahead of the opposition for the first time since the middle of the previous year.[25] The bloody events in Grenada seemed to have reopened many of the anxieties which had inspired strong anti-communist and anti-Cuban feelings in Jamaica in the elections of 1980 in which Manley was defeated by Seaga. The popularity of Jamaican involvement in the invasion, despite strongly-worded criticism of it by the opposition People's National Party (PNP), further reinforced this perception and gave Seaga an electoral opportunity he could not have imagined a few weeks beforehand. Moving to deepen the 'Jamaicanisation' of the Grenada issue, he accused the Soviet embassy in Kingston of being involved in espionage and dismissed a lowly civil servant in the Jamaican foreign ministry for allegedly meeting with a KGB agent. Some two dozen people associated with the PNP and the small Communist Party in Jamaica were also named as having recently visited Cuba, Grenada and the Soviet Union, the implication being that in so doing they might have been involved in 'anti-Jamaican' activities. These various moves were all a prelude to the calling of a snap election in December 1983, even though the two major parties had an agreement that no election would be held until certain electoral reforms, including the completion of a new register, had been effected. On these grounds the PNP refused to enter the contest, in which as a consequence the JLP automatically won all 60 seats in the Jamaican Parliament. The result aroused great controversy in the island, especially as another opinion poll taken in December showed that the JLP gains from developments in Grenada had been neutralised by the opposition's charge of electoral opportunism and that in the electorate as a whole, as opposed to that part of it which was registered, the PNP was in fact 7 per cent ahead of the JLP. Manley has called for new elections as soon as the voters' list is ready, but local comment generally has it that 'having achieved the major objective of additional time to see progress in economic policies that need more time to unfold', Seaga is 'unlikely to yield' to the PNP's demand.[26] In many ways, therefore, the most striking immediate impact of the invasion of Grenada on the rest of the Commonwealth Caribbean has been the boost it has given to Seaga's political fortunes.

However, even with up to five years in office ahead of him, it is doubtful if it would be to Seaga's advantage to seek to break up CARICOM. It is more likely that he will revive the idea of widening the membership and thus of turning it into more of a strategic and economic alliance representing US interests in the region. Whilst such a prospect will be viewed with dismay by many of the regional technocrats and intellectuals who once had such high hopes of the development potential of regional integration, Seaga may not find the political obstacles in his way too difficult to overcome. Although some observers have wondered if the four CARICOM states which opposed the invasion might constitute a regional bloc capable of resisting such a ready acceptance of US hegemony over the Commonwealth Caribbean, that possibility seems less than likely when their particular attitudes and positions are examined separately. In the light of its relationship with Guatemala, which claims a large part of its territory, Belize had every reason to oppose the invasion of anywhere by anybody and knows too that it cannot get into conflict with the United States, which it sees as a major restraining factor on potential Guatemalan aggression. To this end, it has allowed US troops to use its territory to engage in what is euphemistically called 'jungle training'. The Bahamas sees itself as a part-Atlantic, part-Caribbean state and has only recently fully joined the common market arrangements set up within CARICOM. By geographical location, economic linkage and political inclination, it cannot in any sense be said to be anti-US. Guyana under Burnham has affected bouts of anti-Americanism in its foreign policy, but, because of its similar territorial dispute with Venezuela, will not have wanted, any more than Belize, to give legitimacy to the use of the weapon of invasion in Caribbean affairs. Guyana's leadership potential in the region is also vitiated by its appalling economic position and unsatisfactory human rights record. This leaves just Trinidad, which undoubtedly won a lot of friends in Latin America by its opposition to the US action and may be well placed to win the Latin American seat on the UN Security Council which Barbados was lobbying for and surely has lost as a consequence of its part in the invasion. Trinidad will, in all probability, want to develop closer relations with the continental mainland, especially with Venezuela, and has already signalled its desire to maintain links with Cuba. But its economy has moved into recession in the last couple of years and it could not hope to sustain a hostile relationship with the United States even if it wished to. The likelihood is, therefore, that its embrace of US leadership will be distinctly cooler than that of other states in the Commonwealth Caribbean, but that it too will have to accept – by virtue of not being able to challenge – the reality of the new geopolitics of the region.

In these circumstances, CARICOM will survive, albeit in emasculated form compared to the original ambitions of some of its architects. Indeed, meetings of ministers and technocrats have continued after the invasion in a kind of collective pretence that nothing had really happened. Subject to all the usual disagreements and conflicts, the work of the organisation in the economic and functional areas will be able to continue. This is not to be disparaged, but it is not the same as co-ordinating foreign policy with a view to asserting an independent regional voice in respect of the major international issues which beset the region — the goal to which CARICOM aspired when first established in 1973. From this perspective, the ramifications of the disunity shown over Grenada unquestionably add up to a major setback for Commonwealth Caribbean integration.

The Theory and Practice of Caribbean Socialism

The revolution in Grenada was watched with particular interest by socialist movements throughout the Commonwealth Caribbean. It was universally welcomed by them and attracted considerable support, not least because it was thought to represent a decisive breakthrough in the fortunes of revolutionary socialism in the region. Hitherto, socialism had been almost exclusively reformist in character, drawing explicitly upon, and echoing the practice of, the Labour Party in Britain. Movements to the left of this, and specifically Marxist-Leninist ones, had been few in number, had attracted little support and had hardly escaped the confines of discussion groups. The only significant exceptions were the People's Progressive Party in Guyana and the Workers' Liberation League in Jamaica. Even in these cases, given the nature of the political culture in both countries, their influence was limited and their political activity largely reduced to the margins of the respective political systems. As it appeared to one well-informed observer in 1978, the future realisation of socialism in the Commonwealth Caribbean was 'a very remote possibility'.[27]

The March *coup* in Grenada in 1979 shifted the focus of revolutionary socialism in the region from the more developed countries like Jamiaca and Guyana to the less developed countries of the Eastern Caribbean. In so doing, it altered the parameters of the debate on socialism and, more importantly, provided an example. Both came together in an articulation of the theory and practice of non-capitalist development for the Commonwealth Caribbean. Grenada provided a test case in as much as significant elements within the leadership of the New Jewel Movement subscribed to the theory and sought to apply it to Grenadian reality. This, in turn, attracted criticism, both of a general kind aimed at the theory as a whole and of a specific type related to its practice in Grenada. In respect of the latter an important strand came from within the revolution itself, as expressed ultimately in the Bishop-Coard confrontation. To what extent Grenada does, or does not, represent a vanguard example of non-capitalist development in the Caribbean is, of course, a matter of pressing concern to socialists throughout the region. The lessons that can be drawn from the experiment are already a subject of considerable controversy and will continue to be so in the years ahead. What is learnt from the experience will, more than any other factor, determine the agenda of future socialist change in the Caribbean.

'Non-capitalist Development' and Grenada

The theory of non-capitalist development was developed by Soviet scholars during the 1960s. Its principal exponent, Professor Ulyanovsky, is a noted Soviet academician and influential adviser on Soviet foreign policy towards the Third World.[28] As it was first formulated, the theory had a tendency to be associated exclusively with the prospects of socialist transformation in the newly-independent states of Africa and Asia. However, in June 1975 important aspects of it were incorporated into the 'Declaration of Havana', the final document unanimously approved at the Conference of Communist and Workers' Parties of Latin America. A transition to the region was thereby effected and the theory taken up by a number of Commonwealth Caribbean intellectuals who saw in it a very favourable and appropriate route to power.

As succinctly set out by one of them, Ralph Gonsalves,

> the thesis of the non-capitalist path of development has its roots in the science of historical materialism as creatively applied to countries where capitalism is either non-existent or undeveloped as in Africa and the Caribbean and posits that capitalism can be by-passed or interrupted on the route to the construction of socialism.[29]

Critically necessary for the realisation of this is 'a broad class alliance involving the proletariat, the semi-proletarian masses, the revolutionary or democratic strata of the petty-bourgeoisie (including the peasantry) and even the progressive patriotic elements of the emerging national bourgeoisie', governing through 'a revolutionary democratic or national democratic state which links up itself increasingly with the forces of world socialism'.[30] It is clear from the writing of Gonsalves and others that the decisive aspect of non-capitalist development resides in the realm of politics, deriving its force from a 'relative autonomy' of the state evident in many post-colonial countries. It follows that the policies pursued by such states are crucial in determining whether or not they are following the path of non-capitalist development, or 'socialist orientation', as it has increasingly come to be called.

Gonsalves thus lists nine main features of the non-capitalist path as follows: (1) the abolition of imperialism's political domination; (2) the reduction and eventual abolition of imperialism's economic control; (3) the consolidation of the mixed structure of the economy and its development into one in which the state and co-operative economic sectors become dominant; (4) the transformation of the political culture towards socialist values; (5) the engendering of new attitudes towards work and production; (6) the expansion of mass participation in and control of the state administration and state economic enterprises; (7) the removal of plantocratic national bourgeois and imperialist elements from the supreme command of government and the transference of power to revolutionary democrats and scientific socialists; (8) the development of appropriate planning techniques and organisational methods to raise productive forces; and (9) a raising of the cultural, scientific and material level of living for the mass of the people.[31] The non-capitalist road therefore involves both analysis and programme, theory and practice, of 'one possible path' to socialism. If fully implemented, it does not constitute socialism itself, but rather a political, material, social and cultural preparation for the transition to socialism. As two other Soviet scholars, Solodovnikov and Bogoslovsky, put it, 'the non-capitalist way is a form of approach and ultimately of transition to socialism, the connecting link between national liberation revolution and socialist revolution'.[32]

From the outset some theoreticians from within Grenada argued that the revolution was guided by just such a perspective. They claimed that the origins of this commitment lay as far back as the emergence and development of the New Jewel Movement. The 1973 NJM manifesto is cited as evidence of a 'non-capitalist ideological perspective' and the NJM party structure is seen as possessing 'distinctly scientific socialist characteristics'. Additional considerations were the preeminence within the NJM's leadership of 'the progressive young middle-class intelligentsia'; the class character of the emerging political forces opposed to Gairy; 'the need to maintain the neutrality, if not the support, of the middle strata'; and, finally, the frank recognition, given the circumstances in Grenada, that 'to adopt an overtly Marxist-Leninist path . . . is to court alienation and take a deliberately long route to national liberation'.[33] Accordingly, the non-capitalist way emerged as 'the most appropriate intermediate option' — a strategy which permits 'the mobilisation of diverse social elements in the movement towards national liberation and revolutionary change. Once the progressive forces have seized state power by whatever means, the process of transformation begins.'[34]

After the revolution little was said in public in specific terms about the theory of non-capitalist development. However, confirmation that its imperatives were much in the minds of the leadership was occasionally provided. In an interview in July 1979, Bernard Coard stated:

> So fundamentally, at this time, we see our task not as one of building socialism. It is one of restructuring and rebuilding the economy, of getting production going and trying to develop genuine grass-roots democracy, trying to involve the people in every village and every workplace in the process of the reconstruction of the country. In that sense we are in a national democratic revolution involving the broad masses and many strata of the population.[35]

Bishop reiterated this in an interview in July 1981. The Grenadian revolution was at 'the national democratic stage, the anti-imperialist stage of the process we are trying to build'. In the sphere of economics, this involved policies such as building a strong state sector, stimulating the private sector to boost production and disengaging rapidly from imperialism; and in the sphere of politics, the promotion of measures such as the reform of the state apparatus and the development of 'revolutionary democracy'.[36] The class character of such democracy was all important. Those for the revolution were seen as 'the broad masses of our working people' (the urban and rural working class, the small and middle farmers, revolutionary youth and students, and patriotic women) and those against 'a very small minority clique' (the biggest and most unpatriotic landowners and businessmen, corrupt trade union leaders and bureaucrats, some employees of multinational corporations, and the lumpen and criminal elements).[37] The essence of the national democratic state as so established, and that aspect wherein lay its decisive and historic importance, was that the minority were politically subject to the majority. In Ulyanovsky's words, power lay with 'the broad social bloc of the working people' within which 'the national-bourgeois elements ... are deprived of monopoly political power'.[38]

Critiques of Theory and Practice

As might be expected, the theory and practice of non-capitalist development in the Caribbean has attracted a range of critical comment. Among the earliest was that of the Guyanese economist, C.Y. Thomas.[39] In a review of the theory as a whole he specified two areas of particular concern. The first related to the analysis of class, especially a tendency to underplay internal class struggles. Not enough attention was given, Thomas believed, to potential conflicts between the petty bourgeoisie and the worker-peasant alliance. In respect of the petty bourgeoisie, he argued, there was a tendency 'for this social group to see themselves as arbiters and the only real representatives of national interests', i.e. to ascribe to themselves a relationship above class, frequently institutionalised in a developing military-bureaucratic state. The scope for independent working-class action was correspondingly circumscribed to the point, in some instances, of effective prohibition. Thomas here seems to be describing a process typically encountered in sub-Saharan Africa, but to the extent that in Grenada such a petty bourgeois group did emerge, his criticism has wider applicability. Equally so does his remedy, which was to place the working class unambiguously at the forefront of strategic class alliances.

The other issue about which Thomas was concerned was the question of political democracy. Too little recognition was given, he argued, to freedoms which were termed 'bourgeois' and therefore regarded as 'luxuries', but which in fact 'have been won on the basis of mass struggle'. These include a number of individual and collective rights, such as freedom of speech, association and publication, the independence of the judiciary and an insistence on the establishment of institutions representative of the popular will. Not only must these be mentioned, but they must be expanded 'as a pre-condition of socialist construction'. As Thomas put it:

> not only is the state of the class struggle primary, but that struggle itself is inseparable from the general conditions for working-class democracy and participation in national life. Proponents of the non-capitalist way do not often seem to place enough emphasis on the primacy of mass action in any socialist oriented alliance. This point, we feel, holds all the more strongly in so far as effective leadership does not lie among the working class. It is therefore not enough simply to recognise the need for democratic life and pass this over with a general endorsement of the 'progressive' character of these regimes as some non-capitalist theorists do.[40]

The relevance of such considerations to the situation in Grenada surely needs no emphasis. The conclusion suggested is, of course, that the revolution did not so much fail in social and economic terms, as in political ones.

A similar understanding arises from a review of non-capitalist development in the Eastern Caribbean authored by University of the West Indies political scientist, Pat Emmanuel, shortly before he joined the post-invasion interim government in Grenada.[41] In this he identified a number of specific problems of practice, one of the most important of which arose from 'the political requirements of a strategy of mixed economy'. On the one hand, to ensure future socialist orientation, this determines the dismantling of 'the bourgeois-democratic constitutional system'. Whilst on the other, in order also to maintain 'bourgeois collaboration in the form of a parallel private sector development', there is a direct requirement to the contrary, since in the Eastern Caribbean it is precisely 'the letter and culture of Westminster parliamentarism' which enshrines 'the security of property and profit – the bedrock of capitalism'.[42] Emmanuel argued that the contradiction revealed here could be subsumed in the 'anti-imperialist first phase of post revolution struggle' by 'the official declaration of the goal of mixed economy'. However, as the revolution develops and class struggle sharpens, conflicts naturally arise between the bourgeoisie and the national democratic leadership. This elevates 'the issue of constitutionalism . . . to the extent that bourgeois participation in the mixed economy is felt *by the party* to be desirable'[43] in the short run, but is clearly against socialist orientation in the long run. What strategy, in the circumstances, is to prevail is a vexed question – and one which assumed particular prominence in Grenada in mid-1983.

Another problem which Emmanuel identified as arising from the specific context of the Caribbean related to the almost unique 'sociology of property' which has produced 'a peasant state of mind or outlook . . . unreceptive to socialist conceptions of collectivisation'. It is so because in the Caribbean *'the peasantry was born out of proletarian conditions*, and not the other way around'.[44] That is, when emancipation from slavery was achieved, liberty was quintessentially expressed by the establishment of a thriving peasantry which stood in contrast to the continuation of an agro-proletariat tied to the plantations in varying degrees of servitude. Land was thus synonymous with freedom. In the Grenadian context this was revealed in the discussions on agriculture in the NJM Political Bureau which were marked 'confidential' in the knowledge that should any hint reach the outside that the peasantry was to be 'collectivised' (which it was not), then the revolution would be gravely imperilled. Emmanuel's analysis points in the same direction and further elaborates a significant division in the Eastern Caribbean between the Windward Islands (including Grenada) where the peasantry is well established and the Leeward Islands (excluding Montserrat) where it is not. Common to both groups, however, is the fact that in neither has there been 'significant recent experience of proletarian life based on the production of commodities outside of agriculture'.[45] By default, as it were, the petty bourgeoisie (including the peasantry) thus becomes the principal class around which socialism must initially be built.

The problem with this class, as theorists of non-capitalist development and its various critics have recognised, is a tendency to vacillation in the face of revolutionary situations. Only the firmest revolutionary democratic leadership can avoid it, and in so far as this leadership itself may be drawn from the radical intelligentsia, it also can be subject to the same corrosive temptations. As Emmanuel pointed out, the political context of the Eastern Caribbean is particularly conducive to such possibilities arising. Revolutionary socialist parties are of recent origin, are drawn in large part from this class, and have been marked by 'shortcomings' which are variously organisational, financial and ideological. Indeed, he argued:

> the cadres that are expected to undertake ideological work are themselves quite young and recently initiated. An understandable revolutionary enthusiasm too often causes creative revolutionary philosophy to degenerate into a catalogue of abuse and ultraleftism. The fact that party cadres have to be built after, rather than before, revolutionary takeovers can seriously compound this tendency.[46]

Grenada, of course, provides a classic example of this. Paradoxically, however, Emmanuel considered the NJM to be qualitatively superior to the other socialist parties and groupings in the region. An explanation as to what happened in September and October 1983 might therefore have to be sought elsewhere. In this case one other observation of his is worthy of citation. Referring to the tendency for vacillation among the leadership of national democratic regimes, he stated: 'in their anxiety to pass the stern Soviet tests of ideological development, it can so easily occur that petty bourgeois radicals can outdo themselves with new kinds of infantile disorders on the far left'.[47] A more succinct summary of the PRA faction in the NJM Central Committee can scarcely be imagined.

Finally, consideration must be given to a critique embodying a Trotskyist perspective. This has recently been elaborated both at the general level of non-capitalist development theory and in respect of the specific situation in Grenada. In regard to the former, Fitzroy Ambursley and Robin Cohen had argued that 'the theory of non-capitalist development has no real basis in the writings of Marx, Engels and Lenin' and that its origins are to be found in 'the neo-Menshevik theses advanced by Stalin during the 1920s'.[48] In tone and style it is a familiar criticism, targetted at the Soviet Union (and even Cuba), seeing in their policies 'a restraining influence' on 'radical developments in the Caribbean'.[49] This is scarcely credible and derives from the authors holding a set of axioms every bit as rigid as those they seek to denounce. All this is not to imply that there are not many problems with the theory of non-capitalist development as it is currently understood. It does need redevelopment rather than mere reformulation and refinement. In this sense it is not the baby, but the bathwater, that needs pouring away.

At first sight, Ambursley's work on Grenada merits much the same type of judgement. In this he sought to show that as of 1982 Grenada was experiencing 'an interrupted popular revolution' and that the policies of the NJM, 'far from creating the objective conditions for the ultimate transition to socialism', were, in reality, 'deepening the island's subordination to those classes and institutions whose interests are antithetical to the cause of socialism'.[50] He purported to arrive at such a conclusion by way of an analysis of the internal policies of the PRG. No quarter was given as the revolution was described as 'a new Grenadian Bonapartism . . . of the petty bourgeoisie . . . in essence, like Gairyism, a mediated form of oligarchic rule'; economic policies dismissed as 'subordinated to the logic of capital accumulation'; and experiments with 'people's power' lightly brushed aside by designating them as no more than a form of bourgeois democracy, albeit one with certain 'distinctive characteristics'.[51] The combative style of such criticism would invite a reply in kind were it not for the fact that Ambursley himself has recently had second thoughts about his earlier work, stating that his chapter on Grenada 'contained some unfortunate formulations, showed scant appreciation of the subtleties of the NJM's political strategy and was somewhat ultraleft in many of its recommendations'.[52] This is a very commendable change of heart since Ambursley's writing is empirically well grounded and his latest contribution (with Winston James) points in the direction which any serious analysis of the failure of the Grenadian revolution must inevitably go, namely 'the heavy-handed manner in which it treated dissent' and an identification of 'the central contradiction of the Bishop regime' as 'a Marxist leadership with the clear objective of establishing a socialist state of some kind, and yet, at the same time . . . closely tied to the Caribbean and the West in terms of its economic relations'.[53] Ambursley is thus not to be summarily dismissed, but critically read and his many valuable insights into the Grenadian revolution recovered as the common property of Caribbean socialists as they seek to understand, and come to terms with, the lessons of theory and practice revealed by it.

Grenada: Exception or Vanguard?

While matters of theory are obviously important, the most pressing question facing Caribbean socialists is whether Grenada represents an exceptional case or is a vanguard example of the revolution to come. Early reflections on the Grenadian revolution among Caribbean socialists emphasised the latter, seeing in it a liberating experience which others were destined to follow sooner rather than later. This optimism was shared in some measure by the revolutionary leadership in Grenada, who were also quick to draw parallels between their experience and that of the Cuban revolution. As Selwyn Strachan commented in November 1979:

> Our course of development will be more or less the same as the Cuban revolution. There may be one or two minor differences, but nothing dramatic. And that, of course, will go for almost every country in the Caribbean, because we have [all] been underdeveloped by the imperialist world . . . If we have taken a decision to socially transform our society, and we are adopting the correct approach according to the laws of historical development, we would more or less have to go through the same process, with slight differences because of the unevenness, since some countries are more developed than the next. But basically, the approach will be the same, if we are moving to socialism.[54]

However, just as the experience of the 1960s confirmed Cuba's 'exceptional' quality, so the early 1980s confirmed Grenada's. The reality for Grenada, at least as far as the Commonwealth Caribbean was concerned, was one of building the revolution alone.

If the Grenadian experience is to be seen, at least for the present, as 'exceptional', what features have made it so? Four principal factors may be identified spanning the origins, development and final demise of the revolution. The first concerns the nature of the Gairy regime which no less a body than the Foreign Affairs Committee of the House of Commons described as 'corrupt, repressive and sustained only by rigged elections'. Compounding this was 'gross mismanagement of the economy'. Westminster-style politics under Gairy were thus discredited and abused to the point of 'no confidence' in the system as a whole.[55] This explains the ease with which the NJM took power. Such a combination of circumstances has not arisen elsewhere in the Eastern Caribbean and is unlikely to do so in the near future. Indeed, to the contrary, the political culture of the Westminster system appears to be well entrenched, with the consequence that bitterly contested electoral politics rather than ramshackle despotism or revolutionary change represents the most likely future for these islands.

The second factor is simply the consequence of the Grenadian revolution being a 'first' in the Commonwealth Caribbean. This provided both opportunities and constraints. To begin with, novelty allowed the revolution to traverse what proved to be uncharted waters with all the opportunities that this can offer. As Bishop put it, 'our revolution is an attempt to build a new socio-economic model. It is an attempt to solve our problems by new methods.'[56] But the price of novelty is to run the risk of error, either by faulty compass or unanticipated dangers, and the Grenadian revolution encountered both. During the course of 1982, constraints began to overwhelm opportunities and the 'ship' of Grenada, to extend the analogy, took on water, began to founder, and finally in mid-1983 struck the rock on which it sank. These may not be singular occurrences in world revolutionary processes, yet it is hard to believe that in a tempestuous Caribbean, future 'revolutionary navigators' will not taken on board something of the experience of Grenada and so be that much wiser before the event.

The third factor contributing to the 'exceptionality' of Grenada relates to the complexities of building the revolutionary party after the revolution. That this can successfully be achieved is not in doubt since the Cuban revolution has proved it. But the Cuban example also points to the need for purges (the Escalante affairs of 1962 and 1968) and the need for time. It also underlines the importance, in the person of Fidel Castro, of undisputed leadership. In the Grenadian case none of this applied. The 'purge' by Coard was both precipitate and unsuccessful: the proposal for joint leadership, the demonstration of a fateful division. As was made clear earlier, personal ambition played only a small part in this. Far larger was the question of leadership and direction. In considering this it is notable that Caribbean revolutionary socialists had frequently drawn attention to 'the ideological coherence of the leadership' of the NJM, viewing it as exceptional in both a general and a Caribbean sense. The latter is important, for political leadership in the Caribbean, whatever the nature of the political system, is almost invariably a one-man or one-woman affair. Lieutenants, when appointed, are persons of shadow rather than substance. It is the tragedy of the Grenadian revolution that neither Maurice Bishop nor Bernard Coard could ever have been second to anyone. Would-be revolutionary leaders in the Commonwealth Caribbean, at present marked everywhere by the fact that they are singular rather than plural, have no doubt already internalised this fact and are building their parties accordingly.

The final exceptional factor is the immediate context of the US invasion in October 1983. The fact that the US government desired to end the Grenadian revolution is a matter of record. All it lacked was the pretext and the will. The former was presented by the arrest and death of Bishop, the latter by the suicide attack on the US 'peace-keeping force' in the Lebanon. The dangers of just such a conjunction were not unanticipated in Grenada, ironically by Maurice Bishop himself. In an interview in July 1981 he pointed out:

> I think we also have to understand that this period is in many respects the most dangerous period in recent times. The Reagan administration has come up with some new concepts — particularly those of 'linkage' and 'international terrorism' — that are extremely dangerous. This concept of terrorism seeks in one blow to get round the Carter concept of human rights and to give them free reign to call any countries that are opposed to their way of thinking 'terrorists'. In that way they are seeking to rewrite recent history; turn back progressive developments around the world; and to create an image and a climate of hostility against those countries that have fought for their liberation and have been successful, countries of course like Cuba and Nicaragua, like Mozambique and Angola.
>
> The concept of linkage likewise is very dangerous. What this doctrine says is that if something happens in some part of the world of which they disapprove then they reserve the right to take a similar action in another part of the world, in Latin America, for example. That would mean that if anything took place in Europe that America disapproved of, that would give them the right to invade Cuba or Nicaragua, El Salvador or Grenada.[58]

To be proved right after the event is in this instance no consolation. Even so, it is difficult to believe that precisely the same explosive combination that constituted Grenada will be repeated elsewhere in the near future. To that extent the US invasion is 'exceptional' in its timing, if not in its impelling logic.

The exceptional quality of the Grenadian revolution as set out above should not be taken to imply that revolution will not erupt elsewhere in the Caribbean basin. As Castro has recently asserted, 'Cuba cannot export revolution any more than the United States can impede it',[59] pointing to the fact that revolutions are overwhelmingly the product of internal circumstances, not external. To the extent that this is true, then El Salvador and Guatemala in Central America and Guyana and Suriname in the Caribbean present themselves as distinct possibilities. In such cases, the example of Grenada will no doubt be more or less prominently before the actors involved, but in no sense will it direct the course of revolutionary development. As always, events will acquire a pattern of their own.

Conclusion

The conclusions reached in the various parts of this chapter point to a deepening and a widening of United States hegemony in the Caribbean basin, but one which is not yet absolute; a new vulnerability in relations between Commonwealth Caribbean states which, while not immediately destroying their separate regional identity has, in the short run, severely constrained CARICOM and may, in the long run, be so debilitating as to weaken collective expression to the point of virtual extinction; and a setback and a challenge to Caribbean socialism, both in theory and practice, which although not precluding future revolutionary change in the region does identify the Grenadian revolution as exceptional in several regards.

Taken together, these changes may constitute a turning-point. However, there is also a sense in which much of the above was already set in motion — trends which the rise and demise of the Grenadian revolution have confirmed rather than directly contradicted. To that extent the importance of Grenada is not so much to set the Caribbean on a new road as to mark the distance covered and the distance yet to go. In short, it is a conspicuous milestone, deeply etched and firmly set, against which present and future Caribbean generations will endeavour to measure progress.

Notes and References

1. George Walden in House of Commons, *Parliamentary Debates (Hansard)*, vol. 47, no. 35, 26 October 1983, col. 308.
2. For an extensive recent discussion of these themes, see A.J. Payne, *The International Crisis in the Caribbean* (Croom Helm, London, 1984); and A.J. Payne and P.K. Sutton (eds.), *Dependency under Challenge: The Political Economy of the Commonwealth Caribbean* (Manchester University Press, Manchester, 1984).
3. *Fifth Report of the Foreign Affairs Committee of the House of Commons: Caribbean and Central America*, together with an Appendix; part of the Proceedings of the Committee relating to the Report; and the Minutes of Evidence taken before the Committee with Appendices (HMSO, London, 1982).
4. Ibid., pp. 1-66 and 255-95.
5. Ibid., pp. 269-70.
6. See Sir Geoffrey Howe in *Parliamentary Debates*, vol. 47, no. 35, cols. 304 and 329-33.
7. *Fifth Report of the Foreign Affairs Committee*, pp. xi and liii.
8. Ibid., pp. lxiii-lxix.
9. *Observations by the Secretary of State for Foreign and Commonwealth Affairs* on Fifth Report from the Foreign Affairs Committee of the House of Commons: Caribbean and Central America, Cmnd. 8819 (HMSO, London, 1983).
10. *New York Times*, 9 April 1981. cited in V.A. Lewis, 'Commonwealth Caribbean Relations with Hemispheric Middle Powers' in Payne and Sutton (eds.), *Dependency under Challenge*, p. 247.
11. *Caribbean Insight*, November 1981.
12. See 'The Threat to the Caribbean Community' in P.K. Sutton (ed.), *Forged from the Love of Liberty: Selected Speeches of Dr Eric Williams* (Longman, Port of Spain, 1981), pp. 352-60.
13. *Latin America Regional Report: Caribbean*, RC-84-01, 20 January 1984.
14. 'Funeral Address given by Commander in Chief Fidel Castro, First Secretary of the Central Committee of the Communist Party of Cuba and President of the Council of State and of the Council of Ministers, in tribute to the heroes killed in unequal combat in Grenada by Yankee imperialism, 14 November 1983', reprinted in the *Guardian*, 19 November 1983.
15. *Latin America Regional Report: Caribbean*, RC-84-01, 20 January 1984.
16. *Latin American Weekly Report*, WR-84-04, 27 January 1984.
17. W.S. Smith, 'The Grenada Complex and Central America: Action and Negotiation in US Foreign Policy', *Caribbean Review*, vol. XII, no. 4 (1984), p. 65.
18. *Guardian*, 12 January 1984.
19. *Observer*, 5 February 1984.
20. *Jamaica Weekly Gleaner*, 9 November 1983.
21. See A.J. Payne, *The Politics of the Caribbean Community 1961-79: Regional Integration amongst New States* (Manchester University Press, Manchester, 1980).
22. *Press Release. Fifth Meeting of the Standing Committee of Ministers Responsible for Foreign Affairs* (Caribbean Community Secretariat, Georgetown, 1980).
23. *Press Release No. 52/1982. Third Conference of the Heads of Government of the Caribbean Community. Attachment 11. The Ocho Rios Declaration* (Caribbean Community Secretariat, Georgetown, 1982).
24. *Latin America Regional Report: Caribbean*, RC-83-10, 9 December 1983.

25. C. Stone, 'The Jamaican Reaction: Grenada and the Political Stalemate', *Caribbean Review*, p. 60.
26. Ibid., p. 63.
27. A.P. Maingot, 'The Difficult Path to Socialism in the English-Speaking Caribbean' in R. Fagen (ed.), *Capitalism and the State in US-Latin American Relations* (Stanford University Press, Stanford, California, 1979), p. 301.
28. See R. Ulyanovsky, *Socialism and the Newly Independent Nations* (Progress Publishers, Moscow, 1974).
29. R.E. Gonsalves, *The Non-capitalist Path of Development: Africa and the Caribbean* (One Caribbean Publishers, London, 1981), p. 2.
30. Ibid., pp. 2-3.
31. Ibid., pp. 8-14.
32. V. Solodovnikov and V. Bogoslovsky, *Non-capitalist Development: An Historical Outline* (Progress Publishers, Moscow, 1975), p. 247. Their emphasis.
33. W.R. and R.I. Jacobs, *Grenada: The Route to Revolution* (Casa de las Americas, Havana, 1980), pp. 80, 78, 82, 35 and ff.
34. Ibid., pp. 35-6.
35. B. Coard, *Grenada: Let Those who Labour Hold the Reins* (Liberation, London, 1981), p. 12.
36. Interview with Bishop, July 1981, in M. Bishop, *Forward Ever! Three Years of the Grenadian Revolution* (Pathfinder Press, Sydney, 1982), pp. 35-8.
37. 'Freedom of the Press Versus CIA Destabilisation' in ibid., p. 181.
38. Ulyanovsky, *Socialism and the Newly Independent Nations*, p. 82.
39. C.Y. Thomas, ' "The Non-Capitalist Path" as Theory and Practice of Decolonization and Socialist Transformation', *Latin American Perspectives*, vol. V, no. 2 (1978).
40. Ibid., pp. 24-5.
41. P. Emmanuel, 'Revolutionary Theory and Political Reality in the Eastern Caribbean', *Journal of Interamerican Studies and World Affairs*, vol. 25, no. 2 (1983).
42. Ibid., p. 205.
43. Ibid., p. 208. His emphasis.
44. Ibid., p. 210. His emphasis.
45. Ibid., p. 218.
46. Ibid., p. 226.
47. Ibid., p. 203.
48. F. Ambursley and R. Cohen, 'Crisis in the Caribbean: Internal Transformations and External Constraints' in Ambursley and Cohen, *Crisis in the Caribbean* (Heinemann Educational Books, London, 1983), pp. 6-7.
49. Ibid., p. 13.
50. F. Ambursley, 'Grenada: the New Jewel Revolution' in Ambursley and Cohen, *Crisis in the Caribbean*, pp. 191 and 202.
51. Ibid., pp. 205, 208, 215.
52. F. Ambursley and W. James, 'Maurice Bishop and the New Jewel Revolution in Grenada', *New Left Review*, no. 142 (1983), p. 4, footnote 4.
53. Ibid., pp. 93-4.
54. Cited in 'Introduction' by J. Percy to Bishop, *Forward Ever!*, pp. 15-16.
55. *Fifth Report of the Foreign Affairs Committee*, p. xxxvi.
56. 'Grenada is not Alone' in Bishop, *Forward Ever!*, p. 238.
57. Gonsalves, *The Non-capitalist Path of Development*, p. 24.
58. 'We'll Always Choose to Stand Up' in Bishop, *Forward Ever!*, pp. 50-1.
59. *Latin American Monitor: 5: Caribbean*, vol. 1, no. 1 (January 1984), 6.B.

SELECT BIBLIOGRAPHY

Ambursley, F. and Cohen, R. (eds.), *Crisis in the Caribbean* (Heinemann, London, 1983)
Bender, L.-D., *Cuba vs. United States: The Politics of Hostility*, 2nd edn (Inter-American University Press, San Juan, 1981)
Bishop, M., *Selected Speeches, 1979-1981* (Casa de las Americas, Havana, 1982)
——, *Forward Ever! Three Years of the Grenadian Revolution* (Pathfinder Press, Sydney, 1982)
——, *One Caribbean* (Britain/Grenada Friendship Society, London, 1983)
—— and Searle, C., *Education is a Must* (Education Committee of the British Grenadian Friendship Society, London, 1981)
Blasier, C. and Mesa-Lago, C. (eds.), *Cuba in the World* (University of Pittsburgh Press, Pittsburgh, 1979)
Chernick, S.E., *The Commonwealth Caribbean: the Integration Experience* (Johns Hopkins University Press, Washington, 1978)
Coard, B., *Grenada: Let Those who Labour Hold the Reins* (Liberation, London, 1981)
Da Breo, D.S., *The Grenada Revolution* (Management Advertising and Publicity Services, Castries, 1979)
Dominguez, J.I. (ed.), *Cuba: Internal and International Affairs* (Sage, Beverley Hills, 1982)
Emmanuel, P., *Crown Colony Politics in Grenada 1917-1951* (Institute of Social and Economic Research, University of the West Indies, Cave Hill, Barbados, 1978)
EPICA Task Force, *Grenada: The Peaceful Revolution* (EPICA, Washington, 1982)
Feinberg, R.E. (ed.), *Central America: International Dimensions of the Crisis* (Holmes and Meier, New York, 1982)
Gonsalves, R.E., *The Non-capitalist Path of Development: Africa and the Caribbean* (One Caribbean Publishers, London, 1981)
Grenada is Not Alone (Fedon Publishers, St George's, 1982)
Institute of International Relations, University of the West Indies, *Independence for Grenada: Myth or Reality?* (Institute of International Relations, St Augustine, 1974)
In the Spirit of Butler: Trade Unionism in a Free Grenada (Fedon Publishers, St George's, 1981)
Is Freedom We Making! The New Democracy in Grenada (People's Revolutionary Government, St George's, 1982)
Jacobs, W.R. and R.I., *Grenada: The Route to Revolution* (Casa de las Americas, Havana, 1980)
Levine, B.B. (ed.), *The New Cuban Presence in the Caribbean* (Westview Press, Boulder, 1983)
Lewis, V.A. (ed.), *Size, Self-Determination and International Relations: The Caribbean* (Institute of Social and Economic Research, Kingston, 1976)
Millett, R. and Will, W.M. (eds.), *The Restless Caribbean* (Praeger, New York, 1979)
Payne, A.J., *The Politics of the Caribbean Community 1961-79: Regional Integration amongst New States* (Manchester University Press, Manchester, 1980)
——, *The International Crisis in the Caribbean* (Croom Helm, London, 1984)

—— and Sutton, P.K. (eds.), *Dependency under Challenge: The Political Economy of the Commonwealth Caribbean* (Manchester University Press, Manchester, 1984)

Pearce, J., *Under the Eagle: US Intervention in Central America and the Caribbean* (Latin America Bureau, London, 1981)

Searle, C., *Grenada: The Struggle against Destabilization* (Writers and Readers, London, 1983)

—— (ed.), *Carriacou and Petite Martinique: In the Mainstream of the Revolution* (Fedon Publishers, St George's, 1982)

Singham, A.W., *The Hero and the Crowd in a Colonial Polity* (Yale University Press, New Haven, 1968)

Smith, M.G., *Stratification in Grenada* (University of California Press, Berkeley, 1965)

To Construct from Morning: Making the People's Budget in Grenada (Fedon Publishers, St George's, 1982)

Wesson, R. (ed.), *US Influence in Latin America in the 1980s* (Praeger with Hoover Institution Press, Stanford, 1982)

INDEX

Adams, Tom 94, 97-8, 114, 132, 140, 148-57 *passim*, 172-4, 207, 209
Advisory Council 182-96 *passim*
Afghanistan 73, 80, 176
Ambursley, Fitzroy 220-1
Angola 72, 75-6, 82, 223
Antigua and Barbuda 3, 43, 67, 89, 91-3, 96, 154, 207
Associated States 91, 95
　see also constitutional issues
Austin, Hudson 16, 163, 185
　Revolutionary Military Council 136, 138, 140-3, 155
　struggle for power 117-21, 129-34 *passim*

Bahamas, The 43-4, 64, 151-2, 172, 190, 202, 212
Bain, Fitzroy 110, 120-1, 124, 127, 134, 136, 138
Bain, Norris 37, 133-4, 136, 138
bananas 2, 23-4, 50, 111, 114
Barbados 3, 32, 76, 81, 89, 115, 190, 202, 207, 212
　invasion 149-58 *passim*, 175, 185
　relations with PRG 50, 67, 90-8 *passim*, 132-3
Bartholomew, Tan 105, 117-19, 137
Belize 89, 151-2, 172, 212
Bish, Milan 63, 115, 149
Bishop, Maurice 179, 188, 206, 216, 222-3
　development policies 18, 27, 35, 216
　foreign policy 20-1, 202-3
　house arrest and death 131-40, 152, 156, 161, 210
　opposition to Gairy 9, 13, 15-16
　relations with Commonwealth Caribbean 90-100, 148, 207
　relations with Cuba 81-7, 158
　relations with US 49-52, 61-7 *passim*, 114-16
　struggle for power 105-11, 117-22, 126-31, 143-5, 222-3
Black Power Movement, The 8-9

Blaize, Herbert 7, 15, 192
Braithwaite, Nicholas 183, 186, 188, 190-1
Britain 9, 51-2, 91, 97, 114, 174, 199, 204, 207, 213
　colonial policy 1-8 *passim*, 32, 43, 91
　Foreign Affairs Committee 199-201, 221-2
　independence crisis 11-13
　invasion 142, 151-7, 170-1, 175-6, 181-2
　post-invasion arrangements 179, 187, 190
　relations with PRG 22-3, 34, 50, 63, 81
Brizan, George 15, 193
bureaucratic elite 2, 6, 178
　see also non-capitalist development
Burnhams, Forbes 75, 90, 172, 190, 208, 212
Bush, George 115, 149-50
Butler, Uriah 'Buzz' 1-2

Canada 32, 34, 81, 172-3, 187, 190, 202
Caribbean Basin Initiative (CBI) 62-5, 95-6, 115, 187, 202
Caribbean Community (CARICOM) 78, 89, 202, 208-13, 224
　invasion 139, 141, 151-6 *passim*, 171-2
　relations with PRG 92, 95-100 *passim*, 114, 116
Caribbean Development Bank 62, 94-5, 189
Caribbean Free Trade Association (CARIFTA) 89, 208
Caribbean Peace-keeping Force 184, 190
Carter, Jimmy 57, 61
　Caribbean basin policy 46-7
　relations with Cuba 48-9
　relations with Grenada 49-53
Castro, Fidel 40, 85, 222, 224
　foreign policy 71-4, 77-9

229

230 Index

relations with Grenada 82-4, 128, 142, 162
relations with US 48-9, 55, 60, 158, 169, 198, 205
Central Intelligence Agency (CIA) 39-41, 50-2, 58, 61-2, 84, 106, 129, 186, 192
Centre for Popular Education (CPE) 27-8, 35, 110-12, 125
Chambers, George 96, 98-9, 116, 151-2, 171-2, 208
Charles, Eugenia 63-4, 140, 154, 157, 174, 182
Chile 14, 38, 45, 52, 71, 86
Coard, Bernard 29, 38
 capture and imprisonment 184-5, 187, 194, 196
 economic policy 20, 22, 25, 31-2, 83, 86, 216
 opposition to Gairy 9, 14-16
 struggle for power 105-9, 118-33, 140, 143-5
Coard, Phyllis 29, 40, 106, 109, 112, 118-19, 125, 129-30, 132, 184, 194
cocoa 2, 23-4
Colombia 59, 74, 80, 174
commercial elite 2, 6, 11, 20, 36, 178
 see also non-capitalist development
Commonwealth, The 172-4
Compton, John 91-2, 149
constitutional issues
 Associated Statehood 7, 11-12
 constitution commission 36, 39, 179
 invasion 180-3
 Westminster model 9, 18-19, 35-6, 98, 222
Cornwall, Leon 105, 117-20, 130, 135
Costa Rica 55, 80, 175
Creft, Jacqueline 129, 133-4, 136-7
Cuba chapter 3 (71-88), 38, 92, 100, 117, 137, 202-4, 211-12, 220, 223-4
 invasion 153-63 *passim*, 168-9, 184-5
 model for development 8, 27, 221
 relations with Grenada 22, 26, 28, 33, 128-9, 133, 138, 141, 162, 169, 178
 relations with US 43-9 *passim*, 55, 59-60, 64, 66, 96, 115, 164, 199-206 *passim*, 224

Declaration of Ocho Rios 98, 209
dependency 18-19, 34-5
de Riggs, Chris 30, 106, 117, 119-20, 122, 194
destabilization 21, 27, 39, 41, 43, 49-53, 61-8
Dominica 89, 91-3, 96-7, 154, 207
Dominican Republic 43-5, 55, 74, 76, 99, 210

Eastern Caribbean Currency Authority (later Eastern Caribbean Central Bank) 91, 152
elections 6-7, 14-15, 39, 99, 116, 191
 see also constitutional issues
El Salvador 47, 55-8, 63-4, 81, 175-6, 203, 205-6, 223-4
 Democratic Revolutionary Front (FCR/Farabundo Martí Liberation Front (FMLN) 47, 56-7, 86, 206
Emmanuel, Patrick 183, 189, 218-19
Enders, Thomas 56-7, 67
Ethiopia 48, 59, 72, 86
European Economic Community (EEC) 22, 25, 33-4, 62-3, 114, 190

France 1, 25, 34, 87, 169, 175
Free West Indian, the 30, 37, 40, 131

Gairy, Eric 5-16, 22, 24, 34, 51, 81, 86, 90-1, 179, 193-4, 221-2
George, Errol 130-1
German Democratic Republic 39, 86, 114
Gillespie, Charles 186-7, 195
Gonsalves, Ralph 214-15
Governor General, The 90, 158, 160, 179-3
 see also Scoon, Paul
Grenada Chamber of Commerce 12, 22
Grenada Farmers Corporation 23, 110
Grenada National Party (GNP) 7-12 *passim*, 37, 192
Grenada United Labour Party GULP) 6-7, 193
Grenada Union of Teachers 31, 112
Grenadian Voice, the 40, 61, 189,

Index

191
Guadeloupe 1, 67
Guatemala 43, 55, 74, 175, 212, 224
Guyana (formerly British Guiana) 12, 28, 43-4, 67, 89, 207, 209-12, 224
  invasion 151-2, 175, 190
  relations with PRG 75, 81, 90, 93

Habib, Philip 46-8
Haiti 43-4, 55, 74, 99, 210
Honduras 43, 55, 57-8, 63, 76, 175
Howe, Geoffrey 154, 164, 170
Hughes, Alister 40, 132, 139, 191-2

International Monetary Fund (IMF) 25-6, 187, 210

Jacobs, Richard 86
Jamaica 38, 52-3, 75-7, 80, 89, 202, 204, 209-10
  invasion 151, 153-4, 172, 175
  relations with Grenada 81, 90, 93, 97-8, 189-90
  relations with US 43-6, 55, 64, 96
James, Liam 105, 117, 119-21, 127, 137, 139

Kirkpatrick, Jeane 54, 57

landholding 6, 22-3
Layne, Ewart 105, 108, 118-22, 127, 136-7, 163
Lebanon, The 149-50, 161, 223
Libya 34, 55, 185
Louison, Einstein 131-2, 139
Louison, George 10, 119-21, 128-9, 132-3, 139, 194-5
Luce, Richard 63, 200

McKenzie, Rear Admiral R.P. 48, 66
Manley, Michael 75, 77-8, 90, 93, 210-11
Marketing and National Importing Board 22, 113
Marryshow, T. Albert 1-3
medical schools, the
  see St George's University Medical School
Memorandum of Understanding 97, 207
Mexico 25, 34, 44, 55, 59, 74, 76, 78, 80, 174, 199, 201-2
middle classes 4, 7-8, 15, 36, 119

see also non-capitalist development
Militia, the 28, 36, 38, 40, 108, 111-12, 117-18, 120, 123, 134, 161, 163, 184-5
Mongoose Men, the 8, 10, 13, 15, 193
Montserrat 89, 91, 133
Motley, L. 204, 206
Movement for the Assemblies of the People (MAP) 9-10, 35
Munroe, Trevor 128, 132

National Conference of Delegates 37, 123
National In-Service Teacher Education Programme (NISTEP) 26-7, 111-12
National Women's Organization (NWO) 29, 35, 40, 112
National Youth Organization (NYO) 28, 35, 118
New Jewel Movement (NJM) *see* chapter 6 (105-47), 49, 82, 90, 92-3, 175, 178, 180, 192, 194-5, 222
  early development 10-13
  non-capitalist development 213-19 *passim*
  organizational structure 11, 15, 36-9
Nicaragua 43, 47, 57-9, 64, 66, 74-85 *passim*, 169, 175-6, 205-6, 223
  Frente Sandinista de Liberación Nacional (FSLN) 47, 57, 78, 203
Noel, Lloyd 15, 37, 40, 191
Noel, Vincent 30, 134-5, 140
Non-Aligned Movement, The 20, 67, 72-3, 77, 93, 173
non-capitalist development 213-21
North Korea 84, 86, 106, 118, 162, 178
nutmeg 2, 6, 23-4, 67

Operation Amber 65-6
Organization of American States (OAS) 50, 74-6, 116, 157, 174-5
Organization of East Caribbean (OECS) 95, 97, 99, 114, 139, 149, 151-7, 175, 200
Ortiz, Frank 49

Panama 43, 55, 59, 74, 76, 78, 80

Canal 44, 46, 78, 86
Parish Councils 29, 36-7, 119, 123-4
Pearls airport 31-2, 111, 129, 132, 137-8, 142, 158-9, 185
peasantry 2-3, 6, 22, 110
   see also non-capitalist development
people's power 34-9
People's Revolutionary Army (PRA) 16, 28, 40, 83-4, 143, 178, 184-5, 219
   struggle for power 105-6, 117, 120, 128, 130-6 passim
   see also Revolutionary Military Council
People's Revolutionary Government (PRG) chapter 2 (18-42), 16-17, 105, 136, 179, 184-5, 188
   Caribbean media 40, 52-3, 61
   foreign policy 81, 84-7, 106, 114
   relations with US 49, 51, 61, 66, 86
Pierre, Leslie 15, 40, 191
Plessey 33, 68, 187
Point Salines International Airport 31-4, 67-8, 84, 111, 158-9, 162, 185, 187, 191
police 117, 120, 196
private sector 21-2, 112, 140
Puerto Rico 21, 43-4, 65, 77, 86

Radio Free Grenada 40, 50, 133, 137
Radix, Kenrick 9, 61, 109, 131-2, 139, 194
Ramdhanny, Lynden 37, 133
Ramphal, Shridath 173, 190
Reagan, Ronald 30, 35, 53-6
   invasion 148-66
   post-invasion policy 178-80, 187-8
   relations with Central America 56-9
   relations with Commonwealth Caribbean 94, 96, 98
   relations with Cuba 59-60, 73, 80, 206
   relations with Grenada 61-8, 86, 115, 223
Redhead, Lester 128, 134, 136
Revolutionary Military Council, The 136-42, 152-6 passim, 163, 178-85 passim, 190, 194, 196, 208
Roopnarine, Rupert 129, 132, 141

Rushford, Tony 182-3, 186, 189-91

St Bernard, Ian 105, 118, 137, 139
St George's University Medical School 29, 142, 149, 155, 159
St Kitts-Nevis 1, 3, 89, 91, 95-6, 122, 126
St Lucia 12, 43, 67, 89, 91-3, 96, 154, 207, 209
St Paul, Cletus 128-31
St Vincent 4, 29, 89, 91-3, 96, 141, 154, 207
Sanchez, Nestor 55
Scoon, Paul 157, 160, 173, 179-96 passim
   see also Governor General
Seaga, Edward 63, 80, 96-9, 114, 149, 151, 172, 187, 208-11
Shelton, Sally 49-50
Shultz, George 115-16, 148-50
slavery 1-3
Smith, Wayne 60, 206
Soviet Union 77-8, 80, 115-17, 121, 137, 211, 220
   invasion 150, 168, 175, 185
   relations with PRG 24, 34, 37, 65, 67, 84-7, 106, 108, 123, 162-4, 178
   relations with US 44, 48, 54, 59
Strachan, Selwyn 10, 13, 28, 38, 106, 118, 120, 122-3, 126, 129-31, 194, 221
Stroude, Captain 134, 139
Suriname 44, 224

Tanzania 8-9, 36
Thatcher, Margaret 153-4, 171
Thomas, Clive Y. 216-17
Torchlight, The 40, 52, 61, 120
tourism 25, 33-4, 114
trade unions 4-5, 14, 30-1, 35-6, 124
Trinidad and Tobago 2, 30, 43, 67, 75-6, 89, 99, 203, 207, 210, 212
   invasion 151-2, 171-2, 190
   relations with Grenada 1, 8, 12, 23, 91, 93-4, 96, 133, 141

unemployment 14, 23, 123
United Nations 8, 15, 54, 59, 80, 84, 132, 157, 175-6, 212
United States see chapter 3 (43-70) and chapter 7 (148-67) and chapter 8 (168-77) 12, 16, 21-2, 32, 77, 96, 118, 137, 202, 207,

211-12, 223-4
Agency for International Development (AID) 50, 186-8, 193, 195
Caribbean hegemony 198-202
post-invasion policy 178-80, 184-96 *passim*
relations with Commonwealth Caribbean 95, 97-8
relations with Cuba 78, 80-1, 204, 224
relations with Grenada 25, 34, 39, 85, 106-8, 114-15, 142, 144

Venezuela 25, 44, 59, 67, 74, 76, 80-1, 174, 199, 201-4, 212
Ventour, John 118-19, 123
Vieques 65-6, 148
Vietnam 56, 58-9, 82, 86
Village Co-ordinating Bureaus 36-7, 125

West Germany 52, 170-1
West Indies Associated States (WIAS) 91-2
West Indies Federation 32, 89, 208
Whiteman, Unison 9, 13, 15, 98, 110, 114, 119, 120-38 *passim*
Whyte, Winston 15, 39, 192-3, 196
Williams, Dessima 50, 174
Williams, Eric 47, 75, 93, 96, 203
working class 4-5, 7, 9-10, 20, 110, 124-5, 128, 140
    see also non-capitalist development
World Bank 24, 32, 78, 115, 188

Young Pioneers 28, 35

Zimbabwe 174-6, 195
Zonal Councils 36-7, 119, 123-5